DENIS COMPTON

DENIS COMPTON

The Life of a Sporting Hero

Tim Heald

First published 2006 by
Aurum Press Limited
25 Bedford Avenue
London WC1B 3AT
www.aurumpress.co.uk

Portions of this book appeared in an earlier form in Tim Heald's
DENIS COMPTON: The Authorized Biography (1994).

A catalogue record for this book is available from the British
Library.

ISBN 1 84513 089 8

10 9 8 7 6 5 4 3 2 1
2010 2009 2008 2007 2006

Designed and typeset in Adobe Garamond by SX Composing
DTP, Rayleigh, Essex

Printed and bound in Great Britain by CPD Wales Ltd, Ebbw Vale.

CONTENTS

AUTHOR'S NOTE

I am writing this more than eight years after Denis Compton's death, and a dozen since he helped me write my biography of him which was published in 1994. In 1994 Compton's life was still a 'work in progress', and one had to suspend many judgements. Now it is possible not only to write about the whole life but also to attempt a complete evaluation – to say where he stands in the pantheon of sporting heroes and to what extent he was a creature of his time. Towards the end of his life English cricket seemed to be in a possibly permanent decline. Now, in the aftermath of his death, a new generation of charismatic English cricketers have not only regained the Ashes but restored the English game to something approaching the heights of Compton's pomp. And, surprisingly, as his achievements become a part of history, they look even more impressive than they did at the time.

In the intervening years the Compton legend has taken on a well-defined permanence. Readers of my earlier book will therefore find much in these pages that is familiar. The accounts of Denis's glory years remain, properly, much the same, and my perception of him as a sporting genius and a boon companion remains essentially unchanged. Many of those who talked to me back in the 1990s are now dead, so I have not been able – even if I thought it appropriate – to add to what people such as Colin (Lord) Cowdrey, Keith Miller or David (Lord) Sheppard told me then. Nor, of course, can I ask Denis himself for more information or comment.

But after the earlier book's publication a number of people wrote in with observations and recollections, all of which I have considered and some of which I am happy to include, with gratitude. I am particularly grateful to Denis's widow, Christine, and his sons Brian and Patrick, for sharing their memories with me. There are now a number of permanent memorials to Denis, and I have written about these as well as including new material and evaluations of the Compton life. Whereas the original book was a portrait of a living legend, this new book is the story of a whole life, which is now, alas, a part of history.

Tim Heald
February 2006

CHAPTER ONE

Denis Compton always pulled in the crowds during his cricketing career so it was no surprise that he filled Westminster Abbey for his memorial service on 1 July 1997. In fact there was a waiting list.

He always, I think, had a keen eye for the absurdity of his fame. I remembered, that morning at his own Westminster Abbey Memorial, how at the wake for the broadcaster Brian Johnston, commemorated not long before in another Abbey ceremony, I had found Denis, uncharacteristically, without a glass in his own hand.

I asked if I could bring him a drink. 'No thanks old boy,' he said, with an impish grin. 'The Prime Minister's getting me one.' And sure enough, seconds later, John Major hove in view with a glass of red wine for the maestro.

That July morning in 1997 Denis's old friend and cricketing colleague, the one-time Middlesex and England fast bowler J.J. Warr, told the story, which was obviously destined to enter Compton folklore. He got it slightly wrong, which was what always seemed to happened to stories about Denis. They were rolling stones and they gathered lots of moss. Denis was one of those men who attracted anecdote and many had a germ of truth in them at first, but were gradually embellished until they acquired, almost, the character of fairy

1

stories. 'No truth in it at all, old boy,' he used to say when confronted with yet another tale of youthful naughtiness or absent-mindedness. And as the years passed everyone became less and less certain and – to a certain extent – who cared?

'Service of Thanksgiving for the Life of Denis Compton, CBE 1918–1997,' said the inscription on the service sheet, sandwiched between the crest of the Abbey itself and the emblematic old field gun of his Arsenal Football Club and the three sabres of his beloved Middlesex County Cricket Club.

Before play actually started there was organ music by Bach and Mendelssohn, neither of whom one would have immediately associated with Denis during his lifetime, although he did once claim that during Canterbury week when the bands played he always tried to bat in time to the music. There were four suitably rambunctious hymns, culminating, appropriately for this most English Englishman, in 'Jerusalem', and we finally filed out to Elgar's 'Pomp and Circumstance' as the Abbey bells tolled above. Denis would have enjoyed that.

He died, as J.J. Warr reminded us, on St George's Day, 23 April, as eleven years previously had his great friend and partner Bill Edrich. He would have enjoyed that too.

The great and good were well represented at the Abbey: Lord Runcie, the former Archbishop of Canterbury, said three prayers including words of Cardinal Newman and Sir Francis Drake; Peter Hill-Wood, Chairman of the Arsenal, read the famous 'Let us now praise famous men' passage from Ecclesiasticus; 'Jim' Swanton who had partnered Denis in his first game for Middlesex Seconds and gone on to be the doyen of cricket writers and broadcasters read an evocative passage of Neville Cardus about Lord's Cricket Ground, 'The Mecca of Cricket'; Denis's son Richard came from South Africa to deliver the Corinthians lesson about the greatness of love. The Bidding was delivered by the Very Reverend Wesley Carr, newly arrived as the Dean of Westminster. 'All of us,' he said, 'whatever our age and wherever we have come from, players and spectators alike, acknowledge the skills that he was given and which he so flamboyantly employed.'

John Warr, who gave the address, was at one time, in the estimation of another member of the congregation, Denis Silk, cricketer and schoolmaster, 'the finest after-dinner speaker in London'. This time, in Silk's estimation, Warr, who was a medium-fast bowler with Middlesex in the Fifties, was slightly below par. If so, this might have been something to do with his own emotions for Silk later remembered that as 'J.J.' concluded his tribute there was definitely a tear running down one cheek. The final thought, which may have prompted the tear, was that 'In the last few weeks of his life a comet appeared in the sky over Britain. It is said to appear every four thousand years. Well, Compo was a comet in his own right, and we must all pray that it isn't another four thousand years before we see another like him.'

There were many famous cricketers in that congregation and you could have picked a world-beating First XI from their number. Imagine a team composed of John Edrich, Raman Subba Row, Ted Dexter, Colin Cowdrey, Tom Graveney, Keith Miller, Godfrey Evans, Alan Davidson, Fred Titmus, Brian Statham, Alec Bedser. They were all there and that team would take some beating. You could have plucked second and third teams from the Abbey pews and they would have been almost as good. One unexpected visitor was the Labour MP Denis Skinner, aka The Beast of Bolsover. He just happened to be passing, saw the crowds, asked what was happening, expressed enthusiasm and was somehow smuggled in. Among the mainstream mandarins were a former Governor of the Bank of England, Robin Leigh Pemberton, a prime minister, John Major, the Lords Maclaurin and Griffiths, Tim Brooke-Taylor and countless others all united in their love of cricket and of Denis.

A couple of months earlier Warr had also given the address at Denis's funeral at St James's Church, Fulmer, the Buckinghamshire village where Denis lived for many years. Like the great Abbey celebration this more modest service also included 'Jerusalem' and the Corinthians passage about love. Afterwards there was a wake at the Bull Hotel in Gerrards Cross near the ground where Denis played much of his post-first-class cricket.

Denis's body was cremated so that, bizarrely, the only part of him that still remains is the rogue kneecap which caused him so much trouble during his playing career. After being surgically removed it is now preserved in a biscuit tin at the Museum in Lord's Cricket Ground. His ashes were scattered at Lord's, on the turf in front of the pavilion.

There then followed a bizarre quirk of fate which provided an apt final footnote to a life which was sometimes as chaotic as it was cavalier. The Marylebone Cricket Club decided that the playing surface of the old ground needed to be replaced so the sacred turf was cut up and sold off in sods before being replaced with newly sown grass. A largish section was purchased by Denis's beloved Denham Golf Club and laid there as a Compton memorial lawn. It would be comforting to think that the Compton ashes are there too but the reality, alas, is that they could be almost anywhere.

There are other memorials, of course. For instance there is a trust and a medal named after him and his old Australian mate and rival Keith Miller. It goes to the player nominated by the chairmen of both countries' selectors as the outstanding success of the Ashes series. At the Nursery End of his home ground in St John's Wood there is a Compton stand, next door to another dedicated, aptly, to Bill Edrich.

Memorials such as these ensure a permanent place in the game he graced. And still, almost half a century after he retired, there are plenty who remember that inimitable sportsman and the extraordinary effect he once had on the whole nation and much of a world beyond. Gradually those memories are fading and those who share them die. But what is extraordinary, in the aftermath of the great Ashes summer of 2005, is the way in which, when comparisons are made, it is so often the name of Denis that is invoked. It was Denis who hit the winning runs against Australia in the year of the Queen's Coronation. Over fifty years later when the heroic deeds of men such as Warne and Flintoff are celebrated it is Compton who is most called up in comparison.

He would have loved the 2005 Ashes series. Those endless fluctuations would have excited him as much as they did the rest of us. He would have been awed by the Australian triumph in the first Test at Lord's and enthralled by the way England bounced back at Edgbaston, and captivated right up to that last moment in mid-September when the umpires, with consummate theatricality, lifted the bails to signal that the last match had been drawn and the series therefore won by England. He would have been as thrilled as the rest of us at the heroics of players such as the Australians Warne, Lee, McGrath and Ponting and yet more by those of the victorious home team and the deeds of Flintoff, Trescothick, Strauss, Vaughan, Hoggard and Harmison. He would have had a special smile for England's South African prodigy Kevin Pietersen. Above all he would have echoed the words of P.J. Kavanagh, writing in the *Spectator*, and applauded 'a team that liked each other, played for each other, delighted in each other's success; that happy team spirit was one of the delights of the summer'.

Shades of times past.

CHAPTER TWO

Denis Charles Scott Compton was born in Hendon, Middlesex, on 23 May 1918, soon after what should have been the start of the cricket season, though the first-class game was in abeyance that last summer of the First World War. No Hobbs, no Hendren, no Hirst, no Rhodes. These four played on when cricket resumed the following year, but the first war stole some of the best years of their sporting life just as the second was to deprive Denis of some of the best of his.

His brother Leslie, and his sister Hilda had been born in Essex, where most of the Compton clan remained, but his father Harry, a self-employed painter and decorator, had moved to Hendon in the hope of finding more work. He formed a partnership with a man called Hayward. Compton and Hayward. Not, alas, as rich and famous as Compton and Edrich were to be in later years.

Times were hard, and business was seldom good. Years later I met a man who said that he had been born and brought up in Hendon and he remembered Denis's father coming round one day to mend the garden fence. He brought his two sons with him and my informant remembered vaguely that he thought Leslie the nicer of the two. He couldn't remember why but he seemed to think Denis had been a bit bumptious.

In the end the painting, decorating and fence-mending firm foundered and Harry Compton signed on as a lorry driver for a man named Jabis Barker. He often drove through the night and would arrive home exhausted. Mrs Compton, Jessie, had been in service before the war, and sounds like a woman of optimism and ingenuity. If anyone ever had to go short it was not the children. There was always, even at the worst time, a proper cooked breakfast and a hot evening meal for them.

Denis was born at their modest suburban home, a terraced house in Alexandra Road, No. 47. Talking about his early days he sounded, seven decades on, both fond and wistful. 'I would say,' he reflected, sitting over a glass of what in later years became his preferred tipple – chilled Sancerre – 'that I had a very happy childhood.' The words sound simple, but they were delivered very carefully after serious thought and contemplation. The point he was making and deliberating was that it had not, at least in a material sense, been at all an easy childhood. 'Poorish' is the typically understated word he used to describe it.

Pleasures were simple. 'Every Christmas we used to go to Derby Road, Epping Forest, Woodford, Essex.' This was the headquarters of the Compton family. There were so many Compton cousins and uncles and aunts at Christmas that the children slept five or six to a bed, waking early for Father Christmas. There was a lucky dip in a barrel.

Looking back on those days he once mused: 'They were very much more family-oriented in those days.' Pleasures were necessarily simple and homespun. In the summer the big treat was also in Essex, rabbiting in the fields with a favourite uncle.

His father was a keen cricketer; so was Leslie; so were the neighbourhood children; so was everybody worth talking to. When I persuaded Denis to cast his mind back to those early days he was in his seventies and his memory, never brilliant, had grown even foggier with the years. Inevitably, I suppose, it was cricket that loomed largest. His was a precocious talent and it was this, along with other ball-playing skills, that marked him out and made him different. Small wonder if cricket seemed to play an overwhelmingly important part in his life even in retrospect.

Shortly before I spoke to him about his childhood, Denis had been to the funeral of his old Middlesex colleague Jack Young at Finchley Crematorium. Afterwards, with an hour or so to kill, he drove down to Alexandra Road to look at his birthplace. It was all much as he remembered though, as so often, reduced in size, everything smaller than it had seemed as a boy. But the pavement and the lamp-posts were just as they had been, and these were his first pitches and wickets. You chalked three white stump marks up the side of the lamp-posts and then, at weekends and after school, you bowled and batted and fielded with a tennis ball and the most appropriate piece of wood you could find. He remembered half a dozen such roadside nets going on all the time in Alexandra Road alone. 'The street used to be jam-packed. And every game had its own rules. If you hit the ball into someone's garden it was six. Even though it was only a tennis ball windows sometimes got broken if you gave it a real whack.'

His father did everything he could to support and encourage his son's precocious talent at both cricket and soccer, and school – Bell Lane Elementary, just round the corner – was not only a keen sporting institution but also intensely competitive. 'There were evening games against Wessex Gardens and the Hyde,' recalled Denis, 'and hundreds of parents would come along to watch.'

Bell Lane was only an ordinary elementary school, but the staff all seemed to love games and many of them were more than competent coaches. Denis's two principal mentors were a master called James Bond who played football at close to professional standard, and Mr Mitchell, the cricket master, who Denis remembered being extremely strict.

These two were much more important than anyone concerned with academic life. 'On the intellectual side they very quickly gave me up as a bad job because I was always playing games,' he told me. 'But I got by and I passed my exams with a great deal of effort.'

Bell Lane was his only school, and he was there between the ages of five and fourteen. Granted he had a formidable natural sporting talent, it is still difficult to imagine such a school as Bell Lane honing it as effectively in later years. Much has always been made of Denis's natural genius and colleagues such as the Cambridge-educated J.J. Warr often dined out on stories of how if Denis had ever consulted a coaching manual he must have read it upside down. There is some truth in this but Denis himself always gave credit to Mr Bond and Mr Mitchell. They were obviously quick to grasp that their pupil was a potential star sportsman and even if they had the nous not to try to make him conform or to drill him into playing the way everyone else played they plainly encouraged and nurtured their boy. In a typical state school after a period around the 1960s Denis would have been much more likely to have slipped through the net. He might never have played cricket at all and he almost certainly wouldn't have honed his skills in those rough and ready pick-up contests in the street. Nor would hundreds of parents have come along to watch him perform.

There is a photograph of him at the age of fourteen exhibiting not only what even E.W. Swanton conceded was 'nearly a model stance' but also immaculate whites, gloves and pads as well as the slick neatly parted hair which was later to become a famous trademark. It is a picture which speaks volumes about changes in our national school system over the past sixty years. By the time I talked Denis into reminiscence no one in Britain played street cricket. That sort of spontaneous children's game had become largely confined to the Caribbean and the Indian subcontinent, a sociological fact which said much, Denis believed, about what had happened to the game at Test match level too. He never lived to see the resurgence of English cricket and was glum about the game's prospects though wary of seeming to look back through rose-tinted spectacles. He often seemed nostalgic for the past but was savvy enough to realise that to be too obviously so was bad for the image.

E.W. Swanton, who watched Compton practically all his life, wrote a perceptive little monograph about him, called simply *Denis Compton* and published by Sporting Handbooks in 1948 when Compton was at the pinnacle of his achievement. 'Jim' as he was commonly called (his Christian names were actually Ernest William) was for years the *Daily Telegraph* cricket correspondent and a mellifluous BBC radio pundit, and the subject of a recent biography by David Rayvern Allen. He was, in his day, very highly regarded even if he was often considered snobbish and self-important. He was certainly a lifelong admirer of Compton and a genuine expert on the subject.

Rayvern Allen commented that in his account of this first sighting of the young Compton 'Jim's memory was slightly awry'. The Swanton version was that Swanton joined him when the score was 'round about a dozen'. Actually, said Rayvern Allen, the fourth wicket fell at 54. And so on. The only absolutely undeniable fact was that Swanton and Compton were both playing in the same match. The discrepancy poses an interesting question. Does the fact that Swanton remembered the statistics incorrectly invalidate the impression? Does the mistake regarding numbers mean that other verdicts are unreliable?

Swanton said that there was another crucial coincidence which helped the young Compton to 'catch the flavour and the spell of cricket'. This was that the Number 13 bus route began and ended in Hendon, and the Number 13 bus was the one that took spectators to and from Lord's Cricket Ground in St John's Wood. In the event it turned out that this too was 'wrong' though infinitessimally so. It was actually the 113 bus which ran from Edgware, through Hendon and on to St John's Wood. This was the route that Denis Compton took and Swanton must have meant. The 13 ran from Golders Green. It's a tiny point but a genuine error. Denis misremembered it and Swanton perpetuated it. These points not only suggest that memories, especially Compton's, are fallible, but that whereas for some cricketers statistics and figures are all-important, for others they are almost irrelevant.

It wasn't that much further from Lord's to the Kennington Oval, so little Denis could watch Surrey and one of his two particular heroes, Jack Hobbs. The other was Patsy Hendren of Middlesex, with whom he later played. Sadly he never saw Hobbs, 'the Master', put together a big score. 'My father used to take me quite often to the Surrey v. Notts match on August Bank Holiday,' he said. 'It's still played on the August Bank Holiday. One year we went and Surrey won the toss – and I knew they were going to bat because it was the most beautiful day. They did. Hobbs and Sandham. Funny he was bowled for about 16 by a big man called Barratt who stood about six foot six. Nearly broke my heart. Then I saw the most wonderful innings by Andrew Sandham who made around 170. But I didn't see very many first-class matches as a boy.' Sandham, Hobbs's junior partner in both age and ability, nevertheless played for Surrey for a quarter of a century and made over 30,000 runs with an average of more than forty.

There were innumerable breakthroughs in that early career, notably the moment in 1930 when as a twelve-year-old he was first allowed to play for his father's team. At first the other side protested because he was so small, but the protests didn't last long. The adult bowlers, bowling as fast and as guilefully as they knew how, were hit for a fluent 40. A little later he began to be picked for an adult wandering team called Stamford Hill, who played some of the top London clubs such as Finchley and Honor Oak. His father Harry was their regular first-choice umpire.

'The captain was a Jewish bloke called Ted Miller. He had no idea how to play the game but he absolutely adored it and he was so kind to me. He encouraged me and he looked after me. When everyone else was drinking beer he'd make sure I had a lemonade and say, "You'll soon become a beer drinker like the rest of us. But not now. Not yet."'

In 1930, aged twelve, and already captain of the school team, he made 88 for north London schools against south London schools. This was his first appearance at Lord's.

But the moment which really sealed his fate came on 13 September 1932, when he played for the Elementary Schools against a side of public schoolboys raised by Mr C.F. Tufnell. This was a sort of adolescent Gentlemen v. Players. Denis captained the Elementary Schools and opened the batting with a south London boy called Macintyre, later to become the distinguished Surrey wicketkeeper. Together they put on a hundred for the first wicket. Then Denis ran him out. This was one of the first such incidents which have passed into legend. Denis struck the ball firmly in the direction of cover, shouted 'yes', set off, stopped, shouted 'no!' and left the other batsman stranded; Denis then went on to make 114 before being stumped. He declared at 204 for 8 and, putting himself on as fourth change, got two wickets for 5 with his flighted spin. Mr Tufnell's boys were all out for 56.

Denis was presented with a bat by the *Star* newspaper. He also got his scorecard signed by the Bell Lane cricket master, who certainly wasn't going to get carried away with heady praise. He simply wrote, 'Best wishes, M. Mitchell', which seems less than gracious.

Mr Mitchell also gave an interview to the *Star* which sounds more enthusiastic than the laconic autograph on the cricket bat. 'Young Compton,' he was quoted as saying, 'has a natural talent on the sports field, whether it is with a cricket bat in his hand or a ball at his feet. Of all the hundreds of boys who have passed through this school, I have never known one so clearly destined to become a professional sportsman. His reward of a Jack Hobbs bat from your newspaper could not have gone to a more deserving case.'

There was a caveat about academic studies but a nice piece of prescience. 'Frankly,' said Mr Mitchell, 'his schoolwork suffers because he puts so much into sport. But this is one case when I think it is justified. I am sure he is going to be a great credit to our school and I will be surprised if he is not an established professional at both football and cricket before this decade is out.'

The legendary Sir Pelham Warner, former Captain of England and Chairman of the Selectors during the 'Bodyline' tour of Australia, was clearly more impressed. The former England and Middlesex captain watched the match and subsequently invited the young prodigy to join the Lord's ground staff. Denis's mother, who knew nothing whatever about cricket, was unimpressed.

'"Yes sir," said my mother, "but that means he'll only be working for four months of the year. What is the boy going to do for the other eight?"'

This was a perfectly fair question, but Denis was about to experience a second stroke of luck. At least that is the way he used to tell it. In retrospect the Compton sporting career assumed a charmed inevitability, an apparently effortless glide from one triumph to another. At the time, and to him, it didn't seem like that at all.

As luck would have it, I was picked to play for England school-boys against Wales at soccer. And there happened to be an Arsenal scout there, which I didn't know about. Well, he must have gone back with a good report to Herbert Chapman, who was then the Arsenal manager, because he approached my father and mother and said, 'We'd very much like this boy when he's finished school, to come and join the ground staff at Highbury.' And my mother said, 'Well, how long's that for?' And he told her eight months, so she said, 'Well that'll keep him occupied all year.'

Those who saw him play rate his soccer as highly as his cricket. The writer Benny Green once wrote that Compton on the wing in the war years was 'one of the supreme sights of English life'. At Bell Lane school he played centre-half and was, in his own recollection, a chronically one-footed player. 'I kicked the ball with my left foot and just used the other one for standing on.' A typical piece of Compton self-deprecation. 'On the ground staff at Arsenal they used to have shooting boxes. Don't think they do now. You hit the ball into the base part of the box and it came back at different angles. And I learnt to improve anyway hitting the ball with my right foot. They put a slipper on my left foot and a boot on my right. And there was a game we used to play there, which gave you the most wonderful ability to control the ball with your head and your feet. Again they don't play it now. It was called head tennis.' The essence of it was that the ball was not allowed to touch the ground, but had somehow to be juggled between feet and head. 'By God,' said Denis, 'it was competitive.' Oddly enough, though he should by geographical rights have supported a north London side his preferred team was West Ham. He loved them. Then as now they had a cavalier spirit to which he warmed. 'Even today,' he said in the 1990s, 'I look at their results before the Arsenal's.' He was, in truth, the sort of character one would have expected to find playing for a side like West Ham or Fulham who always seemed to care more about panache and flair than actually winning.

The ground staff pay was not lavish. At Lord's, where he started in the summer of 1933, he got ten shillings a week. However, the ground staff were responsible for selling the tuppenny matchcards. The crowds were enormous and each boy set out his stall on Saturday with a hundred dozen cards. If he disposed of them his commission was three times his weekly wage. 'On Saturday nights,' said Denis, 'I'd go home to Hendon on the Number 13 bus feeling like a millionaire.' (Well, actually, it would have been the 113 as I've pointed out. The version according to Denis is often not entirely accurate!)

There were thirty or forty boys on the Lord's ground staff. He particularly remembered Len Muncer, who went on to play for Middlesex and Glamorgan, and Laurie D'Arcy, later a brilliant coach. They reported for work on the dot at 8 a.m. – 'You had to be sharp.' During the day they mowed and rolled under the supervision of Harry White the groundsman ('marvellous old boy'). The heavy roller needed a dozen boys to pull it, and they rolled and rolled for hours on end.

Archie Fowler was his greatest coaching inspiration. Fowler never curbed his natural game and told him not to pay too much attention to those who tried to.

He also said, 'You'll never ever be any good until you really learn to play off the back foot.' That's so different to today. Not against slow bowlers, but against medium-pace or exceptionally fast bowlers you must get on your back foot. And by God he was right. I see these players today playing forward to the fast stuff and no wonder they get hit so often. I was often on the back foot before the ball was bowled. That was one of the advantages of having learned in the street with a tennis ball. The bounce was very high so you learnt to let the ball come on to the bat, and when it did the ball went down. It became an automatic shot.

As a bowler, of course, he was limited by tennis ball street cricket. You couldn't spin it, but at least he learned to bowl a length. When he did graduate to a proper leather seamed ball he began by bowling orthodox off-spin, but quite soon became bored with it. Orthodoxy never had that much appeal for Denis in any shape or form. It was Jack Walsh, the Leicester spinner, who introduced him to fun and games at bowling. Walsh was in the nets at Lord's one day when Denis was bowling. He would have been about sixteen at the time. Walsh watched a while, then came over and had a word. 'Why do you bowl this orthodox stuff?' he asked, 'because I know you love and get a lot of fun out of cricket. Seen you bat and all that. Why don't you have even more fun? I know you could bowl this if you wanted to.' Denis replied that he'd never tried, so Walsh took him aside and gave him a first lesson in leg-spin. 'So,' says Denis, 'I started to learn and I got quite useful at it. It was a lot more fun. Jack said you'll get a lot more stick but you'll get a lot more wickets and you'll never have a dull moment! And he was right.'

Every day the boys had an hour or so of nets at 4 p.m. before the members came for their late afternoon/early evening practice. The boys were required to bowl at MCC members, who came up from their workplaces in the City in absolute droves.

Compton quickly became something of a pet of the great C. Aubrey Smith, otherwise known as 'Round the Corner' Smith. He had briefly captained Sussex and was also an actor of note who starred in *The House of Rothschild* and *The Prisoner of Zenda* as well as being a key figure at the Hollywood Cricket Club. However he was really best known, as R.C. Robertson-Glasgow once wrote, as 'the world ambassador for the English gentleman'. Smith spent his summers in England and came up to Lord's two or three times a week. Like others of the more generous MCC members, Smith would place coins on the stumps instead of bails. If the bowler knocked them off he got the coins.

Encouraged by Fowler, young Compton developed his individual style of play and particularly the sweep shot for which he became famous. The received wisdom now is that he only got away with this inherently dangerous shot because of his unusual gifts of timing and perception. He used to take a contrary view:

I can honestly say that nobody taught me the sweep. It seemed to be something that was an instant reaction to a ball that pitched middle and leg or middle stump. But I swept quite differently from the way they sweep today. Take Mike Gatting for instance. Gatting sweeps with his bat directly across the line and that makes him very vulnerable. If he doesn't get it quite right then he gets a top edge as he so often does. My sweep was different. I never hit it to square leg. I used to let it come on a long way and help it on its way.

People often say that the stroke must have got me out often during my career, but it only happened twice. In the first innings in 1938 against the Australians at Lord's, lbw, bowled O'Reilly for 6, sweeping. I missed him. Dai Davies was the umpire. I was told, tsk, tsk, you must never play that shot again. Anyway I continued to play it and I reaped terrific rewards from it. The other time I was out to it was 1957, Newlands, Cape Town, in the last Test match which we won when Wardle bowled them out. I was caught for 57. Caught Maclean bowled Tayfield. Very unusual because that time I did get a top edge and he had me caught at fine leg. But twice – that's not bad in a whole career.

Denis flourished in the somewhat Dickensian atmosphere

at Lord's. The boys sound like Fagin's pickpockets: lots of cheeky chappies like Denis's friend Harry Sharp who went on to play for Middlesex and become the county scorer until finally retiring in 1993. Denis described him as 'the original cockney'. The head groundsman and therefore their immediate boss when it came to rolling wickets was Harry White, who had a cottage behind the Mound Stand with a vegetable garden and Rhode Island Reds. The Secretary was Billy Findlay who had kept wicket for Oxford and Lancashire. Findlay was friendly but patrician. 'Very correct,' said Denis. It all sounded splendidly old-fashioned and feudal. There was even a special Lord's drink called 'Hatfield' which was a sort of Pimm's.* It has long since disappeared and was, as far as I can gather, unique to Lord's.

By 1934 his precocious talent was really beginning to flower. Arthur Wellard, the Somerset and England spinner and six-hitter, bowled at him in a practice match on the Nursery and was apparently impressed. That year he also played four times for MCC, scoring 222 at an average of 44.40. Against Suffolk he left his gear behind and made nought in kit borrowed from George Brown, the old Lancashire pro. It was much too big for him. But in the second innings he had his own stuff and made 118. He also made 52 against Bishops Stortford and took ten wickets in a two-innings match against East Grinstead.

In 1935 he played 16 matches and made 690 runs at an average of 46. Bill Edrich made fewer runs but averaged 57.

---

* When, in the winter of 2004–05, the Lord's Pavilion underwent a multi-million-pound refurbishment I suggested to Roger Knight, MCC's secretary, that the drink be revived and served to members. He managed to find the original recipe which involved industrial quantities of claret, noyau and brandy topped up with ginger beer. Oddly enough few people seemed to remember the drink until I asked Alan Moss, the Middlesex fast bowler of the Fifties, if he remembered it. 'Hatfield!' he exclaimed. 'Do I remember Hatfield? We used to drink it from silver tankards every lunchtime. Always a pint. Sometimes two.'

The first time they played for MCC together was against Beaumont, the Jesuit school at Old Windsor. The MCC captain was Alec Waugh, brother of Evelyn and a fanatical cricketer (the model for Bobby Southcott in A.G. Macdonell's *England, Their England*). He put them in at 10 and 11 after being told that they were primarily bowlers. The scores are preserved at Lord's. Compton made 45 not out (top score), Edrich was out for 17 and Waugh for 3. When Beaumont batted, Compton got two wickets, Edrich one and Waugh four.

Club beat school by 139 runs. Denis also got a fifty against Surbiton and a century going in first against the Midland Bank. He also went on the club's annual tour of the Channel Islands, where he made 51 out of 114 against Guernsey! In the whole of his life he never went back to the Channel Islands, a fact he contemplated with some incredulity.

Just before Whitsun in 1936 he was chosen to play for Middlesex Second XI against Kent at Folkestone. On the first morning Middlesex opened and lost four wickets to a 'strong chesty fellow' called Cole. The Middlesex opening batsman who survived this onslaught was none other than E.W. Swanton, already something of a veteran cricketer at almost thirty years of age.

His account of what happened next, to which I've already alluded and whose precise accuracy was so harshly criticised by his biographer, is worth reprinting even if he may have gilded the lily a little. Actually if I read his autobiography correctly it seems to me that Jim first played with Compton (and Edrich) in 1934 as a triallist for MCC against the Indian Gymkhana. Never mind, here is Swanton, on first recognising a genius:

At this point there entered a juvenile figure with an oddly relaxed way of walking, somewhat loose round the knees and with a swaying of the shoulders, inclined to let his bat trail after him rather than use it as a stick in the usual fashion. As he had to pass me I thought a word of encouragement would not be out of place, and murmured something about playing up and down the line of the ball and there being nothing to worry about. My new companion thanked me politely and very soon started pushing the ball round the field with every appearance of ease, and running up and down the pitch rather more quickly than his ponderous partner found comfortable. To within a run or two a hundred were put on for the fifth wicket, each of us just missing his fifty. Such was my introduction to Compton (D.).

On his return to Lord's Swanton told the Middlesex captain, R.W.V. Robins, that he had just been playing with the best young cricketer he had ever seen.

Meanwhile there was soccer. The Arsenal ground staff was much smaller than the one at Lord's. There were only ten boys at Highbury. All through the winter months he left home at seven and walked to Hendon station to catch the Underground in order to arrive at eight.

'A ground staff nipper of fourteen, sweeping the shilling terracing' was how he described himself. Whenever the players took the ball onto the pitch and practised shooting at Frank Moss, the goalkeeper, young Denis would contrive to find himself sweeping the terrace immediately behind the goal. Whenever a player kicked the ball over the bar or round the post Denis would fling down his broom and would retrieve the ball. Then, in the evening, he would boast about it to his mates.

'In my imagination,' he said, 'I was nearly a fully fledged Arsenal footballer.'

CHAPTER THREE

Looking at the young Denis walking out to bat alongside his gnarled old partner, Patsy Hendren, you see someone who looks like an athlete and also a hero. One of the things that still strikes me is that Hendren looks like an old pro whereas Compton looks like a fancy-hat amateur. He wasn't, of course, but that's how he looked: Raffles, Peter Wimsey, a member of I Zingari, the aristocratic wandering cricket club founded by a trio of Old Harrovians in the nineteenth century, but definitely not a working-class lad from the wrong side of the tracks.

The most striking point about Compton's appearance compared with the batsmen of a later era is that he is recognisable as a human being and an athlete. You can see his face and figure and they're both matinée-idol quality. That single picture explains at least an element of the Compton story. He was, in a way that endeared him to females everywhere, and strangely, antagonised very few males, 'drop-dead gorgeous'.

Hendren, by contrast, looks like an ageing prizefighter, thick-set and with a potato face which suggests his Irish ancestry and the nickname 'Patsy'. He had joined the Middlesex ground staff in 1905 and was a Middlesex and England legend as well as being a childhood hero of Denis. His final first-class average was over fifty and he approached that figure in Tests as well as being a consummate fielder who took 725 catches. When he and Denis went out to bat together he was already Mister Middlesex. It assisted Denis in his hero worship that 'Patsy' was a good enough footballer to have played for several top clubs including Brentford, Queen's Park Rangers and Manchester City.

'From the first time I clapped eyes on Denis,' Hendren told the *Evening News* years later, 'I knew the boy was going to be one of the game's greats. The fact that it was one of the bats that carried my name helped me warm to him! I autographed it for him and he continued to play with it for quite a few seasons. I was coming to the end of my career when he was just starting out on his, and what I liked about him was his willingness to listen to the old pros and learn from our experiences.'

It is sometimes suggested that Compton was lackadaisical in his approach to the game but the picture Hendren painted of the young tyro was one of huge enthusiasm, a love for the atmosphere of cricket as well as the actual play, and perhaps most surprisingly, a keenness to sit at the feet of his elders and learn from what they said. 'Here was a natural player,' said Hendren, 'who did not need coaching as much as just a few tweaks here and there.' Hendren made no suggestion of arrogance. Just a young man in a hurry.

It is said, perhaps apocryphally, that the only reason Denis was not selected for the 1936 tour of Australia was that he was too young and good-looking. His county captain, Walter Robins, admitted that in the mid-thirties everyone knew that the era of Hobbs and Hendren was past and that the future belonged to young men like Hutton, Compton, Edrich and Washbrook. In 1936, however, there was a view that bedding in one young player – Hutton – represented enough of a challenge. Compton was a risk too far.

G.O.B. 'Gubby' Allen was the captain of England on that tour and years later, too old and sick to appear on Denis's *This Is Your Life* programme, he recorded a handsome public apology. He told Norman Giller, the programme's chief researcher,

> I had the casting vote. It was my view that he was too inexperienced, and I was concerned that a bad tour could wreck his confidence and spoil one of the greatest prospects we had ever produced. In subsequent years as I watched Denis develop and got to know him as a good friend I realised that I had been wrong in my assessment. He had the sort of approach that meant he would have flourished Down Under. The bigger the occasion the better he played. Denis represented England seventy-eight times in his distinguished career. I am very sorry that it was not eighty-three Tests, and I want to offer my profound apologies to Denis.

In the 1970s the fifty-something-year-old Denis, rather portly and creaky by now, was in the Northampton dressing room and the county's opening batsman, Wayne Larkins, asked if he had ever tried on a protective helmet. He hadn't. Denis seldom even wore a cap. He wore his England one at first because he was so proud to have been awarded it, but usually played bare-headed, equally proud, no doubt, of that thick sleek black hair, Brylcreemed or not. Once at Whitsun in bright sun he dropped a skier in front of a packed crowd at Lord's. Robins, the captain, summoned him.

'Compton, you dropped that catch because you were unsighted by the sun. Where's your cap?'

'In the dressing room, sir.'

'Well go and get it and put it on.'

And in front of twenty thousand or so spectators a chastened Compton ran off the field and returned wearing his cap, the long peak doing the job for which it was designed – keeping the sun out of his eyes. On another occasion he was in the dressing room playing shove-halfpenny when a wicket fell unexpectedly and he was next in. Picking up his bat he charged off only to return seconds later, looking rueful. He had forgotten his box.

Naturally a man with such an indifference to protective clothing had never tried on a helmet, but he was curious all those years after his retirement and accepted Larkins's offer. He was astounded to find it such an encumbrance and could hardly move his head. Thinking this rather a good game, the Northants players persuaded Denis to try on the rest of the gear. When he was finally kitted out he felt as if he was a bomb disposal expert in Ulster, so trussed with pads and shields that he could hardly walk. The final straw was the bat. It was unbelievably heavy. 'We were always told,' he recalled, 'that we should treat the bat as if it were a wand. Well you couldn't treat that thing like a wand. It was more like a sledgehammer.'

Even in his seventies he was an immaculate dresser, in a conservative tradition, and in his playing days appearance was even more important. There were silk shirts from Simpsons in Piccadilly, two pairs of flannels, both beautifully creased, one for batting and one for fielding. Some players didn't bother too much with their batting trousers. Denis did. And the boots. At Lord's there were boot-boys to blanco them snowy white and, naturally, the Lord's staff were good at their job. Best of all, however, was Trent Bridge. There in those far-off days the staff used not only to whiten the uppers of the boots, they had little paintbrushes and would carefully paint the soles in black. Denis enjoyed that sort of detail and that sort of style. He was never a trainers and tracksuit figure.

Denis's debut came at the Middlesex v. Sussex match at Lord's during the Whit holiday weekend. Sussex batted first and made 185. Compton had a hand in two wickets, both of which happened to belong to the Parks brothers. He caught

J.H. off the bowling of Smith and always maintained, characteristically, that it was a perfectly ordinary catch. Gubby Allen, England fast bowler and later almost part of the furniture at Lord's cricket ground, always used to say that it was an absolute blinder, a skier which he took running backwards from his position at mid-off. It was Allen himself who helped him take his first wicket as a bowler by catching H.W. Next day *The Times*, no less, remarked that Compton D. was 'a likely looking left-handed recruit'.

Middlesex went in to bat that evening and came up against an apparently rejuvenated Maurice Tate. Tate was coming to the end of a distinguished career as a medium-paced seamer but was still an intimidating prospect. Four wickets went down cheaply and next morning Middlesex struggled. When Denis went in at 1.15 p.m. they were still 24 runs behind and Allen had a dislocated finger. He had originally been pencilled in higher up the order but was demoted further and further through the morning, ending up, perhaps in deference to his youth and inexperience, as last man in.

From the very first he brought a deceptive insouciance to the game and it was fitting that his debut for the Middlesex First XI was marked by the sort of improbable, against-the-odds last-wicket stand for which he was later to become renowned. The difference was that, as a newcomer, he was placed at No. 11 in the order. Despite Swanton's evidence about his batmanship, Robins was apparently taking no more risks than Alec Waugh had done at Beaumont.

Middlesex at that time included tough pros such as Hendren and his great friend J.W. Hearne but they were never as hard and pragmatic as the best northern sides such as Yorkshire and Lancashire. For the first three years of Denis's Middlesex career they came second to Yorkshire. That first year they only failed because of drawing their final two matches but when their captain R.W.V. Robins challenged the champions to a final match on neutral ground, the Yorkshire-men trounced Middlesex by an innings at the Oval. The great problem with this Middlesex side was, as Christopher Martin-Jenkins has shrewdly observed, that they put so much of their trust in amateurs. Robins himself, an accomplished wrist-spinning all-rounder, played regularly but other 'Gentlemen' such as G.O.B. Allen, J.L. Guise, I.A.R. Peebles, H.J. Enthoven and E.T. Killick did not turn out with anything like the same regularity. Amateur Allen and professional Hendren both had war-interrupted careers of almost exactly thirty years. Hendren played 928 innings, Allen just 210. Killick had an average of 35 yet only batted 71 times in thirteen seasons.

Amateurs in those days were distinguished by having their initials listed before their surnames while professionals such as Compton had their names printed in reverse order. This distinction between 'Gentlemen' and 'Players' was mirrored in many different ways. Denis and Patsy Hendren were not only Compton and Hendren, unlike Mr Robins and Mr Allen, they entered the field by different gates, stayed in different hotels and travelled in a different class of railway carriage. There were more professionals in cricket than before the Great War and they generally made a reasonable living though really big benefits were confined to star England players or possibly members of the Yorkshire team. As Martin-Jenkins has pointed out, the professionals of the 1930s were responsible for their own insurance, away-match hotel bills, travel costs and equipment. Even a national hero such as Harold Larwood only received £2000 from his benefit whereas the much less famous Yorkshire all-rounder Roy Kilner made double that amount. When Denis's less celebrated brother Les took his benefit much later, in 1954, he still only netted £6000 and that was reckoned a big success. The career on which Denis Compton was now launched earned one a living but not necessarily a handsome one.

As Compton came in Allen warned him that Tate came off much quicker than he might expect and that whatever else he did he must in any event play forward. Maurice Tate was a legendary fast bowler and the Compton house in Hendon was full of cartoons which always accentuated the enormous Tate boots which were reputed to make the ground tremble as he ran in to bowl. As the boy Compton came in Tate wished him the best of luck but added the proviso that his job was to get him out.

Later Denis told Norman Giller: 'You need to have cricket in your blood to understand how I felt making that first lonely walk out on to what I considered sacred ground. For non-cricketing people I can only describe it as the equivalent of making a solo entrance on to a great stage such as the Palladium or Covent Garden.'

Denis said 'Yes, sir' to Allen, said nothing to Tate, took guard, received a perfect delivery which pitched on off stump. In some confusion he played back and failed to connect. The ball missed middle stump by a whisker and Allen 'expressed himself pretty forcibly'.

Denis apologised and said he'd do better in a moment. To the next ball he again played back and again missed. Then, however, he came to his senses and began to play forward. The third ball was a Tate special which swung in the air like a boomerang. Denis played a classic coaching manual forward defensive smothering it into submission. He later said that was the most satisfying moment he had experienced. He turned the next ball off his legs for a single, and he was off. The score mounted. They got the 24. They even scored 12 more. Then Jim Parks appealed for an lbw against Denis. The umpire's finger went up at once, though in Gubby Allen's opinion it was definitely not out.

Allen, being Allen, remonstrated fiercely. The umpire apologised profusely, agreed that Denis was not out but explained that he was dying for a pee and could contain himself no longer. If he hadn't closed the innings his bladder would have burst. When Denis told me the story in 1993 he identified the official as Bill Bestwick; earlier in his auto-biographical *End of an Innings* he wrote that it was Bill Reeves. His memory *was* often fallible and the incident took place many years before he recalled it to me. Sometimes it is possible to verify such matters from contemporary records; sometimes not. Sometimes the story of Denis Compton's life seems to have two versions: the world according to Denis and the world according to everyone else!

The lead that day, said the man from *The Times*, was 'hard earned and not gained if it had not been for young Compton, one of the most promising of young players'.

Unfortunately rain wiped out play on the final day and ruined the match. Nevertheless the promise was unmistakable. He had been noticed and approved, not only by 'Plum' Warner, Walter Robins and Gubby Allen but by the national press and therefore, by extension, the cricketing public.

The next match was against Nottinghamshire, whose fast bowlers were Larwood and Voce, the heroes (or in some eyes villains) of Douglas Jardine's victorious 'Bodyline' tour of 1932–33. Larwood was at the time the most terrifying fast bowler in the world and, as we've seen, Denis and his colleagues wore minimal protective clothing. Your main pro-tection in those days was the bat.

In a low-scoring game Denis, now batting at No. 8, made 26 and 14. The man from *The Times* was even more impressed than he had been by the last-wicket stand against Maurice Tate. Compton D., he opined, 'was mainly responsible for showing that Larwood was not unplayable'.

It may have been in this match, or it may have been the following, in which he made his first big score (87), that an entirely typical conversation took place between him and his captain Walter Robins who was batting at the other end. Denis had hit the quick bowler (either Larwood or Clark of Northamptonshire) for two consecutive fours, both of them off drives.

Fast bowlers do not like being driven for four, especially twice in succession by a teenager playing in only his second first-class match.

The captain came down the wicket and had a word with the young tyro.

'You know what to look out for now, don't you?' (This is Jim Swanton's version, corroborated by Denis.)

'No, skipper.'

'Well he'll bounce one at you.'

'If he does, I shall hook him.'

And he did. The next ball was an authentic bumper and Denis swivelled and swung and sent it straight into the Mound Stand. The man from *The Times* was ecstatic. His hooking of the fast bowler, he said, 'earned for him the highest praise'. Larwood's reaction is not recorded.

From here he went from strength to strength.

Three weeks after his first appearance for the county Denis scored his maiden century. This was in the return match against Northants. At the beginning of the final day Middlesex were just three runs ahead with five first-innings wickets still standing. As Jim Swanton says, 'The plain need was for some more runs with all possible speed.' Almost immediately three wickets went down, leaving Denis with Sims and then Ian Peebles, one of the game's natural No. 11s – in twenty years of batting for Middlesex he averaged a glorious 8.97 runs per innings.

In later years everyone realised that this sort of impossible circumstance brought out the best in him, but at the time this back-to-the-wall pugnaciousness had not yet been appreciated. *Wisden* sums up the achievement thus: 'By perfect timing

Compton drove, pulled and cut with remarkable power, and took out his bat, with fourteen 4s as his best strokes, in one and three-quarter hours. He and Sims put on 76 for the ninth wicket and there followed a remarkable last partnership of 74 with Peebles, who by sound defence stayed while Compton scored his last 60 runs.'

Unfortunately this grand last stand did not quite buy a famous victory. A thunderstorm stopped play when Northants had lost eight wickets.

Everyone who saw this innings was impressed by the combination of judgement and stroke-play, and it was characteristic of Compton throughout his career that he nearly always scored at speed. This was particularly necessary because England and more especially Middlesex were never strong bowling sides and they therefore needed more time than most to bowl out their opponents. Speedy scoring was also invaluable when your partner was a shaky No. 10 or 11. Time was of the essence.

In order to sustain so many effective lower-order partnerships Denis must have been a very effective farmer of bowling. I find this surprising because of his universally acknowledged limitations in running between the wickets. His colleague John Warr had a famous quip about his first call being an opening bid, the second a negotiation and the third being redundant because the wicket has by then gone down, but if he were really so dreadful would he have been able to protect so many rabbits so effectively?

My own guess is that in playing with inferior batsmen he took on a confidence and assertiveness that he lacked when alongside his peers like Edrich and Hutton. But that is only a guess. Denis himself always seemed unsure but felt that he was a better runner than the myth suggests. Although he was indeed involved in some spectacular run-outs and had to be held responsible for many of them, accomplished players such as Tom Graveney told me that they never had a problem running between the wickets with Denis.

There is some statistical evidence to support this claim. In volume 4 issue 5 of the esoteric but authoritative magazine *Cricket Lore* (which sadly went out of business in 2005) there was an article by Keith Sandford that subjected Compton's partnerships with Len Hutton to a rigorous statistical analysis. Sandford had already done this with the West Indians Rohan Kanhai and Gary Sobers. The Caribbean myth was that these two great players did not make runs together but Sandford was able to demonstrate, to universal amazement, that in fact the two averaged more than fifty in their partnerships together.

He did something similar with Hutton and Compton. The popular belief about Hutton and Compton is similar and it is perfectly true that considering the number of Tests they played together for England they shared in remarkably few stands. However this was not because they failed to gel but because they were seldom at the crease together. Hutton himself was quick to acknowledge this, writing, in 1956, 'I have been associated with him in Test cricket more than any other player. Yet we have figured in so few long partnerships that I can count them on the fingers of one hand. I can offer no satisfactory explanation for this, except that his best years, 1946–1949, did not coincide with mine.'

Compton's recollection and verdict are similar but also flawed. He wrote in his memoir *End of an Innings* that he and Hutton put on 228 once against the West Indies when the total was actually 248. He continued, 'It was one of only two stands: that one in 1939 and the stand of 93 at Nottingham in 1948. It sounds difficult to believe, but if you check the records you'll find it's true.'

Actually if you check the records it's not true at all. For a start the 1948 stand in Nottingham was worth 111 runs not 93 as Denis wrote. No wonder it was so often maintained that statistics were unimportant in Compton's career. In fact both men began their England careers in the same year. Hutton played 79 times for England; Compton 78. Hutton always opened and Compton usually came in at four. In three Test series however they never batted together at all and in several others only a few times. However, and it is a big however, in their twenty-nine stands they added a total of 1620 runs, averaging 62.30. As Sandford demonstrates the two men scored more than 50 together in more than 40 per cent of their partnerships and in all those partnerships there was only one run-out. And, no, it wasn't Denis who was the culprit, it was Hutton who left our hero stranded in mid-wicket on 44.

Hutton and Compton shared six stands of more than a hundred and another six of more than fifty. Uncertain running between the wickets is a recurring theme in any study of the Compton career. If, however, his approach to the game was really as cavalier or even shambolic as some suggested he surely could not have achieved the success he did.

The second point deriving from his debut appearances, and seldom made, is that Denis's enthusiasm was infectious. It wasn't only the spectators who were excited by his example, it was also his team-mates. Peebles played above himself in that Northamptonshire match because Denis was at the other end setting an example. For the best part of two decades other tail-enders responded in kind.

That was his only century that year, but there were plenty of other high scores and he ended the season with over a thousand runs and his county cap. He was second to Hendren in the Middlesex averages and had played some remarkable innings and participated in some splendid stands, not least with another Arsenal footballer, Hulme. These two put on 132 in under two hours against Gloucestershire at Lord's. He also had a spectacular match against Kent, at Maidstone, where he made 87 and 96.

Already, by the end of this first season in the County Championship, he was being judged by high standards. Plum Warner said that he was 'the best young batsman who has come out since Walter Hammond was a boy'.

There was much praise in similar vein. Here, for instance, is *The Times*, on the 87 at Maidstone:

'Compton,' wrote their man, 'went on to play cricket which must have been of profound interest to every knowledgeable spectator on the ground. He is an astonishingly mature cricketer for his age, not only in defence but in the even more important matter of picking out the ball to hit and hitting it in the right way. He has style, he has discretion, and he has the strokes.'

The boy was eighteen. The pulse races.

A little later, however, the *Times* correspondent was musing on a typically buoyant 80 against Sussex at Hove. Denis hit it in an hour and a half and made his runs faster than Hendren. The *Times* man was impressed. Perhaps, already, that went without saying and yet, for the first time, there was a sense of 'if' and 'but'. The criticisms were, in essence, the sort of criticism that Denis had to endure throughout his sporting life – and beyond. Too many risks, too much unorthodoxy, lack of graft and concentration, bit of a Flash Harry. It was rather the sort of thing that a certain sort of critic would many years later say about Ian Botham.

'Compton had a large number of balls which could be hit,' wrote *The Times*, 'and he proceeded to hit them. Not that he is without impetuosity. Too often he prefers, violently and untidily to hit across the flight of the ball, than to drive up and down the line of it.'

There you have it. Gifted? Of course, but the chap is impetuous and he hits across the line of the ball. That sneaky misgiving often surfaced during his career, though in the main the mandarins were charitable. As one said after the Maidstone match when he twice missed hundreds quite narrowly, 'This match has shown him such a good batsman that figures are a mere irrelevance.'

It is bizarre to read about that year of his first-class debut in the contemporary press. There were advertisements still for 'Between maids, Generals and Laundrymaids' and for chauffeurs ('Rolls certificate and private service essential'). *The Times* carried reports on innumerable cricket matches far removed from the truly first-class. There was on 9 July a report as long as that paper would now give to a mid-table championship game, on the Welsh Guards v. the Eton Ramblers.

It was the end of an era and across it gambolled the young Compton like a spring lamb.

CHAPTER FOUR

The following autumn the heady success of that debut summer was emulated on the other side of London at Arsenal. This was one of the world's great clubs enjoying arguably its greatest hour. Under the inspired management of Herbert Chapman they swept all before them.

In fact the Arsenal's greatness was relatively recent. When they were originally founded in 1886 they were the works team for Woolwich Armaments and played on Plumstead Common under the prosaic name of Dial Square. Their first kit and even ball was supplied by Nottingham Forest, two of whose players had recently moved to Woolwich and formed the nucleus of the original team.

After a brief foray into the old First Division, the Woolwich Arsenal, as it was now called, fell back into the Second Division and struggled. Part of the problem was its relative remoteness and inaccessibility. By the outbreak of the Great War the club realised it had to move to survive. A plan to merge with Fulham fell through but they found a base at Highbury not far from Gillespie Road Underground station on the Piccadilly Line. In 1915 they dropped 'Woolwich' from their name and moved north despite objections from Tottenham Hotspur, the established north London club. This set the tone for the continuing enmity between the Spurs and the Gunners which was accentuated further when, in 1919, the First Division was expanded to 22 clubs. Arsenal were included; Tottenham weren't.

During Denis's early childhood Arsenal were an average mid-table First Division side but this changed when Herbert Chapman was signed at a then unheard-of salary of £2000 a year. He came from Huddersfield Town, which under him became the most successful team of the times. In 1926 Chapman guided Arsenal to second place in the First Division, followed by a first-ever Cup Final the following year when they lost 1–0 to Cardiff City.

Chapman was a visionary. He built a new and grandiose Highbury Stadium with marble halls, stands now considered Art Deco masterpieces, under-soil heating for the pitch, floodlights and a youth training scheme, which was how Denis managed to follow his brother Leslie to the club immediately after leaving school. Chapman even managed to get the old Gillespie Road Tube station renamed Arsenal, the only club to have an eponymous train station. He and the club were a phenomenon.

In 1930 the Arsenal beat Huddersfield Town to win the FA Cup. The following year they became the first London club to win the First Division Championship; and in 1932 they almost won Cup and League but were runners-up in both, losing, just, 2–1 to Newcastle in the Cup. They won the League for three years in succession – 1933, 1934 and 1935 – though Chapman, the man who created this record-breaking juggernaut, didn't live to see it all. He caught a cold in the January of 1934 and died as a result. He was just fifty-five and had signed Denis a year earlier.

The names of the team when Denis first joined were a football hall of fame. There was Frank Moss in goal, the incomparable little Scot Alex James, Denis's Middlesex cricketing partner Joe Hulme, and Cliff Bastin, Jimmy

Dunne, Eddie Hapgood, George Male and David Jack. These were the great names of the day – the sort of men whose pictures appeared on cigarette cards and who were idolised by little boys the length of the land.

Now, still only eighteen, Denis had played first-class cricket and been a success. In a man's game he had played a man's part. As a footballer he was just as talented. 'A natural,' said Laurie Scott, his colleague, looking back on the young left-winger from retirement in the lee of the Pennines. On a visit to Highbury in 1993 I met a former fan who remembered watching the young Denis. I asked what he had been like as a footballer and he thought for a moment and then said simply, 'He was good . . . good.' That sounds faint praise, but there was something in the way he said it which made you realise that he didn't just mean good, average, he meant good, special.

Chapman and his successors George Allison and Tom Whittaker all obviously recognised that precocious talent and, in the wake of his first-class cricket baptism, they must have acknowledged that the lad not only had talent but character and maturity as well.

That September, only days after the end of the cricket season, the Arsenal played a friendly match against Glasgow Rangers. It was an annual pipe-opener played alternately at Highbury or Hampden Park. Denis was picked on the left wing and he played well. So well in fact that the next day he was summoned to the manager's office.

'Compton, you played very well against the Glasgow Rangers and they were impressed.'

They were evidently so impressed that they wanted to buy him. Denis later thought the offer was £2000, a substantial transfer fee in those days, especially for one so young. And Rangers, in their way, were as great a club as Arsenal.

George Allison was scrupulous in the way he presented the facts. Rangers had made an offer and therefore he was honour-bound to tell Denis all about it. It was a flattering proposal and he was in no doubt that Denis would enjoy playing for them, that they would look after him well, and that he would prosper. On the other hand the Arsenal had taken Denis on as a lad and watched him grow up. As far as Allison was concerned Denis was part of the family, and he and the club would be sorry to see him go. Nevertheless the offer was enticing and it was up to Denis to decide.

He had no hesitation. Ever since he arrived he had regarded Highbury as a second home, just as the other players did. On the one hand men considered that playing for the club was an honour, on the other they felt that they were looked after in a way that transcended a merely professional or commercial arrangement. Denis always knew that if ever he was in trouble he could go – indeed was expected to go – to the manager or the board. If they could help, they would.

Besides, he was a homebody. He had lived all his life in north London and, at this early stage in his life, he knew no other world. Also, throughout his cricketing and footballing life he had had the comforting presence of his big brother Leslie to keep him company. He wouldn't know anyone in Glasgow. He didn't fancy the idea of living in digs in a foreign city miles from family and friends. So he said no.

He wrote later:

Through my association with Arsenal which began in the autumn of 1933 I came to comprehend fully why they were so successful year after year in the fierce competition of English League and Cup football.

Honestly, I can say that in all the time I played for Arsenal I never heard a player declare that he wanted to leave the club. That is a fine testimony to any body of employers. Although they had been in the reserves and knew they would benefit both financially and from a prestige point of view by moving to another team, even some of the leading players in the land were reluctant to go. My brother provides an excellent example but there have been many others.

Young players of considerable promise, with all the ambition of youth to spur them on, have also preferred to remain at Highbury in the hope of attaining first-team status rather than move to clubs where a place in the League side would have been almost certain.

I am sure this loyalty to Arsenal has been created by the care taken by the club officials to see that every man on the staff is made as happy as possible.

The players at Highbury understand that if they need help or are in difficulties they can, and are expected to go to the manager or the board. If the matter can be put right it will be.

Walking into Highbury was, to me and to the majority of players, like walking into a second home. Nothing there is too much for the player's well-being. In the dressing-room every-where is spotless and everything is done on the most up-to-date and generous scale. Each man has his own locker. Two men are employed to keep the boots in first-class condition and as much attention is paid to making the training equipment clean, dry and free from holes as is paid to the playing kit.

Arsenal even go to the extent of providing centrally heated floors so that the player's feet will not become cold while he changes.

Magnificent bathrooms and the most modern electrical and sun-ray appliances contribute to a man's knowledge that the club has spared nothing to send him out to play at his fittest and happiest.

Small wonder, then, that the thought which runs through the mind of every Arsenal player is: 'I am playing for Arsenal. Therefore, I must do everything I can to keep them on top of the football world. Victory is expected of us and we simply must win. It will be no fault of mine, anyway, if we don't.

In an era of massive salaries and transfer fees when the power and status of star players eclipses those of the most gifted footballers of the 1930s and '40s such sentiments seem almost servile. In comparison with these mercenary and egalitarian times the relationships between men like Compton and their employers appear paternalistic if not quite feudal. Imagine telling someone like David Beckham that he is lucky to have his own locker! Yet such sentiments accurately reflect the character of those times. Players were thankful to be in regular employment and they were grateful for modern amenities and sympathetic bosses. To a modern generation such attitudes will seem absurd, simple and pathetically deferential but that was what sporting life was like then. Virtually unrecognisable.

Compton's loyalty in turning down the blandishments of Glasgow Rangers was rewarded at once, for he was named to play in Arsenal's next home game. 'Arsenal know their business best,' wrote one not untypical commentator, 'but it seems rather a bold policy.' The headline emphasised the doubt: 'Bold Arsenal Policy: D. Compton faces Derby County'.

The game was played on 26 September 1936 in front of a crowd of 65,000 and ended in a 2–2 draw. Denis was a success. 'Cool as a veteran,' said one headline. In his 'Daily Sportlight' in the *Express*, Trevor Wignall rather eloquently summed up the majority view:

> Because he was taking part in his first league match, because his nervous system was not upset by the roars and the presence of nearly 70,000 people, because he is only 18 years of age, and because he scored the first of the four goals, Dennis [sic] Compton must be judged the success of the afternoon.
>
> He fitted into the Arsenal scheme with such ease that he must be called a typical Arsenal man, and I know that Bastin is willing to admit that he has never received better short passes. Compton's sense of position, his trapping of the ball, and his

disregard for mere showiness were all excellent . . . Compton, cool and collected as a veteran, slapped the ball into the net. Throughout the boy was top class and those who declare that he will play both football and cricket for England may not be far wrong. The Arsenal unquestionably took a chance in playing him in such an important game, but Compton came through with colours flying so high that, if George Allison wishes it, he has his outside-left position adequately filled for the rest of the season.

It is difficult to think how anyone could have been more ecstatic, and these sentiments were echoed by almost everyone. One observer, however, detected a flaw. The 'Special Correspondent' of the *Sunday Times* acknowledged that the boy done well, but he went on to say: 'Of course, he still has quite a lot to learn. His chief fault is trying to do too much with the ball instead of getting rid of it to better purpose.'

More than half a century later Denis would give a rueful laugh and look a shade embarrassed. He recognised the truth of this criticism and that it was largely justified throughout his career. 'I loved to play with the ball.' He made sinuous sliding movements with his hands suggesting a weaving run round opposing players like a downhill skier performing the perfect slalom. 'I loved to beat my man.'

Most people, however, were simply dazzled by the brilliance and maturity of that first performance. And the fault – if fault it was – lay not in selfishness, lack of team spirit or even a desire to show off, but in simple exuberance and *joie de vivre*. He wanted to make the ball do magic things and he liked nothing better than literally to run rings round other people. Not for the applause, but simply for its own sake. In doing so he might not always have played the best team game but, as with his joyous batting at cricket, he communicated an unmistakable and infectious sense of fun.

The next game, a week later, was against Manchester United at Old Trafford. Arsenal played like drains and lost 2–0. The exception was Denis, who played beautifully. That distinguished correspondent Henry Rose, later to die in the Munich air crash with the young stars of Manchester United, wrote of him: 'One spot of sunshine in the Arsenal gloom. They have a future England player in Compton. He is a grand outside-left with plenty of tricks. He outshone stars like Bastin and Drake.'

This was no mean feat, for Bastin and Drake were both full internationals at the peak of their careers.

The team did not perform well in their next match, which was at home to Sheffield Wednesday in front of what by the standards of the day was a relatively small Highbury crowd of 47,000. Once again, however, Denis stood out. He was variously 'a find' and 'one of very few players to hold the ball and use it intelligently'. Nibloe, the opposing full-back, by all accounts a somewhat pedestrian player no longer in the full flush of youth, had a wretched afternoon. Denis completely mesmerised him with his 'deft feet', and half the time poor Nibloe didn't seem to have any idea where Denis was going.

The downside of this brilliance, however, was that Denis was showing alarming signs of holding on to the ball too long. This time more than one commentator remarked on it. 'Tries to do too much with the ball,' said one. 'Wasted time by beating men when a direct centre would have been more to the purpose.'

After these poor matches the manager decided on a drastic measure. He dropped Cliff Bastin and brought back the old legend Alex James, Denis's hero, for the game against Charlton Athletic at the Valley. This is a game which Denis remembered with radiant affection. In the bus on the way to the match he asked his idol what he was to do that afternoon. He addressed him respectfully as 'Mr James' and 'sir', and was in such awe that he would have done anything the great man wanted.

James's advice was short and to the point. 'Just watch me,' he said. 'When you see I have the ball just run.'

And he did. Every time James got the ball in midfield Denis would belt hell for leather up the left wing and seconds later James's beautifully timed and directed pass would send the ball straight to his toes as if magnetised. It was magic, and Denis regarded the game in retrospect as one of the finest he played. It was watched moreover by a staggering 77,000 people, the gate swollen by those who had come to celebrate Alex James's return. Arsenal won 2–0.

Not everyone, however, saw it Denis's way. Indeed none other than Trevor Wignall, who had so eulogised him in his 'Daily Sportlight' column a few weeks earlier, now turned and excoriated him. 'Young Compton,' he wrote, in a somewhat patronising tone, 'must have made many think, as he made me, that his future will be better assured if he is immediately taken from the first team and given another run with the reserves. He has already developed the beginnings of a habit of fiddling about, his shooting at goal has practically gone to pieces, and he is cultivating tricks and customs that are not pleasant to see in one so youthful.'

Denis was a romantic about his football, and playing for Arsenal was thrilling, especially for an eighteen-year-old from a background like his. He and his team-mates might not have been paid the prodigious wages that modern stars attract, but they felt pampered and cosseted, which by the standards of the day they were. Nevertheless the regime was strict. There was no smoking in the dressing room, and no visitors. Once the players actually began to change, even those players not in the first team had to leave. Apart from the eleven the only others allowed to stay were the manager, the trainer and the masseur.

Denis was always superstitious, and his preparations for football were as meticulous as they were for cricket. Everything had to be done just so, in exactly the same way each time. He always liked to have a final rub-down from the masseur before strapping his ankles up with cotton wool, binding on any necessary bandages and then, when kitted out, taking a football into the bathroom and kicking it several times against a hot pipe. This, he believed, helped to give him a feel for the ball.

Back in the dressing room he would have eucalyptus oil rubbed in by the trainer as a precaution against cold, and he would take a sniff of 'inhalant' – probably Vick – to clear his head. The manager, Chapman, Allison or later Whittaker, would make his way round the team giving each individual a final word of encouragement and advice about the particular attributes and deficiencies of the opposition. Then the referee would enter and tell them they were due on the field. Denis never minded where he ran in the order, but his brother Leslie, who was even more superstitious than he was, always insisted on running out last of all unless he was captain for the day, in which case he led them out, ball in hand. Remarkably, the Compton brothers not only played cricket together in the same Middlesex team but also represented the Arsenal together in the same XI.

These little rituals of preparation were almost as much a part of the experience as the game itself. Nothing, however, could match the sky-splitting roar of the huge crowds as the teams ran out. From the very beginning Denis thrived on this. He loved to hear the bullfight surge of sound as he wrong-footed an opponent or shot for goal. He was nervous, fidgety even, and the big occasion made the adrenalin surge. But he never suffered stage fright. Those first few games demonstrated that the lad not only had talent in buckets but also an enviable sangfroid.

CHAPTER FIVE

One of the most remarkable and beautiful of all cricket books is a volume of essays by T.C.F. Prittie called *Mainly Middlesex*, first published in 1947. What makes it unique is not just the elegiac quality of the prose but the fact that it was all written while he was a prisoner of war in Germany. In his foreword Sir Pelham Warner wrote, 'From whatever dungeon he was occupying beyond the Rhine at the time, he managed to send an article to the *Cricketer* on the game as played within the severely limited boundaries of a thirty-foot medieval moat. This showed that the old spirit lived and it delighted me. I have learned since that the German cipher experts lost some sleep by assuming that it was all an elaborate code.'

'No man,' wrote Prittie 'is Compton's superior in adversity. No man is fuller of latent antagonism, of an oppositionism that is almost Irish.'

Prittie, the cricket correspondent of the *Manchester Guardian*, was – despite this Mancunian affiliation – a Middlesex man through and through. He was entranced by the young Denis, but the man he really worshipped was Patsy Hendren. On his very first visit to Lord's, as a schoolboy, he had watched Hendren score a dashing and masterful century and was then 'by some higher Providence' allowed into the professionals' dressing room, where he and his brother met their hero. Not even Hendren, famous for his uncondescending grace with schoolboys, could put the two at their ease, and in the taxi home they 'remembered the supreme failure of our momentous interview. We had not even asked Hendren for his autograph.'

Hendren, along with Hearne, who was to him as Edrich to Compton, effectively carried the Middlesex batting between the wars, and he was in many ways Compton's mentor and model. 1937, his last full season in first-class cricket, was Denis's first. You get a sense of this transition from that famous photograph of the two of them going out to bat. Hendren ('no oil painting' in Denis's words) a gnarled old veteran, Denis a lissom youth. They are Falstaff and young Hal. Hendren, after all, was old enough at forty-eight to be Denis's father.

'Crusoe' Robertson-Glasgow wrote a typically perceptive, elegant and entertaining essay about 'Patsy', whose real name was Elias. He was known as Patsy for the simple reason that he was Irish. Without actually saying so, Robertson-Glasgow gives an indication of arguably the most important Hendren characteristic, which was only marginally to do with cricket. Or to put it another way, it was to do with an approach to life as a whole, of which cricket was an integral part.

I think that he most enjoyed doing something outrageous when the scene was all majesty and strain. Perhaps it was the crisis of some Test match. He saw the serious doctors bending anxiously over the patient. He saw rows of faces in the crowd like flock upon flock of sheep, absorbing the wonted pabulum, relieved by some incredible ass in a horned handkerchief, who was plainly doomed to bore whole families for weeks with bleating stories of the wonderful. He saw the pavilion members, righteously conscious of the privileged accommodation, some affecting knowledge, others sobriety; next to them, the gentlemen of the Press, poising the knowing pencil, forging a paragraph from a no-ball, making a sermon of a cut. And his demon whispered to him: 'Hendren, for heaven's sake do something funny.' And he'd do it.

This sounds familiar.

'He taught me to relax,' said the old Compton. 'I was very young and although I was that way inclined I needed someone to reassure me and make me less tense. Patsy gave the impression he was always joking. Batting with him was a giggle a minute. He was always roaring with laughter. He used to come down the wicket and say "Enjoy yourself." And, above all, "Don't let those bloody bowlers think you're worried."'

This sort of message was music to the Compton ears.

'When he stopped playing for Middlesex,' wrote Robinson-Glasgow, 'cricket must have missed its imp, its laughing familiar, as Lord's missed its hero.'

He could just as well have been writing about Denis. Taking over the Hendren mantle involved more than just being the best batsman in the Middlesex team, it also meant being the embodiment of cheeky insouciance. Not just making loads of runs, but also becoming 'the laughing familiar' of Lord's. Denis had the temperament and the ability to do both.

The two men not only shared the same cricketing gifts and the same attitude to life, they were also, out of season, football outside-lefts. Hendren was a footballer, before Denis's time. Denis never saw him play. Hendren's cricketing swansong and Denis's full-time debut were equally remarkable. The forty-eight-year-old veteran ended up with a spate of centuries and the young tyro had three hundreds, an aggregate of almost 2000. He also, more significantly, made his debut for England in the final Test against New Zealand, and in doing so became, at 19 years and 84 days, the youngest ever English Test cricketer. This record was beaten by Brian Close who, after the war, was first selected when still only eighteen.

It is interesting and depressing to compare this precocious Test debut with the English selection policy of more recent years. What would have happened to a talent like Compton's if it had emerged in the 1980s or '90s? Would it have been stifled at birth with year after year of Second XI cricket? Would he have been dismissed by the selectors as 'only a one-day player'? Such hypothetical questions are unanswerable, though I have my suspicions . . . Yet at the same time he does seem, gazing back at the Thirties, to have been very much a child of those times.

As so often he got off to a relatively slow start in the 1937 season, but despite this he was chosen to play for the South against the North at the end of May. This was a Test trial as well as being part of the 150th anniversary celebrations of MCC. Denis made 70 and 14 not out, batting almost as well, according to eyewitnesses, as Walter Hammond, who made 80 in the first innings and a not-out century in the second. This was high praise, for Hammond was in his prime, which meant, in Robertson-Glasgow's opinion, that his hitting, 'mostly straight and through the covers, was of a combined power and grace that I have never seen in any other man'.

Denis was later, of course, to play under Hammond's captaincy – and not much enjoy the experience. Despite Hammond's all-round abilities as a player there was a caution in his temperament which did not suit Denis. He was also one of those rare people who tried to interfere with his natural game.

However it was another performance in this trial which signalled the beginning of a new era. This was the 102 which a young Pudsey player named Len Hutton made for the North.

For the next twenty years Hutton's name was bracketed with Compton's. In Middlesex terms it was to be Compton and Edrich but, fine cricketer though he was, Edrich was widely acknowledged to be a notch or two below Compton; Hutton, though a very different style of player, was generally agreed to be Denis's peer. As Cyril Washbrook, Hutton's opening partner, once remarked, 'Len and I both had a fairly serious outlook on the game and we played it in a sound way. We didn't play shots like Denis did, those sort of shots weren't in our habit at all.'

'Denis plays every stroke in the textbook,' wrote Hutton, in his autobiography. 'Many too which are *not* there – and makes the sweep shot consistently better than anyone I know. Many times I have seen him sweep the ball clean off his middle stump, and I just cannot remember a time when he has failed to connect. Even so, I confess that, when I have been batting with him, he has given me a queasy stomach every time he has made the stroke.'

Those two verdicts speak volumes. Washbrook and Hutton were northerners and they had the serious, some would say dour, approach characteristic of men from that part of England. Denis was not like that, either as a cricketer or as a person.

One story Denis liked to tell sums up this difference better than any other. Years later, in 1951, Denis, as vice-captain, was in charge of the MCC team on their return journey from Australia. In Honolulu he got a telegram from the actor Nigel Bruce, best known as a brilliant, silly-ass Watson, to Basil Rathbone's Sherlock Holmes.

Bruce had learned that Denis and his men were heading his way and his cable was an invitation to make a slight diversion and play a game of cricket against the Hollywood Cricket Club. It would only be a light-hearted occasion, taking up an afternoon. Afterwards Bruce and his fellow expatriate thespians promised the team a day and a half of the best entertainment Tinseltown could offer.

Denis, as one can imagine, was extremely keen to accept. Once in London he had met Danny Kaye who had told him to ring up if ever he was in the States. Denis was genuinely thrilled. Terrific party; lovely ladies. There was even the prospect of locking swords with his old friend from Nursery days at Lord's, C. Aubrey Smith. Smith was a pillar of Californian cricket.

However, when Denis put this tantalising proposition to his colleagues, he found to his horror that the majority were not in favour. The ones who most resisted the idea were Hutton and Washbrook. They were quite untempted by such frivolity. They had been away from home quite long enough, and they just wanted to get back as fast as possible.

Denis was aghast, and to the end of his life regretted the lost opportunity. In his autobiography he wrote that he was 'most disappointed and very puzzled by their decision'. Even in his seventies he was still disappointed and still puzzled. It was simply not in his nature to turn down an invitation to have fun.

The episode epitomises the Hutton and the Compton approaches to life. This difference swiftly communicated itself to cricket lovers throughout the country. There has always been an intense rivalry between north and south, and indeed an almost greater one between Yorkshire and the rest. During their careers Hutton and Compton seemed to exemplify everything about the two parts of England. I was a small boy during this rivalry's second half and I remember that at prep school we used to take sides in much the same way as we did for the Oxford and Cambridge boat race. You were either for Hutton or for Compton. And your autographed cricket bat – Denis's was a Slazenger, Hutton's a Gradidge – was a symbol of your allegiance. 'Are you Compton or Hutton?' was the burning question of the day.

The great Yorkshire fast bowler Freddie Trueman always felt that the enmity with Middlesex was out of hand. Men like Wardle and Appleyard on the Yorkshire side and Walter Robbins and Denis were in danger of getting carried away by the rivalry.

'It was a disgraceful relationship,' Trueman told me later. 'And it went right back to the days of Plum Warner and Lord Hawke.' Fred, who entered international cricket as a tyro when Denis was a veteran, did what he could to patch things up and forged good relationships with several of the Middlesex side, notably Peter Parfitt who continued to be a close friend well into retirement. Other peacemakers included Brian Close, Ray Illingworth and Frank Lowson from the North and John Murray and Freddie Titmus from the South.

Trueman wrote in his memoirs:

The senior pros were crafty so-and-sos. They had scores to settle with certain opposing players and, being naïve, it took me a while before I realized that having made the bullets, they then used me to fire them. For example there was a lot of rivalry and bitterness between Yorkshire and Middlesex which dated back to the pre-war years. When I came on the scene, against certain Middlesex batsmen I was encouraged to 'let one fly' or 'shave his ears'. The senior pros of both clubs were jealous as hell of each other, but it didn't take me long to realize I was being used. When I did, I simply ignored the overtures of my seniors in the Yorkshire team to 'rattle' so-and-so in the Middlesex team. When I cottoned on to what was happening I told them to do their own dirty work and started to stay out of everyone's way and tried to avoid trouble.

Because of this mutual Yorkshire–Middlesex hostility it was often assumed that Hutton and Compton were enemies, but this was emphatically not the case. Len never became the sort of boon companion that men like Keith Miller or Colin

Ingleby-Mackenzie were, but he and Denis liked and admired each other and were adult enough to appreciate that despite their differences they shared a genius for the game which lifted them above even the most gifted of their fellow players. Latterly Len moved to Kingston in Surrey and became a sort of honorary southerner. Until he died in 1990 he and Denis used to talk at least once a week on the phone. The usual subject of conversation was the state of contemporary cricket. Both he and Denis shared a passion for the game which never deserted them. To be sure they reminisced and exchanged memories, but they were just as likely to be discussing the deficiencies of Graeme Hick against really fast bowling as memories of the Oval in 1938. Interestingly both men later became journalists – Len with the *London Evening News* and later the *Observer*, Compton with the *Sunday Express*. They also sent sons to fee-paying schools and it was ironic that in the early years of the twenty-first century Denis's grandson Nick was playing for Middlesex under the captaincy of Len's grandson Ben. Ben was educated at Radley; Nick at Harrow. A long way from the state schools in Hendon and Pudsey which were the alma maters of their legendary grandfathers.

Hutton obviously impressed the selectors more than Denis, because he was picked for the first Test against New Zealand and Denis wasn't. He only made one run in the two innings of that game but scored a century in the second Test and never looked back, becoming a permanent fixture until his eventual retirement a year before Denis. Denis had to wait until the third and final Test at the Oval, after which he too became an indispensable part of the England side.

The emergence of Hutton and Compton as Test players was arguably the most significant cricket event of 1937, though in a way it was just as important for Denis that he was able finally to consolidate his place in a Middlesex team which came tantalisingly close to winning the championship.

In the early weeks of the season he did not really excel. However, against Gloucestershire at Lord's he made the first really big score of his life. It was also, characteristically, made at speed: 177 runs out of 279 coming in three hours. He was particularly severe on Goddard's off-spin and the amiable medium pace of an amateur named Tyler who, as Peter West remarks, 'had surprisingly acquired five wickets for 37 before Denis ran amok'. Tyler's short-lived career for his county amounted to a total of 33 wickets at a cost of 34 each, so he can hardly be reckoned a terror.

In the end Denis scored just short of 2000 runs in first-class cricket that season, averaging just over 47 and hitting three hundreds and no fewer than 16 fifties. Many years later he signed a photograph of himself for my fiftieth birthday with the words 'Whenever I reached fifty I always went on to make a hundred.' This speaks volumes about his attitude, but statistically it was not always the case – particularly in 1937.

In his debut Test he made 65 before being run out 'characteristically' – said Denis in his own book playing up to the legend about his run-outs. In fact it was not in the least bit characteristic and it had nothing to do with his faulty calling or running between the wickets.

Against a rather weak New Zealand side England had started badly. Chasing a total of 249 they had slumped to 36 for 3 with Hutton and Washbrook (also a debutant) among them. Then Denis and Joe Hardstaff put on 125 in a couple of hours. *Wisden* thought Denis batted 'extremely well' and showed particularly good judgement in choosing which balls to hit hard. The bible also commented favourably on their running between the wickets. They did it 'splendidly'. Until, alas, the final moment. Giff Vivian was bowling slow left arm at Hardstaff. Hardstaff hit one very hard straight down the pitch. Denis, typically, was backing up with enthusiasm and started to scamper off when he saw the ball hit so true. Sadly for him, however, Vivian got a hand to the drive. He failed to make a clean stop but the ball ricocheted off him and straight into the stumps, with Denis stranded well out of his ground.

There was more trouble from Hardstaff late in the season when he prevented Middlesex beating Nottinghamshire with an innings of 234. Years later Joe's son, a retired Air Commodore, was secretary of Middlesex CCC, of which Denis was President. So the family connection was maintained.

They were the right side for Denis, Middlesex in 1937. Cardus, at the end of that season, wrote that they were the most interesting team in the land. Indeed he hoped, 'for art and the infinite variety of the game', they would win the championship. In the end they did not. Yorkshire, with Hutton an integral cog in the clockwork, proved too strong.

Cardus respected their 'solidarity' and 'northern shrewdness', but he still favoured Middlesex.

Cricket is not *all* grim contention; it is a game which, more than any other, possesses amenities. And these must be served in the colour and personality of cricket, the changes and contrasts of character. Nearly all aspects of the game are honoured in the Middlesex team; only the left-handed slow bowler is missing [Denis had yet to develop this skill]. There are quick scorers, steady ones, a big hitter (name of Smith), two England batsmen of tomorrow [Cardus presumably meant Compton and Edrich], all inspired by the England captain. And there are quick bowlers and an army of slow leg-spinners, headed by Owen-Smith, who is a genius. All the talents, you might say, displayed at Lord's, with the splendour of London all around, on a summer day. What more could a cricketer's heart desire?

Sad to say there will be no Hendren again. I can hardly believe it. Some evening next June, when the sun is mellowing, his smile will be observed manifesting itself against the background of the pavilion. As time goes on, Patsy's records no doubt will be surpassed; but nobody will approach, either in size or in lovable humanity, his smile.

Although it was Hendren's last season of county cricket the old boy wasn't quite finished. In retirement he went off to Harrow School as coach. Under his tutelage Harrow defeated Eton at Lord's for the first time in decades. Afterwards they insisted that Patsy came out onto the pavilion balcony to receive the plaudits of the crowd for one last time.

Wisden named Denis as one of the five cricketers of 1938. The others were Hugh Bartlett of Surrey, the Australian Bill Brown, Ken Farnes, the Essex fast bowler, and Arthur Wood, the Yorkshire wicketkeeper. 'A ready-made England batsman for years to come' was the perspicacious *Wisden* verdict on Compton, though it was only saying what was perfectly obvious to anyone remotely interested in cricket.

'An adaptable player with a touch of genius,' wrote *Wisden*, 'Compton possesses a sound defence, a wonderful eye and the right stroke for every ball. Among the young batsmen of the day there is no one better worth watching. He is particularly strong on the leg side and his confidence, coolness and resource are remarkable for so young a player. He has never concentrated upon bowling but he often secures valuable wickets with slow left-arm deliveries.'

This really was the year that Denis came of age as a cricketer. He was chosen for the Players against the Gentlemen and for England against the Rest, though he failed to score many runs in either match. He and Bill Edrich were already the mainstay of the Middlesex batting though once more the team failed to take the championship, again coming second to Yorkshire. This was partly due to the absence of Denis and Bill Edrich on

Test duty. Middlesex lost to Yorkshire, Kent and Somerset (of all people) while the 'twins' were away playing against the Australians. It was perhaps significant that while Bill outscored Denis in county cricket Denis was immeasurably more successful on the Test scene. Poor Edrich only made 67 runs in six England innings, whereas Denis made over 200. The selectors received serious flak for persevering with Edrich, though ultimately, of course, their loyalty was rewarded.

There was little room in Denis's life at this time for much outside cricket and football. The hours were long and the pay modest. Distractions were few and he had little time or money to indulge himself. His home circumstances were far from affluent and although he was already something of a star his feet remained firmly on the ground. He still lived at home and beyond visits to the cinema there was not much, apart from games, in the way of fun. He was already, and obviously, attractive to girls and he was interested in them. In this, as in much else, however, he remained curiously innocent and naive. Despite his precociousness as a cricketer and footballer he was in many respects 'young for his age' and remained so for much of the rest of his life.

As far as the record book goes the most impressive innings of 1938 was in his first Test against Australia. He had already played against the old enemy twice. The first occasion was for MCC when he made a modest 23 and 12 not out, though he also took the wicket of the future captain Lindsay Hassett. Six hours of that game were spent watching Don Bradman make a virtually faultless 278. A highly educative experience. For Middlesex he did rather better, making 65 in two and a half hours on a rain-affected wicket before being bowled by 'Tiger' O'Reilly, who was to become a persistent menace. O'Reilly dismissed Denis no fewer than five times that summer. Denis also took a brilliant catch to get rid of the Don, running all the way from slip to short leg before pouching a skier. He had a bounding natural athleticism in those days and an apparently boundless optimism. If there was even the remotest chance going he would take it. Providing, of course, that he was paying attention.

Writing in 1957, Denis's great friend and Middlesex colleague Ian Peebles looked back fondly on the Compton of the early years:

> In the field, when young, his thoughts would sometimes wander far from the immediate scene, and being a character incapable of deception, these flights were immediately manifested in a profound scholarly detachment, most appropriate to some calm cloister but a trifle *outré* at first slip.
>
> Fierce reprimands from his captain, Robins, whose thoughts were always very much on the game, were received with disarming good humour and never did anything to mar a great friendship.

At Trent Bridge in the opening match of the Test series England batted first on an excellent pitch. Hutton and Barnett put on over 200 for the first wicket, Hutton making a century in his first Test against Australia. Denis, batting at No. 6, came in when the score was 281 for 4 and proceeded to emulate Hutton by also making a hundred on his debut against Australia and putting on 206 with Paynter for the fifth wicket, thus breaking a record which had stood since 1903. When he was out soon after completing the hundred, Walter Hammond, in a somewhat curmudgeonly fashion, told him that after making a century against Australia the correct procedure was to take guard again and make another. It's hardly surprising that Denis had reservations about him.

Compton and Paynter scored at a fine rate, adding 141 in the last hour and a half of the first day's play. It was a cavalier innings with characteristic strengths. *Wisden* commented on aggressive leg-side play as well as cuts and drives. Sixty of his runs came in fours, but almost the most interesting aspect of the partnership is the comment that 'Some fine running between wickets featured in this stand.'

This is not the first time that attention has been drawn to Denis's running between the wickets. One can't help wondering about this tendency. He himself was inclined to be defensive about it though he was the first to concede that there were some disastrous run-outs which were entirely due to him. From a physical point of view his outside-left footballing skills would have made him speedy, nimble and quick on the turn, at least until the notorious knee began to cause problems, and there is no question that with the right partner his judgement was perfectly adequate. When he and Bill Edrich were together, however, things fell apart. Some think, and Denis was inclined to agree, that this was because they were both laughing so much. In any event the question of inter-wicket skills is persistent throughout his career.

In the second Test at Lord's he hit 76 not out in the second innings. This was in many ways a better performance than his Trent Bridge century for it was played on a wicket which rain had rendered soft on top and hard underneath. Half the England side were out for 76, but Denis rallied the troops and coped with O'Reilly and McCormick with more panache than anyone. Already he was demonstrating that he was at his best in a crisis. The only man who scored faster was the redoubtable Somerset hitter Arthur Wellard, who made 38 in a stand with Denis of 74. One of his sixes, off McCabe, went into the Grandstand balcony.

Years later, on his seventy-fifth birthday, Denis told Jim Swanton that his 76 at Lord's was 'probably my best knock'. Actually Denis was inconsistent about 'best knocks' as he was about a number of things and I have a slight suspicion that he only agreed with Swanton because he thought it best to humour him. Swanton's words in his *Daily Telegraph* column were:

Denis' 76 not out in the second innings against Australia which first saved England from defeat and finally opened up the possibility of victory, was the innings which convinced me that here was a genius at work.

Heavy rain had left the pitch soft on top and hard underneath. McCormick made the ball fly while for the great O'Reilly it turned and lifted, and at 76 for five Hutton, Barnett, Edrich, Hammond and Verity were all gone.

The 20-year-old, playing in his third Test match showed the coolness and the judgement of a master. First Paynter, then Wellard helped him dissolve the crisis.

In the first innings, however, Denis had fallen to O'Reilly, lbw for only 6. And he really blotted his escutcheon by dropping Fleetwood-Smith in the slips, thus depriving Farnes of a hat-trick.

Old Trafford that year was rained off, with not a ball being bowled, and at Headingley O'Reilly had him for 14 in the first innings and 15 in the second. The latter was bad luck, for he was caught off his wrist. England lost by five wickets, which meant that Australia retained the Ashes. Denis, incidentally, thought Tiger O'Reilly the finest spin bowler ever but that was before the arrival of Shane Warne.

The Oval Test, of course, was Hutton's hour of triumph. Sitting in the pavilion as the runs piled up, Denis bet Eddie Paynter, who was enjoying a hugely successful series, that the two of them would not get more than ten between them. The sum at stake is generally agreed to be a pound, but it is one of those stories that has been so often repeated that one can't be too sure. Indeed it is not entirely clear whether it was Denis or

Eddie Paynter who actually made the bet. My money is on Denis, if only because he always liked a flutter.

Hutton, en route to his 364, had been in over nine hours by the time Paynter came to the wicket. He was promptly deceived by an O'Reilly leg-break which caught him leg before. Then there was half an hour of rain and almost immediately after play restarted Denis was clean bowled by a man called Waite. It was the only Test wicket Waite ever took. His overall Test analysis that year was one for 190. Subsequently whenever Denis was in Australia Waite would ring him up and buy him a beer on the strength of it.

There were several high points in this Compton season, including five centuries. Arguably, however, it was an extraordinary 87 not out against Essex which was probably his finest batting performance. The innings was the highlight of an absolute thriller which fluctuated frantically from first to last. This was the sort of occasion he enjoyed and which almost always brought out the best in him. Essex batted first and made exactly 300. Middlesex were all out for 281, and then Essex collapsed, with the opening pair mustering barely 30 and the next three batsmen going for 0, 2 and 0. Then their No. 8 batsman, a fast bowler called Smith, scored 101 and the score went up to 221, leaving Middlesex with what looked like a reasonable target. At lunch on the final day they had only lost four wickets and needed a mere 69 to win. Then came a collapse. When the last man entered Denis was holding up his end but Middlesex were still 23 behind. The pitch was wearing badly. Smith, the heroic No. 8 batsman who had scored the unexpected century, was taking full advantage of this and had already captured eight wickets. There seemed no hope, for Mr A.D. Baxter, the Middlesex No. 11, never scored more than seven runs all summer. He was the ultimate rabbit.

Denis, however, not for the first or last time, farmed the bowling with the utmost skill, shielded Mr Baxter from the fearsome Smith, and finally steered his side home by a single wicket.

Sometimes one is led to believe that Denis was all swash and buckle, a cavalier who was always on the charge no matter what. But it was never like that. The only times that he became careless were when, as in the wake of Hutton's 364, it simply didn't matter very much whether he made nought or a hundred. But when the chips were down Denis was your man.

On the strength of his performance that summer he was asked to tour South Africa. It must have been a tempting prospect but he was still set on a dual sporting career and under contract to the Arsenal. This time the Gunners won out and he spent the winter playing football, though surprisingly and disappointingly he failed to gain a regular first-team place.

The final summer of the peace in 1939 was full of the harbingers of war. In March, as wickets were being groomed and pavilions painted, Hitler marched into Czechoslovakia; in May conscription was announced, and on the 8th of that month General Franco removed Spain from the League of Nations. It was the second day of the Middlesex v. Essex match, a game which seemed crucial to the outcome of the championship and one which included one of Denis's very best pre-war hundreds.

Terence Prittie recalled the game in detail from his German prison camp, using its golden memory to lighten the dark days of his confinement. Early summer may sound early for a crucial match but whereas Yorkshire, the pre-eminent team of the 1930s, were always strong in the finish and could therefore make early mistakes, Middlesex tended to blow up in the final straight. They lacked a convincing pace attack and their overworked fast bowler, Jim Smith, was nearly always jaded by the end of August. Because of this, wrote Prittie, 'Middlesex's only hope lay in the possibility of making so good a start as to build up an unassailable lead which the champions, despite their far greater staying-power, would be unable to cut down.'

A win against Essex was therefore imperative, but unfortunately for Middlesex their opponents won the toss and batted first, in a manner that was 'sound but undistinguished, typical enough, indeed, of the side as a whole'. You can tell Prittie was a Middlesex man. It is touching to realise how much the rosy memories of his team must have lightened the tedium of wartime imprisonment. By the same token he obviously hated Essex, who were the absolute antithesis of the Compton style . . . 'laborious, unimaginative', while one Essex player was 'one of the most disappointing batsmen of modern times'. They made over 400 but Prittie described this as 'plodding supremacy, a grim, realistic, unbeautiful display'.

Actually Edrich 'failed to inspire confidence'. He was having a bad time, having failed badly against Australia the previous summer. Robertson, by contrast, was all 'languid charm'. His innings was 'as short and perfect as an essay by Charles Lamb'.

When Denis came in the score was 63 for 2, and wickets began to fall with disturbing regularity. Denis defended resolutely but he looked a bit desperate. Prittie thought he had rarely been so pinned down. The two Essex Smiths had him in serious trouble, one only just missing his wicket with a ball that broke back sharply and the other bowling him a maiden and hitting his pads twice. A young colt called Thompson (whatever became of Thompson?) was in with him and, if anything, seemed the more confident. But then Denis knew that everything depended on him and that if his wicket went down all was lost.

Then Thompson got in a tangle and was bowled for 18. Middlesex were still almost 300 runs behind and five wickets were down. Denis was there, 'watchful and determined' but also 'terribly constricted'. Always a slow starter, he was having the sort of unproductive May that was usual for him. And the Essex bowling was tight and truculent.

The new batsman, Price, seemed unruffled, but Denis, while making no mistakes, was playing 'the dourest innings of his life'. Perhaps this relative inactivity affected Price, for he suddenly flicked at a short ball from Captain Stephenson and was out caught. It was now 140 for 6, with only tail-enders remaining to keep Denis company. He was still only 35 not out. Most onlookers thought Middlesex were already doomed to an innings defeat.

Now, however, came a bowling change and for the first time Denis opened his shoulders and let rip, first a 'glorious skimming off-drive' and then a force past mid-on executed off the back foot, balance perfect, elbows tucked in. Prittie said it was his most characteristic shot (what about the sweep?) and not often attempted by anyone else, particularly as it was played off a good-length ball dead on leg stump. It sounds dangerous.

After tea Denis seemed steadier. He was still only twenty-two but Prittie, perhaps over-romantic in his German prison, thought he had something 'of the Horatian hero of whom Addison wrote:

> Should the whole frame of nature round him break,
> In ruin and confusion hurled,
> He, unconcerned, would hear the mighty crack,
> And stand secure amidst a falling world.'

There is a fine irony in such classically lyrical thoughts being inspired by an unassuming bloke whose formal education ceased at fourteen. Prittie considered that at the time only Hammond and Sutcliffe shared the same 'natural and unshakeable superiority complex'. The only modern English cricketer I can think of who possessed it is Botham, though it was once almost universal among the West Indians and then the modern Australians. Perhaps Flintoff has traces of it. Even in old age you could detect it in Denis. It is not at all the same thing as arrogance; simply a deep-seated knowledge that you are better than practically everybody else at your best subject and as good as anybody. Denis was essentially a modest man, but he knew that on his day he had no reason to be afraid.

So far in this innings he had played with 'Teutonic' (a bitter prison camp word!) thoroughness, no indiscretion, no frivolity, just absolute concentration. The loose balls were hit hard but they were skilfully placed. There were no risks.

His fifty took two hours. Sims at the other end was erratic and at 19 was caught at slip. It was now 181 for 7.

This partnership had put on 41 in half an hour but they still needed 75 to save the follow-on and the incoming batsman, Jim Smith, had been out for a duck three times in his only four innings of the year.

Prittie now quoted Dryden. 'Beware the fury of a patient man.' It's an apt quote, and he went on to make the point, apparent to his contemporaries, but not always to his latter-day eulogists, that Compton thrived on battles against the odds. Even in old age there was still a bloody-minded tilt of the Compton head and glint in the Compton eye which gave more than a hint of a Churchillian determination to remain unbowed no matter what.

Jim Smith was a prodigious hitter and not the sort of batsman to hang around. He tried to hit the first ball out of the ground, almost fell over, missed by a foot and in doing so produced 'a cloud of dust and a loud cheer'. Smith was a Character.

It was luck as much as judgement, but in no time at all Big Jim had made 16 and rattled the score past 200. That sort of hitter has more or less vanished from the first-class game, but in those days most counties had at least one in the lower orders and they could be extremely effective. Smith rode his luck to huge effect but before long he had made enough bad strokes to get a whole side out. It was obvious that he could not possibly last much longer and that Denis must now force the pace himself.

This he proceeded to do majestically. Up to now Ray Smith had taken 2 for 20 and looked almost unplayable. In two overs Compton hit him out of the game. He drove him through the covers, he swept him past square leg, forced him off his legs twice, then 'with terrific force' slashed him past cover's left hand. This indeed was the 'fury of a patient man'. And then he farmed the bowling by taking a single at the end of each over.

Prittie's prose keeps pace with Compton's batting. He paid particular praise to his footwork. 'This, more than anything else, marks him out as one of cricket's aristocrats. He is the Chevalier Bayard of the bat in his youthful daring and the chivalry of his every gesture.' Then, apropos Smith, he quotes Mrs Malaprop because, though facing only three balls in five overs, the great slogger was 'as headstrong as an allegory on the banks of the Nile'.

His hitting was obviously tremendous. When he had made 32 Captain Stephenson brought back Nichols. Twice running Smith skied him to long-on where Captain Stephenson stood waiting. Twice running the Captain dropped the catch. At last he was bowled by Nichols while 'lurching like some Frankenstein monster with wildly waving bat, and the wickets smashing with unwonted abandon and twice their normal violence behind him'.

It was now 246 for 8, and 100 runs had come in an hour. The new batsman was Ian Peebles, a fine spinner of the ball, and subsequently a stylish and amusing cricket writer, but not nearly as good a batsman as he sometimes looked.

He stayed a while, indeed almost long enough to see Denis

to his century, but with Compton on 99, Peebles was caught by Nichols for 7.

That seemed to be that: 270 for 9 and the last man, Gray, another typical number 11.

Nevertheless he played out the five remaining balls of Nichols's over and in the next Denis duly proceeded to his hundred. It had taken almost three hours, though the second fifty had come in just three-quarters of an hour.

Now he had made his hundred and the follow-on was saved, so he could abandon his statesmanlike Bismarck role and have some fun. 'Care was now cast aside.'

It is always said that Denis seldom drove straight. There is the often-repeated story of the tea interval when one of his colleagues remarked on this and Denis said watch for the third ball of the next over and proceeded to crash the said third ball into the pavilion for a huge straight-driven six. I do not believe the story to be apocryphal, but the remark always seems to have been made by a different player during a different match and it is always a different ball of the first over after tea.

In any event, Denis proceeded to charge down the pitch at the hitherto menacing Nichols. The first blow hit Nichols on the foot, the next two went for four either side of the sightscreen. Nicols, demoralised, started to drop the ball short so Compton went onto his back foot, glanced him to leg, forced him through the covers and hooked him as suddenly and ferociously as Hendren in his prime. Nichols was promptly removed.

Ray Smith at the other end suffered even more and was slashed hard either side of cover for four. Prittie describes this as an inimitably Compton stroke with the ball hit on the rise 'with a last-second twist of body and turning wrists'. There was nothing uppish about the shots though. He was playing with tremendous aggression but taking very few risks.

At 5.15 p.m. they passed 300. Five minutes later there were another twelve on the board. Peter Smith was brought back and now Compton did hit high, lofting him all over the ground but always placing the ball safely out of reach of the fielders.

As a last resort Captain Stephenson brought back a veteran off-spinner called Eastman who successfully contained Denis for a few balls but was then hit for 22 runs off five balls – a straight four and 'three glorious, towering sixes, the first to mid-wicket, the second into the pavilion, the third hitting the boxes over long-on, and each one cumulatively more tremendous than the last'.

It could not go on for ever, though when this feast did finish it was not through lack of skill – or even faulty calling. Off the last ball of an over Denis hit the ball perfectly well and set off for the single which would enable him to keep the strike. By now, however, he was exhausted, he ran too slowly, and he was run out.

He had batted three and three-quarter hours for 181 and his last 131 had come in 100 minutes. He hit four sixes and 17 fours and, apparently, played no false stroke. Terence Prittie called it 'the innings of a lifetime', not knowing that there were rivals yet to come.

The previous year, he considered, had shown Denis to be 'a fine forcing batsman, of romantic appeal and vivid charm'. 1939, thought Prittie, was the year which put him in a different class alongside Hutton and Hammond and elevated him to 'that regal tradition of those born to command'.

I like to think of the prisoner of war in Germany escaping, metaphorically, to Lord's that afternoon. Prittie reckoned that it was the day on which Compton 'blossomed to completest maturity', and reading his report it is difficult to doubt that he was right. His account is one of the finest sustained and detailed descriptions of a single innings that I know of, and it is, I think, a brilliant demonstration of most of what made Denis Compton so very special. The innings has everything –

bravery, determination, obduracy, skill amounting to genius, a fine instinct for playing the right game at the right time, unorthodoxy, you name it. More than that, it demonstrates the essence of Denis, for it shows how he could communicate the sheer joy of what he did to those who only watched. Prittie's is an inspired piece of writing and only Denis could have inspired it.

In the end Middlesex actually went on to win the match by making 225 for 8 in 110 minutes, with the irrepressible Big Jim Smith hitting 45 runs in 18 minutes 'by means of strokes which can be found nowhere in Knight's *Complete Cricketer*'. Alas, in the end, they failed to pip Yorkshire for the title, and finished second for the third year in succession.

In all Denis scored almost 2500 runs and he made eight hundreds. There were many other high spots: 120 against Constantine and Martindale – whom he reckoned the fastest bowler he faced before the war – in his first Test against the West Indies; a partnership of 248 with Len Hutton; his first double century – against Derbyshire.

On 3 September Chamberlain declared war on Germany and the first air-raid sirens sounded. The West Indian tour was curtailed and the last seven matches cancelled. Hitler played havoc and before long the Germans captured T.C.F. Prittie and locked him up with his memories of Denis Compton to keep him sane. How terribly terribly English that he should have spent his war reflecting on 'that afternoon of the 8th of May when a single man, by a single innings, put Middlesex once more on the high-road to the Championship'.

The day Hitler invaded Poland Neville Cardus was in the Long Room at Denis Compton's cricketing home of Lord's. He was watching a game being played under barrage balloons. Denis would have been out on the grass. In his autobiography, published in 1947, Cardus wrote:

As I watched the ghostly movements of the players outside, a beautifully preserved member of Lord's, spats and rolled umbrella, stood near me inspecting the game. We did not speak of course; we had not been introduced. Suddenly two workmen entered the Long Room in green aprons and carrying a bag. They took down the bust of W.G. Grace, put it into the bag and departed with it. The noble lord at my side watched their every movement; then he turned to me. 'Did you see, sir?' he asked. I told him I had seen. 'That means war,' he said.

CHAPTER SIX

Arsenal's professional footballers had their contracts officially terminated after the third match of the 1939 season. The game was against Sunderland. Afterwards they all found letters waiting for them in the dressing room. These told the players that – in effect – they had lost their jobs owing to the outbreak of hostilities. The Football League had closed down for the duration, and although all the players were retained by the club there was no obligation to pay their salaries. In view of Denis's professed admiration for the club's friendly and enlightened attitude towards its playing staff this action seems extraordinary. It certainly belongs to a different era.

Highbury itself was turned over to the air-raid wardens and remained an armed fortress throughout the war. Such games as were played took place at White Hart Lane, the home of their old north London rivals, Tottenham Hotspur.

Denis and Leslie enrolled as Special Constables. Pictures of the Compton brothers in 1939 look as if they are from a Gilbert and Sullivan operetta. Very dashing, positively Victorian, and not exactly in the front line.

It was dull work pacing the beat. Nothing ever seemed to happen. It was a 'phoney war' to start with. Luckily, however, Denis was a highly recognisable figure and he recalled that he was often asked in for a cup of tea by adoring housewives. On the whole, however, he found it boring and was relieved when at the end of December he was called up and posted to East Grinstead with an anti-aircraft regiment of the Royal Artillery. This was not an interesting or demanding assignment, but at least it was not too far from London and at weekends he was usually able to get hold of enough petrol coupons to manage the journey into town for a game of football.

True, the Football League had come to an end and Arsenal's ground had become a victim of the war effort. But that didn't mean that all football had ceased. Spurs invited Arsenal to share White Hart Lane for as long as they needed it. The authorities imposed severe restrictions on crowd size, so that only 22,000 spectators were allowed into a ground which normally held more than 60,000. As Bernard Joy says, the wartime competitions were a little half-hearted, not least because so many players were posted overseas. Nevertheless there was soccer throughout the war; some of it was very good; and some of the best was played by Denis.

The writer Benny Green remembered leaning against the rusty stanchions of White Hart Lane in the winter of 1942–43 and first being exposed to what he called 'the sorcery of Denis Compton'. Green considered that there was 'no rival who remotely approached him' and that 'greatness remains greatness no matter what the context. Compton out on the wing at White Hart Lane in those mid-war years was one of the supreme sights of English life.'

Green remembered the prodigious left foot, though he also recalled Denis nudging the ball past the West Ham goalkeeper with his right. Denis himself used to become rather defensive when people denigrated his right foot. All those hours in training in the shooting box with no boot on his left foot must have paid dividends. I asked the great Stanley Matthews, who frequently played on the other wing for the wartime England

XI, what he thought about Compton's feet and he replied that the right was perfectly OK for passing and dribbling but that, of course, the serious thunderbolts always came from the left.

His old team-mate Bernard Joy found it impossible to say where Denis would have got to in football without the war. During that period he played twelve times for England – but wartime caps didn't count. Brian Glanville, the football writer and novelist, thought it ridiculous. Of course Denis deserved full caps. Throughout that wartime period he was without doubt the best outside-left in English football. But for Hitler he would have had caps galore. Both Billy Wright and Joe Mercer said that, on top form, he had no equal in his day.

'He brought the same carefree outlook to his football as to his cricket,' said Bernard Joy, though I think he is slightly misled by the appearance of insouciance. I think Denis cared more than he showed. Joy recalled that 'I have known him stroll into the dressing room ten minutes before kick-off when everyone else was wondering where he had got to. Even then he would continue chatting while trainer Billy Milne helped him to dress.' Certainly his sense of time was erratic and apparently always was. But 'carefree' I doubt.

Bernard Joy identified three winning Compton attributes: 'He had as deadly a left foot as anyone on his day, good ball control and a flair for the big occasion.'

As we have seen, Denis was meticulous in his preparation for the big game even about such apparently trivial things as 'taking a ball out into the large bathroom to kick it against the hot pipe a few times'. None of this quite fits in with the Bernard Joy recollection of a carefree Compton rolling in to the changing room just ten minutes before play began. On the other hand, one has to admit that the Compton account was written for public consumption and the public would not have appreciated too much nonchalance. Or that would have been the advice of Denis's PR advisers. Denis said:

These matters may seem small and unimportant but they were part of a set routine and, with possibly sixty thousand people outside waiting to split the skies to cheer as we appeared, they were exciting in themselves.

By the time the referee informed us that we were due on the field, Tom would have been round to nearly every player, offering a few words of advice and encouragement.

'Keep on top of that winger, Bill, he's very fast' or 'Play that full-back's left side, Arthur, he's not as strong there as on the right'. These and other last-minute instructions would be given – and heeded.

The Compton words have the ring of truth. The superstitious belief in ritual is very much a part of most sportsmen's baggage. Denis may have looked 'carefree' to Bernard Joy and other team-mates but he could not have done what he did on the field if his attitude had really been as cavalier as it sometimes seemed. As a player Denis exuded superiority but we all know that that sort of superiority is seldom as effortless as it looks. As an Arsenal player in the years before and after the war Denis played in 59 first-team matches and scored 16 goals. In other words he was far from being a regular. In 1937–38 he played only seven first-team matches. In 1939 he played only once, at the end of April against Derby County.

During the Arsenal v. Charlton Athletic match in 1938 he collided with Sid Hobbins, the Charlton goalkeeper. It was an accident, one of those things that happen in a fiercely fought physical contest, but Hobbins nevertheless harboured a sense of guilt.

Years later, when 'Compton's Knee' had become a national talking point, Denis got a letter from Hobbins. He lost it long ago but to the best of his recollection it said something like 'Dear Mr Compton, I am terribly sorry for the trouble that I must have caused you over these years. It must have started with the injury in 1938, and now I see all the trouble you are having. I am very sorry indeed. Sincerely, Sid Hobbins.'

Mike Parkinson quoted Denis as saying 'It wasn't his fault but it obviously nagged him all those years.' Parkinson continued, 'There can be little mystery to Hobbins's remorse. What happened was that in 1938 he collided with a fellow pro. But at the end of the 1940s after Compton's golden summer of 1947 he was aware he had lamed a hero.'

Actually there is slightly more mystery to it than that, as revealed by Norman Giller in his anthology of Compton anecdotes based on his researches for the Eamon Andrews *This Is Your Life* programme. Giller remembered once sitting between Denis and Sam Bartram, once the famous Charlton Athletic first-choice goalkeeper. They were in the press box at the Valley, Charlton's ground, where Giller was reporting for the *Daily Express*, Denis for the *Sunday Express* and Sam for the *People*. At one point Sam pointed to the spot where, he said, he had once sent Denis sprawling when making a save at the Compton feet. Denis nodded sagely and agreed. 'That,' he said, 'was the start of my knee trouble.'

Giller, an expert football reporter, knew that Bartram had played more than five hundred games for Charlton whereas Hobbins was basically his reserve and only played twice for the first team. Giller consulted the archive and came to the conclusion that Denis did indeed collide with Bartram during a first-team game between the Gunners and Athletic, which left him hobbling. However, the really serious injury came in a reserve match when Denis and Sid Hobbins collided and Denis was carried off for surgery in hospital.

It wasn't Sid's fault that the knee had gone, nor Sam's, though one can understand their feelings. It was certainly a football clash that had precipitated the original crisis and led to the first of many operations. But it was an accident. Just one of those things. I now believe that, like so many long-term sporting injuries, it was a cumulative injury. A player of Denis's panache and brio would have often been sent sprawling by intrepid goalkeepers and after a while this would have been bound to have a bad effect. One or two such collisions might not have done too much damage but a whole career of awkward goalmouth tumbles would have been disastrous. As indeed it proved.

By a sad coincidence a fellow patient in University College Hospital was Tom Whittaker, his old Arsenal manager. Whittaker left hospital shortly after they operated on Denis's knee, but he was soon back again, this time to die.

In the war years Denis made 127 appearances for the Arsenal, scoring 72 goals. Oddly therefore he played more first-class football during wartime than peace.

Few people nowadays would compare Denis Compton, the footballer, with the great Stanley Matthews, who played out on the opposite wing. Yet Benny Green did so when writing about Arsenal, the southern champions, taking on their northern counterparts, Blackpool, at Stamford Bridge. In an earlier match against Queen's Park Rangers, Green wrote, Denis had scored 'one of the great goals of my experience by dribbling the ball along the goal-line, past one defender after another and, while the crowd bayed and screamed for him to push the ball back to one of the oncoming forwards, consummating this brilliant episode by hooking the ball past the goalkeeper into the net with the sort of stylish nonchalance which left the entire opposition desolate'.

The north–south final against Blackpool was widely assumed to be a showcase for Stanley Matthews, Denis's opposite number. But according to Green, 'Denis stole the day with a most astonishing one-man exhibition. After taking an early two-goal lead, Arsenal were at last outplayed by the opposition, lost 2–4 and took away with them the consolation of Compton's unforgettable virtuosity on the left wing.'

The authorities soon realised that the East Grinstead appointment was a mistake. He was languishing there as not much more than a not very glorified stoker. So they moved him to Aldershot to train on the Physical Training Instructors' Course alongside dozens of other top-notch professional sportsmen. Here he came under the command of Colonel R.S. Rait-Kerr, another exile from Lord's. The MCC Secretary was not over-impressed with Compton's soldiering ability nor indeed his fitness, though Denis continued, in his spare time, to play both his main games to the highest standards.

He should by rights have been impossibly big-headed and yet conceit seems to have been alien to his nature then as later. In his seventies I found him remarkably diffident, but one might reasonably put that down to the wisdom that is supposed to come with maturity. However even at the height of his powers his dashing sense of superiority only seems to have shown up on the field of play. One of his contemporaries at Aldershot was a Sergeant K.W.J. Wood of the Army Bomb Disposal Unit. Wood had been a spectator at Lord's the day of Denis's first-class debut when he made the famous 14 with Gubby Allen.

The innings had made a great impression on Wood because Denis was only a year or so older than himself. 1940 was 'pretty hectic' for Bomb Disposal, and he spent little time socialising in the Mess, although he did drop in for meals from time to time. Looking back on it, he thought he probably only exchanged half a dozen words with Denis. 'My overall impression was that he was very quiet, shy almost.'

L.R. Sharrar from Southampton remembered an incident which parallels Sergeant Wood's recollection. 'It was a tense wartime cup game at Griffin Park, Brentford,' he wrote. 'A penalty was awarded to Arsenal – hotly disputed. The coolest man on the pitch, calmly picking the mud from his boots, well away from the crowd of players, was Compton, who, when the ref gained control, strolled up and smacked the ball past Bill Brown in goal for the only goal of the game.'

I'm not sure Denis could ever have been really shy but it seems clear that in those days he had a definite capacity for being quiet and self-contained. He was always different and, while always cheerful and gregarious, also something of a man apart.

Those wartime games must have offered a cheering respite from the grim days of war. The programme for the England v. Scotland match on 17 January 1942 affords a glimpse of that wartime world. The game was played at what was still referred to very firmly as the 'Empire Stadium, Wembley', a reminder that there still was such a thing as the Empire, indeed that the British forces throughout the world included contingents from those many parts of the globe still coloured pink.

All but one of the England side were in the forces, the exception being Willingham of Huddersfield Town. It was an extremely strong side, captained by Eddie Hapgood (Arsenal and RAF) at left back. Stan Cullis (Wolverhampton Wanderers and Army) was at 'centre half back', and the forward line still makes the spine tingle more than half a century later:

'S. Matthews (Stoke City and RAF), W. Mannion (Middlesbrough and Army), T. Lawton (Everton and Army), J. Hagan (Sheffield United and Army), D. Compton (Arsenal and Army).' It's difficult to think of a more dazzling line-up in the history of the English game. At least one contemporary commentator thought it the best England team in twenty years.

For some reason the Scots had five non-servicemen, but the left and right 'half-backs' went on to become the most famous managers in post-war football: 'M. Busby (Capt. – Hibernian and Army) and W. Shankly (Preston North End and RAF)'.

The match was held to raise money for 'Mrs Churchill's "Aid to Russia" Fund', and Clemmie herself was present to meet the players and see England win 1–0. The official programme (thin) cost sixpence and there was a special note about 'Air Raid Precautions', which read:

In the event of an Air Raid Alert, in the course of which information is given by the Spotters that Enemy Aircraft are in the immediate vicinity of the Stadium, an announcement will be made over the loudspeakers.

Spectators will then be requested to leave the enclosures and make their way quietly to the Circulating Corridors under the Stands, as directed by the Stewards and Officials.

Those wishing to leave the Stadium may do so by any of the usual Exits.

The message sounds like an edict from Captain Mainwaring in *Dad's Army*.

At least in the early years of the war England put together a team which in the words of Frank Carruthers, who wrote the 'Arbiter' column in the *Daily Mail*, was 'almost as strong as could have been chosen in normal times'. Hapgood, Mercer, Matthews and Cullis were among the regulars, as was Denis, at least until 1943. Alas, they only played Scotland and Wales, but they enjoyed some thumping victories. Within three weeks during the autumn of 1943 they beat Wales 8–3 and Scotland 8–0. After the second game Denis was described as 'the finest match-winner in the country'.

While England were consistently well up to pre-war standard, Arsenal were a great deal patchier, especially towards the end. Some of the matches were farcical. They were so depleted that both Leslie Compton and Ted Drake had games in goal. Against an Aldershot side which included Britton, Cullis, Mercer, Lawton and Hagan they were losing 4–1 with very little time left. The Aldershot trainer was so confident of victory that he went off early to run the baths in the dressing room. When he returned he asked the score, and was told 'six–four.'

'Who scored our other two?' he wanted to know.

'*Your* two?' asked Billy Milne, the Arsenal trainer. '*We've* scored five.' Indeed they had. Reg Lewis scored a hat-trick and they even added a seventh goal by full time.

It was during these years too that the Compton brothers perfected their double act. This consisted of Denis taking a corner from the left, using that trusty left boot. Leslie would lie quite deep but run onto the ball more or less as Denis hit it and surprise the opposition by coinciding with the ball as it lofted into the goalmouth. Leslie was a big man and brilliant in the air. In one match at White Hart Lane Arsenal beat Clapton Orient 15–2, and big Les scored ten goals, six with his head. Orient, the second-oldest League club in south-east England, were renamed Leyton Orient soon after the Second World War. They were still playing under that name in the early twenty-first century.

Big Les was in many ways a far more typical sportsman of his times than his little brother, Denis. Although he was a fine, uncompromising footballer and an accomplished county wicketkeeper, he lacked Denis's genius and charisma. In retirement he kept a pub like so many of his generation of retired professional sportsmen. This was in Highgate, north London, and here he became known as a genial gentle host who never lost his slightly high-pitched north London accent or abandoned his working-class roots. Denis, by contrast, not only became a legend but also came to speak with an almost fruity rich voice, moved into smart houses in green belt Bucks, and sent his sons to public school.

Many of the Arsenal men worked as ARP wardens at the Highbury Stadium while others, like Denis, were close at hand at Aldershot. Arsenal only failed to win the Regional League in 1941 and went to Wembley for wartime cup finals in 1941 and 1943. Denis played in the '43 final, which Arsenal won 7–1. Lewis scored four, Drake two, but Frank Carruthers in the *Express* wrote, 'I think it will be obvious that Kirchen and Denis Compton have been the match winners': Denis, according to Carruthers, had acquired 'much of the trickery of Stanley Matthews and the confidence which inspired him to crack the first ball he received from O'Reilly in his first Test match for 4'.

Not everyone approved of Compton and Matthews. One critic, Frank Butler, even went so far as to say, 'I am rather doubtful about England's wingers, Stan Matthews and Denis Compton. They are grand to watch but both are individualists.' Dear, oh dear!

Victor Eldridge, who was taught history by Bernard Joy in his first year at grammar school in 1940, wrote:

I witnessed nearly all of the games you mention. Although only a schoolboy at the time I can corroborate the remarks of Benny Green and Bernard Joy as to the prowess of Denis Compton as a footballer.

In particular during the match against Blackpool at Stamford Bridge, I have never seen a better display of dribbling in my life, and that includes seeing the great Stanley Matthews at his peak. I'm sure the secret of his success was his great footwork and sense of balance which of course applies to his marvellous cricket career. This seemed to enable him to do everything at a leisurely pace.

His wartime cricket somehow seems less spectacular. This is partly, I think, because it *was* less spectacular, but also because he achieved a greatness as a peacetime cricketer which really eluded him as a footballer. Most critics agree that Denis played the football of his life at White Hart Lane in the early Forties. By the time the war ended he was sadly past his prime as a footballer, but as a cricketer the best was yet to come.

Just as the Football League was put on ice during hostilities, so was the cricket County Championship. There were some representative games between British and Commonwealth forces and eventually a series of 'Victory Tests'. Generally speaking, however, cricket was a pretty ramshackle affair although unlike the Oval, which was converted for use as a prisoner of war camp, Lord's was not commandeered for military purposes.

Some odd outfits played there, notably a club called the Buccaneers, the creation of a keen amateur called Geoffrey Moore. Denis played against them in a strong London Counties side which also included his brother Leslie. The club's history records that 'Sergeant Denis Compton rattled up 74 in 95 minutes.' The Buccaneers side included Laurie Fishlock, the Bedser twins and Gubby Allen. The left-handed Fishlock made more than 20,000 runs for Surrey between 1931 and 1952 while Alec Bedser's less celebrated brother Eric scored over 14,000 runs and took 797 wickets with his off-spin.

It's intriguing that MCC and the counties themselves did not stay open for business as the great football clubs did. Some of the counties did attempt to play, but their efforts were fairly forlorn. One explanation is that most of the MCC staff were drafted into the forces. Denis's old mentor, 'Plum' Warner, came out of retirement to be the club's temporary Secretary, and the London Counties XI and British Empire XI did perform regularly. In August 1940 Frank Woolley was coaxed out of retirement and had Sergeant D. Compton caught for 60. The legendary Woolley had retired from Kent in 1938 after thirty-two years and six 'doubles' of a thousand runs and a hundred wickets in a season. E.W. Swanton, a loyal man of Kent, once wrote of Woolley, 'I admit no flaw in Frank's cricket'. In return Denis, who took 6 for 81 off only ten overs, had the old man caught and bowled for 38. A crowd of 13,000 watched, but it was a one-day match and not quite, one can't help feeling, the real thing. Robertson-Glasgow confirms this view but puts it in perspective:

> It would be an error to rate our wartime cricket on technical values. The fact that a match is played and that the friends of cricket and the cricketers gather to watch the match is of far more interest than that Hutton, after scoring 20, was out in an un-Huttonian manner or that Denis Compton was late for a yorker, or that Nichols' slips not only stood rather too deep but stopped rather too slowly. For most of us the mere sight of such players is enough. It reminds us of what has been and what soon will be again . . . it has been cricket without competition; a snack not a meal.

There were naturally some snacks to savour. It would have been fun to watch the 101 Denis cracked for Plum Warner's XI against the Club Cricket Conference in seventy minutes – including a six and fourteen fours. He came top of the London Counties batting with averages in the eighties and nineties. His style was regularly described as 'masterly' and 'aggressive'. He gave great pleasure at a time when pleasure was in short supply. But whereas the football of these years seems some-times serious and sublime, the cricket is redolent of tip and run and the Sunday afternoon slog.

Some time around now Denis married. All his life Denis was attracted to women and they to him. It sometimes got him into trouble though even rivals used to agree that there was nothing predatory about his sexual behaviour. He didn't seem to make much effort where the opposite sex was concerned, not least because he didn't appear to need to. His bride and the mother of his first child, Brian, was a beautiful dancer and pianist named Doris. In later years Denis used to dismiss the marriage as one of those doomed wartime romances destined to 'fizzle out' when everyone came to their senses. In fact he did this so often that years later, long after they were divorced, 'Doy', as she was called, wrote to protest that their relationship had never been like that and Denis knew it perfectly well. Denis said nothing but was noticeably less inclined, thereafter, to dismiss his first marriage as if it had never been.

Doy never lost her Sadlers Wells slimness and poise and was described by friends and family as 'petite and immaculate'. On form and in the mood she could be wonderfully funny and entertaining. At other times, particularly in old age when she'd retired to Cape Town, South Africa, she could seem sad, introspective and slightly lonely. Doy married a second time but lost money in ill-advised business ventures. Doy was never very good with money. Although she moved to Africa in the 1960s to be close to Brian, who was privately educated at prep school in Seaford and at Clifton College, the two never shared a home or lived in each other's pockets. She was a lifelong serious smoker and it was cancer that eventually killed her several years after Denis's death. Some observers thought she never really got over him.

In the early years of the war, however, the couple seemed close and contented. Doy was good for Denis who, though talented and successful, was not yet a celebrity. She took him in hand, sharpened him up, taught him how to hold a knife and fork and speak 'received' English. Photographs of the time make them look a glamorous and devoted couple. They appeared on the brink of living happily ever after.

Suddenly, in 1943, something happened. In the words of Benny Green, 'Without warning a catastrophe hit our world. Denis disappeared from it. The Army required his services in India.'

He went to the subcontinent as a sergeant-major. 'Imagine me as a sergeant-major!' he laughed years later, his shoulders heaving as he raised his eyebrows in disbelief. 'Discipline . . . me!' It wasn't only that he was supposed to impose a discipline on his charges – a task for which he was manifestly unsuited. He was supposed to be getting his men fit. Denis's views on physical fitness were never tremendously rigorous.

The best wartime illustration of the Compton fitness theory was when a detachment of commandos was sent to the camp at an Indian garrison town called Mhow, where Denis was stationed. They were to prepare for a top-secret operation against the Japanese, and Denis was given the task of getting them into tip-top physical condition.

The Compton line of reasoning was that if these men had come through Arnhem they were more than fit enough for the Japanese, besides which they had obviously been having a grim time and were due for a break. Accordingly the sergeant-major drew up a programme and made arrangements. Every day a supply of beer was set up a short distance from base. Then under the severe supervision of Denis the men set off on a supposedly long and arduous training run. After a minute or two they would arrive at the beer and enjoy a party, and later they would run back again, with Denis urging them to put on as convincing a display of exhaustion as possible.

The commandos were effective actors and did Denis a favour by regularly complaining to the officers about the rigours of his training methods. 'My God sir, that Sergeant-Major Compton's a very hard man. He's really putting us through it.' As a result Denis's stock rose in all quarters.

He had been transferred to Rangoon by the end of the war. Then he was summoned to Delhi and told he was required for sporting purposes. There were two tasks. One was to raise a football team and the other was to play some cricket matches.

The football team went to Burma to play against battalions of Field Marshal Slim's 'Forgotten Army' sweating it out in the jungle. It was a rough but thoroughly exhilarating month. Denis and his team-mates found conditions primitive, and the pitches on which they played were literally hacked out of the forest. However the effect on morale was terrific. 'Gave everyone enormous pleasure,' said Denis in the 1990s. 'I still get wonderful letters from men who watched or played in those games.'

One of the cricket matches was for 'an Indian XI' against an Australian Forces XI which was returning home from a series of Victory Test matches in England. This outfit included old friends like Lindsay Hassett and Keith Miller, so it was a happy reunion. The affair was only slightly marred by an anti-imperialist riot in the course of play which very nearly prevented Denis scoring a hundred.

He was on 96 when he became aware that the crowd was becoming restive. In fact they were more than 'restive', they were developing into what Denis referred to as 'an unruly mob'. Getting a ball outside the off stump, Denis aimed to drive it but got an outside edge and watched the ball fly at an easily catchable height to first slip. First slip's attention, how-ever, had already been distracted by the disorderly spectators and he didn't even see the ball, let alone catch it. This meant four runs and the gift of yet another Compton hundred.

He didn't get any more runs, that day, because moments later the mob came onto the pitch and headed for the middle. Most of the players made a speedy exit but Denis, armed with his bat, stood his ground. So, predictably, did his friend Keith Miller.

The leader of the riot marched purposefully up to the nervous Denis and said, decisively, 'Mr Compton, you very good player but the game must stop.' For the rest of their lives this line became a private joke between the two men. Whether on the field of play at some social gathering, or even on the phone from Australia, conversations between the two of them would frequently begin with Keith Miller saying, in a Peter Sellers Indian accent: 'Mr Compton, you very good player but the game must stop.'

The records show that Denis played seventeen first-class matches in India during the war, averaging almost 90, but the only other one he remembered was the final of the Ranji Trophy between Holkar and Bombay. This turned out to be the highest-scoring match in the history of first-class cricket with 2078 runs being made. Denis made 249 of them and was not out. This was, at the time, his highest score. A Holkar businessman had promised to pay him 50 rupees for every run over a hundred. In the end this worked out at about 7500 rupees, or £600. It is no real surprise to learn that when the time came to ante up the punter from Holkar had done a runner.

Denis remembered little else about the game except that it was exceedingly hot. Afterwards he packed his bags and left for home. For the unlikely and somewhat reluctant sergeant-major the war was over and it was time to get on with the game.

CHAPTER SEVEN

Back at Lord's after losing six of the best years of his life, Denis picked up where he left off. He signed a three-year contract with Middlesex which brought in about £300 a year, plus £8 for every Middlesex match and £36 for a Test. The famous Brylcreem advertisements began a little later and made him a thousand a year, thanks, apparently, to Doy's businesslike intervention. He was also under contract to use a Wisden bat. In the post-war years a farm labourer would have been paid between £45 and £50 a week and a junior teacher about £500 a year. A three-bedroom house in London would have cost roughly £1500. Compton was therefore, by the standards of the day, tolerably prosperous but, perhaps more to the point, becoming genuinely famous.

As far as run-making goes, the summer of 1946 was as successful as the one of 1939. Indeed in terms of statistics it was remarkably similar. In 1946 he hit nine hundreds, as against eight in 1939. His total aggregate in all first-class games was 2403, as against 2468. He topped the Middlesex averages, just as he had done in that last year before the war, and just as he had done then he came third in the national averages. In '39 he was behind Hammond and Hutton; in '46 he was behind Hammond and Washbrook.

Yet you wouldn't class it as a vintage Compton year, nor a

vintage year in cricket. The tourists were the elder Nawab of Pataudi's Indian side and although they had some fine cricketers in men like Merchant and Mankad, Hazare and Amarnath, they were not a great team, especially when compared with Bradman's Australians. England only played three Tests against them, won the first at Lord's by ten wickets and drew the next two. Denis's best performance was a defiant and unbeaten 71 on a rain-affected sticky wicket at Old Trafford.

In truth he seems to have been a bit dejected. The marriage to Doris was not, according to him, going well and, after Rangoon and Delhi, London was drab and deprived. Around the end of May his form was so poor that he scored only 26 runs in seven innings: 10, 0, 7, 0, 8, 0 and 1. One of the ducks was at Lord's in the first Test.

That was the lowest point of all. Denis had allowed himself to sink into a depression and this contributed to a severe loss of form. The two fed on each other. The more depressed he became the fewer runs he got; the fewer runs, the greater the depression. Looking back on it he thought he should have been philosophical and just shrugged it off, but that is always easier said than done and for Denis this was a novel experience. He had never before had a long run of failure, and it disconcerted him. He even began to wonder whether the six-year lay-off had impaired his ability for ever. Perhaps he would never be the same again.

Lord's was his first Test since the war. What, particularly with Patsy Hendren or Bill Edrich, had once seemed a jaunty saunter to the wicket in the ground which was a second home to him, now seemed lonely and full of foreboding. Then he was bowled first ball by Amarnath, getting his bat caught in his pads. So he had to endure the same trudge back, dismally aware of his failure, a failure made worse by the more than four hundred runs amassed by his team-mates and in particular the 205 of his friend Joe Hardstaff.

It is a matter of history that Denis snapped out of this black dog. At the end of June he was playing against Warwickshire at Lord's. Out he went, 'hardly knowing which end of the bat to hold, and with my confidence absolutely nil'. He played at a ball from Eric Hollies, got an inside edge and watched the ball trickle gently into his wicket. It hit the stumps and the bails shook. To his considerable surprise the bails remained in place.

As we have seen, Denis was very superstitious. He always put his right pad on before his left and his right glove on before his left. When going out to bat with someone else he always expected his colleague to go through the gate first and to walk on his right side. Reflecting on this I had another look at the famous picture of him and Patsy Hendren walking out to bat and noticed with amusement that Denis is on the right and Hendren on his left. So much for Comptonisms!

In between deliveries he always twiddled his bat, which was fatiguing but necessary if the gods were to be propitiated. So when he saw the miracle of the ball hitting the stumps without dislodging the bails he decided that his fortunes had finally changed and everything was going to be all right.

Thus fortified, he threw his bat at the next ball and had the satisfaction of seeing it sail into the Grandstand balcony. Or so he says. Peter West in his biography says it went for four, which rather rules out the Grandstand balcony. Details such as this do tend to be obscured by the mists of time, but the point is that Denis went on to make 122 and by the end of the innings felt his confidence fully restored. That much is not in dispute.

From then on he batted well and made a number of big scores, including 235 against Surrey when he and Bill Edrich put on 296 in three and three-quarter hours. Much of the old exuberance seemed to have returned. In the Oval Test, the third against the Indians in 1946, he even ran out Vinoo

Merchant by kicking the ball into the stumps with the famous left foot, just as he might have rammed in a winning goal for Arsenal up the road at Highbury.

So by 31 August, when he embarked on the *Stirling Castle* to tour Australia, he was back to something like his pre-war best. It had taken time to get into the groove, and in the context of his career as a whole this was not one of his greatest summers. Most other batsmen would have been proud of it, but for Denis there had been more excitement in the past when he was developing that youthful promise and losing his cricketing virginity. And, of course, for Denis, the best was yet to come.

They sailed from Southampton and it is difficult now to understand what that sort of voyage meant to a cricket team. Nowadays, you acclimatise and get to know each other by training at Bisham Abbey and perhaps having a week in the Algarve. Then you fly out and play your first match within a few days of landing.

In those far-off days, however, it was like a story by W. Somerset Maugham: week upon week of deck tennis and dancing. The pace was different. Life was so much more leisurely and relaxed, so much more like fun. This part of touring suited Denis to a T.

I taxed Richie Benaud with this, suggesting that Denis's generation had more fun than modern cricketers. 'I can't agree,' he replied, 'that the cavalier, quixotic and larger-than-life approach to the game, and to things in general is lacking these days. It is there, perhaps in another guise, and often necessarily shielded because of intrusive reporting.'

He amplified this by explaining 'modern-day players definitely have just as much fun as the players years ago but they have it in a different fashion. First-class travel on ocean liners, second-sitting meals, black tie in the evenings and chauffeur-driven cars compared with the jet plane, the Hard

Rock Café, jeans and tracksuits, plus team blazers and ties where necessary, and the team bus with its stereo music and every player to his own Walkman.'

The 1946–47 tour of Australia was unsatisfactory. This was probably inevitable, coming so soon after the war. The MCC, still very much in charge of English cricket, had been reluctant to send a team, but the Australians were insistent and good public relations prevailed. In that sense the tour was satisfactory. Off the field Wally Hammond's men were a huge success. The gesture was appreciated. The sour aftermath of the 'Bodyline' tour, which still lingered, was effectively dissipated. The crowds were enormous. The money flowed in and ensured a profit to MCC of £50,000. As E.W. Swanton who covered the tour pointed out, 345,361 spectators watched the Melbourne test and the team's overheads were relatively small. A suite in the Hotel Australia in Sydney was just £2 a night.

There was a big but. After the First World War MCC sent a team to Australia in 1920 and failed to win a single Test. In 1946–47 the same thing happened. Australia were stronger than anticipated. The English bowling was weak; the fielding, especially the catching, was sketchy; and it took a long time for the two English batting stars, Denis and Len Hutton, to find their pre-war form. The weather was an unexpected nightmare and seventeen of the games were disrupted by rain. Denis himself had spent the latter half of the war away from home and was now wrenched away again. He felt dislocated and ill at ease. And Hammond was, for him, an awkward captain. Norman Preston, writing about the tour in *Wisden*, conceded that Hammond was far from being the inspiration that he had been in 1938 at home.

Hammond's own disastrous form – he averaged a mere 21 in the Tests – contributed to this. But in any case he was too lugubrious and too doctrinaire for Denis's free spirit, which only really thrived under the more laid-back style of leaders like Robins, Mann and Freddie Brown. Denis needed a loose rein and an easy smile, and that was not Hammond's way. There was also trouble with umpires – and bad blood between Hammond and his opposing captain Bradman. Almost worst of all, in Denis's eyes, was the business of the Jaguar. Hammond had been given a Jaguar motor car as a present. Denis accepted this, but not the fact that Hammond and the manager used it to drive flashily from match to match while the rest of the team chugged along by train. This did nothing for team spirit.

Hammond supporters don't always agree. One, also a great Compton fan, wrote,

> Denis Compton arrived like Apollo to challenge Jove, who to my mind was Walter Hammond. And reading your book makes me anxious that one hero/god should seem to cast shadows on another. What such men do on the field is all poetry to us but of course in their own private moments they can be as prosaic as the rest of us. I am always reading of Hammond's moody ways, yet some recently discovered letters suggest, as his published writings do, a much sunnier sort of disposition.

David Grant of Axminster pointed out that in his book *Cricket's Secret History* Hammond 'mentions Denis with admiration more than any other cricketer except Bradman'. He makes a good case but, for whatever reason, Denis felt unhappy with Hammond's captaincy. 'Perhaps,' he wrote, 'I was unfortunate in my relations with Hammond.'

Denis began brilliantly though in truth the opposition was weak. Because the team arrived early, two extra games were arranged, and in the first of these Denis made 84 against an outfit called 'Northern and Country Districts'. He missed the next two games but then made a careful face-saving 98 with

Cyril Washbrook before trying to reach his century with one of his charges down the wicket and being stumped. This was against a strong 'Combined XI'.

After that there was a century against a very weak South Australia Country XI and a free-hitting 71 against South Australia. This was the first time the team had encountered Bradman. He was 39 now and had not been well. He seemed frail and out of practice. He had actually been invalided out of the Australian forces in 1942 and spent the rest of the war as an air raid warden. Rumours of his ill health were rife, and there seemed an even chance that he would decide not to play first-class cricket again. On the evidence of this match it looked as if retirement might be the safer option. This was a drawn game, but MCC (as the England team was still known in all but Test matches) had much the better of it.

In the next match they thrashed Victoria, who were widely regarded as the strongest of the State sides. Denis made a good three-hour century in the first innings, and Hutton an even better one in the second. The brilliant young all-rounder Keith Miller made relatively few runs and did not bowl at all, which should have given pause for thought. After the win morale was understandably high, but as it turned out this was the only first-class match the tourists won.

Three rather dull-sounding drawn games followed in which Denis's top score was 55, and then it was time for the first Test at Brisbane. Denis always believed that one particular incident in this game had a vital effect on the whole series and in particular on Don Bradman himself.

Even the judicious *Wisden* seems to share Denis's view. Australia batted first and, losing Barnes and Morris with only 46 runs on the board, seemed to be heading for a low total. This seemed all the more likely because the Don, coming in at No. 3, looked just as out of sorts as he had done when playing for South Australia. Denis thought that Hammond was (as usual) far too negative in his field placing. The way Bradman was poking around, he would have been bound to get out if Hammond had only surrounded him with a predatory set of close fielders. But Hammond was too nervous. Or so Denis believed. In mitigation, as Denis later admitted, Hammond was hampered by having an attack in which the relatively inexperienced Alec Bedser was the most lethal weapon. And he only bowled fast-medium.

Denis watched with something approaching pity as the veteran Australian captain stuttered along. Bradman was in terrible trouble against Bedser and had two bad mishits in the very first over. After forty minutes he had made only seven runs.

After a while Denis was fielding at long leg watching the bowling of Larwood's old partner, Bill Voce – one of several veterans who Denis felt were too old to make the tour.

Voce, however, was too good for Bradman at this stage, and sure enough, on 28, Bradman played a poor shot, got a thick edge which flew straight to the reliable hands of Jack Ikin in the slips. Ikin made the catch. Ikin was in no doubt that the catch was good. Nor was Denis. Nor were any of the England players.

However the Don did not walk. For what seemed like an eternity the England side stood waiting silently for him to do the decent thing. But still he stood and did not move. Finally the England players appealed and to their amazement and to Hammond's obvious and visible fury the umpire said 'Not out'. Denis used to say that it remained 'one of the most extraordinary decisions I have ever heard'.

Even the Australians, though they might not have admitted it at the time, knew that Bradman was out. Honest Jack Fingleton, Test cricketer, author and commentator, subsequently wrote: 'In the calmness of afterwards, when the flurry and skirl of controversy die down, no harm is done in admitting to posterity that Bradman *was* out at 28, caught by

Ikin in the slips and given not out. This was a mistake which the best of umpires have made from time immemorial, but it probably had a profound influence upon Bradman's career after the war.'

At the time, neither Denis nor any of his team-mates was amused. Hammond, in particular, was incandescent, and relations between the two captains never recovered.

Fingleton and Denis were in complete agreement about the significance of the error. After the reprieve Bradman went on to recover all his lost confidence and make another 187 runs. He and Hassett put on a record 276 runs and Australia made 645, their highest score in Australia.

This was galling, but what made it even worse was the fact that the weather intervened crucially. There was a violent thunderstorm and England were then caught on a fearful rain-damaged wicket. As Fingleton wrote, 'Taking the rest of his [Bradman's] innings away this would have meant that Bradman, of a certainty, would have had to bat some time on that terrible Brisbane sticky pitch that came for England.'

If Bradman had batted on a sticky dog, Fingleton and Denis both consider that he would have failed. He seldom batted well on such surfaces. If that had happened, both these two commentators think that he would have retired forthwith and England would have gone into the next Test against an infinitely less experienced captain.

Denis remained certain that the umpire's decision was a wrong one, but on the other hand, charitable as ever, he said that if it kept Bradman in the game for a few years more, then he was glad. Perhaps so. But no Englishman thought so at the time.

The remainder of the match was punctuated by thunder, lightning and hailstones as big as golf balls. Nearly all Lindwall's deliveries rose head-high. He was, though only at the beginning of his career, one of the great Australian fast bowlers. Several Englishmen, including Denis, batted with skill and bravery but it was impossible and they were all out for 141. Mercifully Lindwall was kept out of the second innings after coming down with chickenpox, but there were still Miller and Toshack to contend with, and England only managed 172. The last fifteen wickets fell in three and a half hours.

An Englishman can't help feeling somewhat cheated, even after all this time. Hammond obviously did, and the resentment soured his captaincy as well as his relationship with Bradman. Denis on the other hand seemed to manage to keep his private views on Bradman as a person quite distinct from his feelings about Bradman as a cricketer. On the field, the Don could seem obdurate. However, he liked Bradman personally and was enchanted, for instance, when during the second Test the great man asked him round for dinner at his hotel and even gave him a few tips on technique. Denis appreciated them, for he knew that some of his strokes weren't quite right.

He also gave Denis a lecture on confidence, which he regarded as all-important. Without it you would fail. Indeed he himself was a case in point, for until the fateful Ikin decision he was manifestly very short of it. Fingleton went so far as to say that he was 'suffering intense mental stress'. Denis took the lesson to heart and appreciated it. As a player in both cricket and football Denis nearly always seemed to have boundless confidence but it did sometimes desert him.

Denis considered Bradman the best batsman he ever saw, and in retirement the two became the best of friends. Indeed Denis, at seventy-five and not in the best of health, still made the long trek to Australia to help Bradman celebrate his eighty-fifth birthday. It was a very select occasion and Denis was the only Englishman there.

Denis only made four in the next match, which was upcountry at a place called Gympie, and where the hospitality was wonderful even by Australian standards. The social side of this tour was outstandingly successful, and the lavish hospitality of their hosts particularly appreciated so soon after the war, when conditions back home were still deplorable.

Denis did not excel in the second Test, though he managed a fifty in the second innings and with Bill Edrich put on England's first century partnership of the series. But the Australians again won by an innings, with Barnes and the now merciless Bradman making exactly the same score – 234.

Three more country games followed, with Denis beginning to run into his true form. He made over seventy in two crowd-pleasing innings and in the second match put on 118 in under an hour with his captain.

This form did not follow him into the Melbourne Test, however, and he was out cheaply in both innings. England suffered fearful luck, losing James Langridge to an injury before play even began. Then, when Australia batted, two England bowlers, Edrich and Voce, had to leave the field. Edrich returned, limping after being hit in the shin from a hook by Barnes, and even took wickets.

The umpires also took a hand, giving Edrich out lbw when he had manifestly hit the ball onto his pads and then compounding the error by delivering the same verdict on Denis when he padded up to a ball well outside the leg stump. In the second innings he was run out for 14. But at least, despite ill luck, the match was honourably drawn.

Now, at last, Denis caught fire. In the second innings against a 'Combined XI' in Tasmania he belted out 124 in under two hours. This was more like the true Compton. Significantly perhaps, Norman Yardley, whose captaincy Denis much preferred to Hammond's, was in charge for this match, and for the next one, when Denis and Joe Hardstaff shared a stand of 282 in three hours.

He sat out the next match but returned for the Adelaide

Test, where he made a century in each innings. 'Perpetual heat and dense humidity' were a feature of this game, and these were conditions which never bothered Denis, especially after his time in the subcontinent.

This was also a game in which Denis came up against the mean side in Bradman's character, a side Denis positively disliked. In latter years, said Denis, the Don mellowed even to the extent, much to Denis's delight, of enjoying the odd dram. But in those days he was often ruthless, displaying a win-at-all-costs attitude exemplified by his refusal to 'walk' in the first Test.

Denis's first-innings hundred was chanceless and indubitably his best of the tour so far. Ray Lindwall eventually had him caught and bowled for 147, but not before Denis had emerged victorious from one of the first of what were to be many exciting duels with his ferocious friends Ray Lindwall and Keith Miller. These two were very quick, very dangerous and very hostile, but Denis met fire with fire.

It was in the second innings that Denis had his revealing little spat with Bradman. In the first Australia led England by a mere 27 runs, but in the second England did not do well. Hutton and Washbrook got off to a good start, putting on a hundred for the first wicket. Then, however, there was a collapse, and England had only 255 on the board for the loss of eight wickets. Only Denis, of the recognised batsmen, was left.

Enter now the chirpy figure of Godfrey Evans. Evans was an ebullient batsman but not, generally speaking, a man to stick around. This time, however, he achieved a miracle. It was over an hour and a half before he scored a single run, which for a man like him was an extraordinary example of self-restraint. Eventually the two of them remained together, undefeated, for two and a quarter hours. During this time Denis successfully farmed the bowling to protect his weaker partner, and they put on 85, of which Evans scored 10, facing 98 balls but scoring off only seven.

Bradman was singularly unamused by this. Obviously he wanted his bowlers to be able to have a crack at Evans. He therefore placed his fielders on the boundary, thus inviting Denis to take the single and get Evans down to the striker's end. Denis wasn't falling for this and refused the invitation until as near the end of the over as possible.

After a while Bradman came up to Denis and said peevishly that this was not cricket. A good crowd had paid good money to see proper cricket and here was Denis just patting the ball down the wicket and refusing to run. 'What you are doing,' said Bradman, 'is not the way cricket should be played.'

Denis agreed that it was dull stuff but there was a simple solution. If Bradman were to bring his fielders in and play a normal game then Denis would also play a normal game. This seemed a satisfactory solution, so Bradman called in his fielders – and Denis promptly whacked the next ball for four.

Bradman was now even less amused. Again he approached the batsman and told Denis, in no uncertain terms, that he was not going to make him a present of free runs. Denis replied that in that case they'd revert to what Denis describes as 'the same procedure'. So Bradman placed his fielders back on the boundary, as Denis puts it, 'regardless of whether it was cricket or not'.

A little later Bradman came over for another talk. Denis was wearing spikes in his boots and he was also indulging his usual habit of charging the slow bowlers. A side-effect of this was that he was marking the pitch.

Bradman complained.

Denis apologised.

'But we have to bat on this,' said Bradman.

'I am *terribly* sorry,' said Denis, 'but I'm playing for our side.' End of conversation.

In the event this too was a drawn game. Australia were set a sporting challenge of 314 in three and a quarter hours, but Bradman refused it. This was a bit niggardly in view of England's feeble attack.

Denis was presented with a watch from the South Australian Cricket Association for his achievement in scoring two hundreds in the game. Arthur Morris got one for doing the same. It was the first time two men had achieved the feat in the same Test. And Ray Lindwall received a third for taking three wickets in four balls, all bowled.

Denis had now hit four consecutive hundreds in first-class matches and he very nearly managed a fifth in the next. He was on 93 not out against Victoria. Keith Miller was bowling and Denis hit it straight back at him, hard. Miller failed to take the catch cleanly but knocked it up and got it at the second attempt. You might think that Miller would have let his mate go after the record, but they didn't play their cricket like that. The rivalry on the field was intense, while on a rest day they would go off to the races and have a few beers together. Neither man would have wished it any other way.

The match against New South Wales was a sporting affair spoiled by rain. Denis, who had made 75 in the first innings, came together with Len Hutton, chasing a target of 339 in four hours. In one of their rare partnerships the two rivals added 85 in 38 minutes but alas, rain stopped play with MCC well on target.

The Ashes were won and lost but the last Test, at Sydney, produced the best cricket of the series on a rain-affected wicket. (On Sunday there were mushrooms on the field of play!) England once again experienced what *Wisden* described as 'wretched luck'. Hutton made a hundred but then had to go to hospital with tonsilitis. Hammond, Hardstaff and Langridge were all unfit, and Yardley was captain for the first time.

Lindwall and Miller bowled short and fast and in the first innings Denis, trying to protect his face from a rearing bouncer, unluckily trod on his wicket. In the second innings he was the only England batsman to 'prove equal to the occasion'. He batted bravely, making 76 in 2 hours 53 minutes and showing once more that, when necessary, he could put his head down and graft. His heroics were not enough, however, and England totalled only 186, leaving a target which Australia achieved with five wickets to spare.

The team now left by flying boat for New Zealand, and arrived in Wellington after a road journey from Auckland feeling jaded and 'travel weary'. In the first three matches Denis achieved little of note, but in the final match against Auckland he enjoyed an unprecedented all-round success on the now familiar sticky wicket. First of all he ran out of partners while making 97 not out, his brilliant driving producing a six and 11 fours. Then he came on to bowl, found a length immediately, broke the opening stand and took 7 for 36. He was effectively unplayable, and the last eight wickets went down in an hour after lunch. In the second innings Yardley didn't bring him on until halfway through, whereupon he took four of the last five wickets, ending with 4 for 13.

It was a high note on which to end his first tour of the Antipodes. He was top of the bowling averages and should probably have bowled more. He almost certainly would have done if Yardley had been captain, but his style of bowling did not suit Hammond in the cautious dusk of his career. In the Tests against Australia he averaged over 50, just behind Len Hutton. Overall he was third behind Hutton and Langridge but, with 1660 runs, scored many more than anyone else.

It had been something of a baptism of fire, for he had never faced an attack as fast as Lindwall and Miller. The combination of their speed and the strange Australian wickets meant that he had to work hard on his game and adjusting his technique.

The statistics suggest that he succeeded, though he conceded that, while managing to compete with these two, he never mastered them. Then again, although they always tested him, they never mastered him either.

The relationship between them became one of the great rivalries and one of the great friendships of Denis's career. On the anvil of their pace that winter Denis forged an enhancement of his genius. His game was profoundly improved. In the domestic season of 1947 there would be no fast bowling to come close to that of Lindwall and Miller. Nor would there be many pitches quite as terrifyingly inconsistent.

The omens for Denis looked good.

CHAPTER EIGHT

Peter Hennessy, in his history of post-war Britain, awards Denis two whole pages for the year 1947, largely because of the inestimable good that he and Bill Edrich did for a flagging national morale. Hennessy writing in 1993 quoted Lord Bancroft, head of the Home Civil Service, who in 1947 was a young Treasury tyro:

> There wasn't much in the shops and there was even less money around to spend in them. But to be young, alive and unwounded was a joyous experience and there was, too, a great deal of hope. There was a great relief at the war being won and coming through alive. The weather seemed pretty good too. Every Saturday, in that golden summer of 1947, we would go to Lord's with our packets of sandwiches to watch Compton and Edrich.

In truth the British were in a sorry state. Rationing, in 1947, was at its meanest and tightest. Someone at the time was asked to do a calculation to see what the daily British ration would be if, as seemed probable, we ran out of American dollars. The answer was 1700 calories a day, which was over 1000 calories less than the minimum during the war. Hennessy quotes a young ex-serviceman of the day, shivering through an unbelievably hard winter, who because of power cuts is unable even to listen to the radio or turn on his electric fire. 'I wish I were back in Egypt,' he told Mass Observation. 'I wish I were anywhere but in this goddamned country where there is nothing but queues and restrictions and forms and shortages and no food and cold. Flu and the fuel crisis is the last straw.'

Jim Swanton remembered how the South African tourists earned extra popularity.

They brought over a good deal of tinned food as a gesture of sympathy for the ration situation, but despite the tins, the captain's efforts over the summer – and he was slim in the first place – cost him a couple of stone. Such hardships, all but forgotten now, were real enough at the time, and they struck no one more forcibly than our visitors from overseas. It was the Tory Government in 1951 that abolished ration cards. We needed petrol coupons even longer.

Into this austere grey world Compton's cricket injected a much-needed ray of sunshine – though in fairness it should be said that God did his bit too and compensated for the frightfulness of the winter by providing some extremely good weather that summer. Swanton, who had spent most of the war in a Japanese prison camp and was in particular need of cheering up, said, 'The brilliance of Denis's batting, day after day . . . was something I have never seen matched. Denis made his runs gaily, and with a smile. His happy demeanour and his good looks completed a picture of the beau ideal of a sports-man. I doubt if any game at any period has thrown up anyone to match his popular appeal in the England of 1947–1949.'

If this sounds over the top it is doubtless because throughout his life, ever since their first encounter on the field of play in Folkestone, Swanton had a soft spot for Compton. Hennessy, who, like me, only caught Denis in the early Fifties, says he knows what his eulogists mean and believes they tell the truth.

As a social and political commentator he also knows that this was one of those rare moments in sport when a game transcended itself and had quite a profound effect on real life.

Sport, particularly when played the way Denis played, brought people together. 'In the early post war years,' wrote Hennessy, 'crowds were huge and almost entirely violence free.' Spectator sports were almost like worship. In that first decade after the war there were no banners, no shouting – everyone even looked the same. As Hennessy remarked, 'Young men dressed like their fathers and grandfathers – jackets, mackintoshes and caps. Young boys wore school uniform. Not until the first glimmerings of affluence put money into young pockets in the mid-Fifties did the external expressions of a youth culture come to distinguish the generations in a sporting crowd.'

As Cardus wrote in a memorable passage,

> Never have I been so deeply touched on a cricket ground as I was in this heavenly summer, when I went to Lord's to see a pale-faced crowd, existing on rations, the rocket bomb still in the ears of most folk – to see this worn, dowdy crowd watching Compton. The strain of long years of anxiety and affliction passed from all hearts and shoulders at the sight of Compton in full flow, sending the ball here, there and everywhere, each stroke a flick of delight, a propulsion of happy, sane, healthy life. There is no rationing in an innings by Compton.

The actual facts that led grown men to wax so lyrical are extraordinary, for that summer Denis made more runs and hit more centuries than any man before or since. Yet, as so often with him, it was not the making of runs that counted so much as the manner of their making. The statistics are unique, but to have been there to see how they were compiled must have been very heaven. Robin Marlar, who later bowled against the maestro – 'To be able to lock horns with such a man! What a thrill!' – was sixteen that year and made his first appearance at Lord's for Harrow against Eton. 'Every day that summer,' he enthused in retrospect, 'seemed bathed in sunshine.'

The beginnings, however, were not auspicious.

A thousand runs in May was one of the aspirations of a top-class batsman in those days. It was one of the 'cricket records' listed in *Wisden* and came immediately after 'Largest Aggregates outside England'. Grace, Hammond and Hallows all did it, and Hayward, Bradman (twice) and Bill Edrich all got a thousand before June, though they 'cheated' by starting to score runs in April. You would have thought, considering all the other records he broke that year, that Denis would have done it easily in 1947. In fact, he scored only 832 runs (363 in the championship) before the Glorious First.

His very first innings of the summer was good enough – 73 for MCC against Yorkshire, the champion county, on a difficult wicket. In the next seven innings, however, he only once made more than fifty.

It is difficult to be entirely sure why this should have been so. Denis tended to start the season slowly, even though he often made runs in his very first match. He himself said that he really perked up when the South Africans arrived – and as he took no fewer than six hundreds off them this sounds plausible.

Above all he thrived on sunshine. That summer was so hot that the South Africans complained about it. 'I loved it,' he told me. 'I feel a different person, and find cricket almost a different and certainly a more pleasurable game, when the sun is shining down hotly and the perspiration begins to run down the back of my neck. That's when I really want to play cricket. The sun agrees with me.' As the Indians had observed when he was the only 'white' man to play in the Ranji trophy competition, Denis tanned deeply – so much so that he went almost black. Odder still, he went a darker shade of brown under the relatively insipid English sun, so that by the end of 1947 he was dark enough to have fallen foul of South Africa's apartheid laws – had they yet been introduced.

So he seems to have changed gear when the sun shone. That is the theory, but as so often the facts sometimes get in the way. He found form against Worcester towards the end of May, making 88 not out and 112. But it wasn't sunny, not at all. In his book about him, Peter West has a typical Denis anecdote about him charging down the wicket to the leg-spin of Roly Jenkins. Jenkins told Denis he didn't mind being advanced upon in this fashion, but was he supposed to shake hands?

Marlar, who bowled at much the same pace as Jenkins, had a similar recollection of Denis's approach to spin bowling. 'Not for him the tactics of stay at home and pick off the inevitable bad ball. Not for him the stay at home and swing a bat so heavy that even the mishit should clear the fence. Compton would lift his bat and start to dance towards you; if you reacted by dropping short, he would dance back again and cut or pull you to ribbons.'

Denis confirmed this. It was, in effect, a function of boredom. If a bowler hit a length he tried to put him off it by dancing down the wicket. As Marlar suggests, he was usually nimble and adroit enough to counter the inevitable reaction by dancing back to the crease. This had the effect of turning the delivery into a rank bad, short ball which, as Marlar says, Denis would cut or pull to ribbons. Or shreds.

Sussex came next. David Sheppard, later Bishop of Liverpool, and sometime – though not by 1947 – captain of Sussex, told me ruefully that Denis's average against his county that year was 120. No mean batsman himself, the Bishop also remarked, just as wryly, that as a schoolboy, which he then was, 'I thought that if I worked very hard and did everything absolutely right I might one day bat like Len Hutton. But I could never bat like Denis Compton.' As it happened Sheppard had a pretty good 1947 himself, for he topped the Sherborne School batting with an average of 78.

This time Middlesex thrashed Sussex by ten wickets, with Compton and Edrich putting on 223 together, of which Denis made 110. It was, apparently, 'the one complete batting mastery of the match'. In addition Denis got a couple of wickets, one of them a stumping by Leslie and the other a catch by Leslie. People always remember Compton and Edrich, but Compton and Compton had their moments too. It was in this fixture, of course, that Denis had made his debut against Maurice Tate. On this occasion, as then, Lord's was an appropriate and packed amphitheatre for his talents. On Whit Monday there were 30,000 spectators in the ground.

When June finally arrived he saw it in in fine style. Middlesex played the South Africans on the last day of May and the 2nd and 3rd of June (The Glorious First being a Sunday). Denis's first innings was a four-hour faultless century. He hit 19 fours, mainly drives and pulls, and he shared partnerships of 147 with Edrich and 103 with his brother Leslie. In the end, however, the South Africans were dominant and in the second innings, on what *Wisden* described as 'wearing turf', only Bill Edrich, with a defiant 133 not out, stood between them and victory. Denis was second-highest scorer with 34.

The bat was beginning to sing now. Denis recalls that most people assumed that the bat was a Wisden. It looked like a Wisden, and he was under contract to Wisden to use one of their bats whenever he played. However, Denis didn't like his Wisden bat and said so to Harry Warsop, whose little north London factory traditionally turned out all the Middlesex bats. 'No problem,' said Warsop. And he produced one of his own bats for Denis to use, the only difference being that he didn't stamp it with his own logo but instead produced a blank blade which he then somehow contrived to emboss with the name and trademark of Wisden. The world thought Denis flayed the bowlers of '47 with a Wisden, but actually it was a Warsop.

Hampshire came to Lord's after the South Africa match and were beaten by an innings. Jack Robertson was the star, with a double century, and Middlesex made 429 for 6 on the first day. Denis and Robertson put on 193 at two a minute, though Denis made 'only' 88. Not for the first or last time he was stumped. That cavalier spirit and those dancing feet did let him down sometimes.

He missed the next two games, one of which against Glamorgan was severely affected by rain. This plum in the middle of June.

The next match was against Yorkshire. Hutton v. Compton. In a sense they emerged with honours even, for the match was drawn and both men made half-centuries. However, Middlesex had much the better of proceedings and Denis had the considerable satisfaction of catching out his great rival off his own bowling. The catch, one-handed, was a remarkable one even by his own standards. Once again Denis's not-out cameo was made at extreme speed – he and Bill Edrich put on 90 in 50 minutes – and, once again contrary to legend, the match was interfered with by rain.

The team then left headquarters for a month, playing six matches, three of which they lost, including one against Oxford University who beat them by a clear eight wickets in the Parks. Denis, unsurprisingly, was absent from this encounter. He and Edrich were also away on Test duty for the game against Essex and this too was lost – by ten wickets this time.

The twins were back for the return match against Yorkshire at Headingley. This was Bill Bowes's benefit but it was really Edrich's match. On a rain-affected wicket he made 172 in two innings while Denis only managed 19. Nevertheless the wicket suited Denis's extravagant leg-spin, and he and Jack Young skittled Yorkshire out for only 85. Denis took four wickets for only 23 and in the second innings 3 for 28. This haul included two catches by Leslie, one the match-winner, a particularly fine effort in the deep rather than, as usual, behind the wicket.

In the next match Hampshire were convincingly beaten despite the absence of the Test players, but they were back again for the Leicester game which was one of the most exciting of an eventful season. This game really does give the lie to anyone who believes that a certain sort of frisson can only be induced by the one-day slog. It was Bill Edrich's first game as captain. Denis made 151 in the first innings though Edrich eclipsed him with 257. In just over two hours between lunch and tea the two of them put on an astonishing 310 runs.

At lunch on the final day Leicester led by 17 runs and had only lost four wickets. The game looked set for a tame draw. Yet again, enter Denis. The last six wickets fell for only 48 runs in 35 minutes. Three were victims of Denis, who took 5 for 108. Even so a draw seemed inevitable because Middlesex needed 66 with only 25 minutes left. Scurrying off the field, Edrich told Compton that they'd get them together. And they did. The pair hit the runs off seven overs and Middlesex finished as victors with four minutes to spare. 'A more thrilling finish would be difficult to imagine,' said *Wisden*. Not only that. In all 1405 runs were scored in three days – 663 on the second. Is it any wonder that old men shake their heads at the state of modern cricket?

The Test players were absent again for the next match against Somerset at Taunton, and the West Country men recorded a remarkable double, beating the eventual county champions by 24 runs. It was comparable to Chelsea beating Manchester United at Old Trafford and Stamford Bridge in the 1993–94 season. (By 2005 you would have reversed these two club names – a telling reminder of the vicissitudes of sport!) This was only the second game that Middlesex lost without their Test players. The other seven were all won. In terms of skill and ability the substitutes were never the equal of the men they replaced, but when Bill and Denis were away regulars like Leslie or Sid Brown seemed to become inspired and play above themselves. The spirit in the dressing room, nurtured by shove-halfpenny skills almost as great as the cricketing ones, was noticeably high.

Back at Lord's, Middlesex came up against the Essex team who had earlier beaten their depleted side by ten wickets. This time Denis was in the side and responded well to the challenge. He made 129 in the first innings and in the second was stumped again, two short of his half-century. Almost as extraordinary as the amount of runs he made was the speed at which he made them. He and his captain, Robins, added 150 runs in ten minutes over the hour, and his 129 included a six and 14 fours. He was at the wicket for just two hours. It was now mid-July and the records were coming into sight. In this game Edrich became the first batsman to reach 2000 runs. They must have been an extraordinary incentive to each other.

In 1994 I heard from a woman on the Isle of Arran. I don't think what she wrote was untypical:

I was lucky enough to be walking past Lord's early in the summer of '47. It was near close of play, the gates were open and my sister and I walked in to see what all the noise was about. Compton was batting at one end and Godfrey Evans at the other. It was most entertaining and we were at once hooked on the game. For three years every spare moment was spent watching Middlesex. I think all the girls were wildly in love with Denis and now after forty-five years still remember him and his delightful cricket with the greatest affection.

Now came another period away from home. For the rest of July and the first half of August they were on the road – or to be more accurate the railway track. There were no sponsored BMWs with players' names written on them. The team travelled as a team. They played their bridge together and they drank their beer together. The amateurs may have stayed marginally aloof, but war had blurred those Gentleman and Player distinctions, as had a Labour government. Labour and the Players were the masters now, and the success and celebrity of a working-class boy such as Denis provided the proof that this was so.

So to Northampton and Nottingham; Hove and Canterbury; and finally just south of the river to Kennington for the Oval and Surrey. What contrasts there were in these destinations. The week in the Midlands essentially industrial and workmanlike with echoes of boots and shoes, pharmaceuticals and lace. Then the gentle breeze of genteel Hove, all Regency crescents and striped deckchairs, followed by the sylvan elegance of Canterbury with the marquees and the bands Denis loved. When a later generation of players demanded that the band should not play during the cricket because it interfered with their concentration Denis threw up his hands in a mixture of horror and disbelief.

'I always tried to bat in time to the music,' he claimed.

Middlesex won all these games except the one against Kent, which they drew. They were big victories too: eight wickets, 287 runs, nine wickets, an innings and 11 runs. To beat Surrey by an innings and 11 was very heaven. It was even easier than it sounds, for Middlesex only lost two wickets in the entire match. Even by the standards of this extraordinary year Denis had a field day – three of them in fact. First of all he scored 137 not out, sharing a partnership with the inevitable Edrich of 287 in two and three-quarter hours. Then, when Surrey batted, he struck irresistible form with that left-arm unorthodox over-the-wicket mixture of googlies and Chinamen. In the first innings he took 6 for 94 and in the second 6 for 80. Two of the wickets were caught and bowled and he also managed to catch Stuart Surridge off the bowling of Robins. To put the gilt on the gingerbread two of his victims were caught behind by his brother and one stumped. Over 47,000 people watched this match and they had to close the gates on Saturday.

The other matches were pretty enjoyable too. He hit 110 off Northants, sharing a stand of 211 with Edrich, then took six wickets in the first innings and three in the second. He didn't play at Trent Bridge, but at Hove in James Langridge's benefit he made 100 not out and took 4 for 90 in the first innings as well as pouching three catches in the second. This was his tenth century of the summer and there were plenty more to come. Denis was uncharacteristically mean to the poor beneficiary. He had him lbw for 2. Incidentally his successful bowling once more took place on a rain-affected wicket. The more closely you look at 1947, the more you see that the modern idea that the summer was completely damp-free is far from the truth.

In the drawn match at Canterbury he made 106 out of 225. This was a slower-paced innings than usual, but once more he played according to what was required. His colleagues were in all sorts of trouble against Doug Wright's deceptively quick leg breaks and the situation demanded patience and application. Wright took 6 for 87 and he finally had Denis caught behind by his future friend and colleague the wicketkeeper Godfrey Evans. But by then Denis had done the business.

It was a strange match, for Kent made over four hundred in the first innings and were able to enforce the follow-on. Then Middlesex, despite a rare single-figure score from Denis, managed also to rake up more than four hundred and thus set Kent 232 to win. In the end Kent got to 181 for 6, although Denis, unexpectedly against a side going all out for its strokes, failed to take a wicket and was much less effective than Jack Young. The crowds during this festival were enormous –

more or less double the average number that attended before the war. This really was the apogee of county cricket in more ways than one. Nothing could make a stronger case for the three-day game; for the excitement of regular spin bowling, much of it unorthodox; and, not least important, for leaving wickets uncovered and susceptible to interesting treatment from the elements.

After the tremendous all-round achievement at the Oval they again played Kent, for the second time in a week, though this time, of course, on home turf. Kent won another nail-biting contest, by 75 runs with five minutes to spare. Denis took four rather expensive wickets and in the first innings was diddled by Doug Wright again when on only 16. In the second innings Middlesex had to score 397 to win at about 90 an hour. This was just the sort of challenge Denis relished, and he rose to it as he rose to practically everything in this charmed moment. Wright had bowled brilliantly in the first innings, taking 7 for 92. In the second he crucially caught and bowled Bill Edrich for only 31, and with Brown and Robertson also out cheaply the Middlesex prospects looked dim. However George Mann gave Denis some stalwart support and together they added 161 in just over an hour and a half. I have to pinch myself sometimes when I read the scoring rates of all those years ago. Could a game have been so totally different? Was the bowling so much easier to hit? Were batsmen more courageous? Incidentally, these runs were not made against an attacking field. Most of the Kent side were positioned on the boundary to cut off fours.

Often today even when, usually in limited-overs cricket, speedy scores are made, they are relatively low. But then men like Compton and Edrich, and even Robertson and Brown, consistently put together hundred and fifties and double centuries. And big partnerships were commonplace as well. I cannot think when I saw two men together make 161 in an hour and a half. Indeed I cannot imagine a modern side making a serious attempt to score almost four hundred at ninety an hour. The shutters would be up at once. Denis didn't like to be heard agreeing with this view, for there were few things he disliked more than old buffers like him rubbishing modern youth. Nevertheless you knew that deep down he was affronted by the paralysis that, for a time, affected his best-loved game. In any case you only have to look at the record of his career and then compare and contrast. He would have loved the acceleration of tempo in the modern game and responded with enthusiasm to the speed at which men like Flintoff and Pietersen make their runs.

It was Wright, of course, who broke the stand at Canterbury. He was not only wily throughout, he managed to maintain a remarkably consistent and nagging length. Shortly after he bowled Mann, Denis, now running short of partners, attempted a big hit off the demon Wright and was caught. After that things fell apart, there being no centre to hold them together, and the last five wickets only realised 25 runs and only lasted 25 minutes.

The fifth Test was on when Middlesex went west to Cheltenham, where they won a famous Comptonless victory which put the County Championship firmly in their sights. Denis was also absent when, immediately afterwards, his teammates trounced Derbyshire despite a hat-trick by the Derby captain – a rare oddity this since the man, Gothard by name, had previously only ever taken one first-class wicket and only took six in the entire season. Even without Denis, the Compton family were once again in the thick of it, for his brother Leslie made his maiden first-class hundred in this match. I am sorry to go on about the speed with which men scored their runs in 1947, but I feel I should record that Leslie took only 87 minutes to make this maiden century and that he and Sid Brown took only 95 minutes to add 181.

The star was back for the return match against Surrey at Lord's. Once more the golden memories are not altogether accurate, for on the first day 35 minutes were lost because of bad light. Nevertheless Middlesex still managed to knock up 462 runs. Denis made 178 in the first innings and then 19 not out in the second. In the first George Mann made a maiden century and he and Denis redeemed an indifferent Middlesex start with a partnership of 304 which yet again was made at an astonishing rate. It took them three and a quarter hours.

Normally the Surrey wicketkeeper would have been Denis's old school contemporary Arthur McIntyre, whom he ran out when they opened the innings for the Elementary Schools on that memorable day which first brought Denis to Plum Warner's attention. However McIntyre was indisposed and a substitute was drafted in by name of Garth Wheatley.

Later he remembered the dramatic batting of the day, naturally, but there was one vignette etched in his memory.

I remember Jim Laker bowling from the pavilion end, and getting a little turn down the slope. Not surprisingly Compton was sweeping. Surprisingly, Surrey had no long leg. Alf Gover, by then approaching the veteran stage, was at short leg and had the job of retrieving the ball from the boundary. After one such trip he said, 'For —'s sake, Denis, remember I'm an old man.'

For two or three overs Compton drew back and placed the ball on the off side. Then came another sweep. When Gover returned, Compton said, 'I'm terribly sorry, Alf, I forgot.' Gover was not troubled again.

I doubt if anyone except the wicketkeeper overheard the little exchange, but it typified the spirit in which Compton played his cricket.

When I reminded Denis of this incident he grinned a little sheepishly and then said, 'Ah yes. But what he doesn't say is

The Comptons: Father, Mother, Denis, Hilda, Leslie.

London Schools cricket, 1932. Denis is sixth from the left in the front row.
The rakish tilt of the quartered cap owes something to Jack Hobbs.
Unless otherwise stated, all pictures by courtesy of Christine Compton.

Denis Compton walking out to bat with Patsy Hendren in 1937.
Getty Images

Denis and Leslie Compton as Special Constables, flanking Fred Price,
the Middlesex wicketkeeper, in St John's Wood, September 1939.

Four Middlesex cricket stars receiving their instructions as newly recruited Military Police in September 1939. Left to right: Fred Price, Ted Roberts, Leslie Compton, Denis. *Popperfoto*

On 1 March 1941 Denis married Doris Rich (Doy). Here he talks to Sir Pelham Warner (left) at the reception, held in the Tavern at Lord's. In the middle is Fred Price.

Denis with Doy.

Herbert Chapman's historic Arsenal side. Compton is in the second row, third from right.

Back to school. Denis and Leslie with their old mentor Mark Mitchell, 'a tough old bird'.

Deputy Prime Minister Clement Attlee meets a wartime England football team. Denis is at the far right.

PLAN OF THE FIELD OF PLAY

ENGLAND (i) 3

Colours: White shirts, dark blue knickers

1. *Goalkeeper*
W. G. MARKS
(Arsenal and R.A.F.)

2. *Right Back*
J. BACUZZI
(Fulham and Army)

3. *Left Back*
E. A. HAPGOOD (*Capt.*)
(Arsenal and R.A.F.)

4. *Right Half-back*
K. WILLINGHAM
(Huddersfield Town)

5. *Centre Half-back*
S. CULLIS
(Wolverhampton Wanderers and Army)

6. *Left Half-back*
D. WELSH
(Charlton Athletic and Army)

7. *Outside Right*
S. MATTHEWS
(Stoke City and R.A.F.)

8. *Inside Right*
W. MANNION
(Middlesbrough and Army)

9. *Centre Forward*
T. LAWTON
(Everton and Army)

10. *Inside Left*
J. HAGAN
(Sheffield United and Army)

11. *Outside Left*
D. COMPTON
(Arsenal and Army)

From the match programme for another wartime international. The England forward line is most impressive.

Churchill being introduced to Denis. Eddie Hapgood is making the introduction. Stanley Matthews is in the background.

Denis training at Highbury.

Denis with an enthusiastic Rank Organisation starlet during the filming of *The Arsenal Stadium Mystery*.

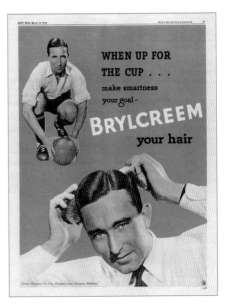

WHEN UP FOR THE CUP . . .

make smartness your goal –

BRYLCREEM

your hair

A typical press advertisement featuring Denis as the Brylcreem Boy.

Denis with John Arlott – they were not always the best of friends. Here they are modelling men's fashions in aid of the International Wool Secretariat. Arlott was often mistaken for Denis.

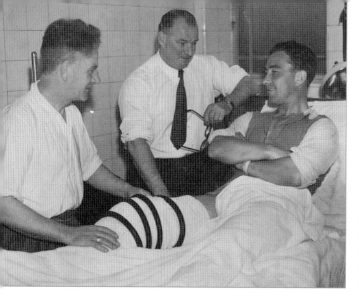

The battle of Compton's knee: here Denis receives treatment from the Arsenal physio Billy Milne. The manager, Tom Whittaker, is also in attendance.

Convalescing with the help of a couple of friends.

WILL YOU PLEASE STOP TRYING TO SHOW ME JUST WHERE COMPTON'S KNEE HURTS!

BERRYMAN.

One of the many contemporary cartoons that addressed this issue of national importance.

The Hastings Festival, 1947, where Denis made his seventeenth century of the season, breaking Jack Hobbs' record of 1925. This picturesque town-centre ground has since been buried beneath a shopping precinct.

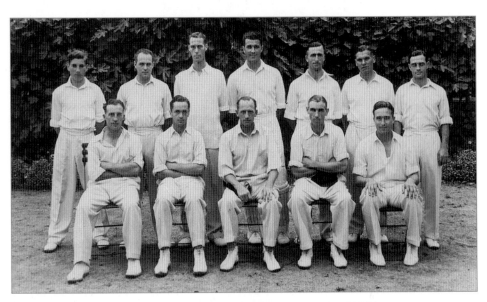

Middlesex's County Championship-winning side of 1947.

Denis hit by a ball from Australian fast bowler Ray Lindwall during the Old Trafford Test in 1948.
Getty Images

Denis and his second wife,
Valerie, with baby son.

Denis and, to his left,
Godfrey Evans, enjoy a
cocktail or several.

Packing for the 1950-51 MCC tour of Australia,
when Denis was vice-captain of the team.
They sailed on the liner *Stratheden* on
11 September 1950. A bat, a pair of shoes and
a single white shirt for a three-month tour
would appear to be travelling exceedingly light...

Filming *The Final Test* at the Oval in 1952, with Bedser, Washbrook, Hutton, Gover, Jack Warner, Laker and Evans.

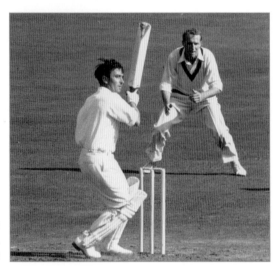

Regaining the Ashes. Denis at the Oval in 1953.
Getty Images

The Ashes regained. Edrich and Compton running the gauntlet of the Oval crowd.
Getty Images

Beach cricket in British Guiana. Denis is taking strike, Peter May is at slip, Reg Hayter behind the stumps.

The post-kneecap-removal comeback. Batting against Eton, 1956.
Getty Images

Denis playing in 1973.
Getty Images

Denis and Christine on their wedding day in 1972.

Reunited with his old friend Keith Miller
on London Weekend Television's *This Is Your Life* in February 1987.

Denis and his oldest son, Brian, on *This Is your Life.*

Denis and son Richard on *This Is your Life.*

With son Patrick on *This Is Your Life.*

A rare family and friends grouping at the end of the programme. Christine is holding their younger daughter, Victoria, with Charlotte standing in front of Denis. Visible at the back to the right of Denis are Fred Trueman, Joe Mercer, Trevor Bailey and, at the far right, Alec Bedser.

Digging the foundations for the future Compton Stand at Lord's.

About to open the new stand during the Texaco Trophy match against West Indies at Lord's in 1991. *Patrick Eagar*

Formally declaring the new Compton Stand open. *Patrick Eagar*

Denis cuts his birthday
cake in the President's
Box at Lord's for his 75th
birthday in 1993.
Patrick Eagar

Acknowledging many happy returns on his 75th from the crowd , 23 May 1993.
Patrick Eagar

An earnest
conversation over
a drink with Rolling
Stone Ronnie Wood
in 1995.

why on earth Errol Holmes [the Surrey captain] didn't put someone down at long leg.'

All the same I am grateful to Garth Wheatley for the story and I think the point he makes is right. He also added, again with justice, 'In a day reduced to 5 hours 25 minutes, Surrey bowled 119 overs and Middlesex made 462 for 7 – better entertainment than a four-day plod.' I would hate to be boring about the wonders of ancient cricket, but I'm glad he made the point. Note also the contribution of the bowling side. And the speed with which they got through the overs was not all to do with their using spin. Gover bowled 20 overs and Alec Bedser 31. But, like the Middlesex batsmen, they got on with it.

Later Mr Wheatley recalled keeping wicket in a quartered hat. ('When did a Harlequin hat last appear in a county match?' he asked.)

He added, 'I also kept wicket behind him while he made 130-odd for MCC against Oxford. Earlier in the year I was behind while Hammond made 100. I saw Compton's 240 in the Champion County match. Apart from nineteen not out versus Surrey in the second innings I do not remember seeing him make less than a hundred in the '46/'47 era and I must have watched him six or seven times at least.'

By his own standards the next game – against Northampton at home – was almost anticlimactic. True, he and Brown had a stand of 122 in an hour, and he scored 60 in the first innings and 85 in the second as well as managing a couple of catches. But there were no centuries and no wickets. In the context of the time this was the next-best thing to failure. Nevertheless the victory meant that Middlesex had clinched the championship.

By now the footballing injury to his knee was beginning to trouble him. 'Compton's knee' was to become a matter of national concern. Ominously on the first day of the Lancashire match, the last day of August, Denis had to leave the field for what *Wisden* rather portentously described as 'a manipulative operation'. In effect this meant that Bill Tucker wrenched it around a bit. Despite this he took four wickets in the first innings, including three batsmen who played for England – Ikin, Cranston and Wharton. By way of retaliation Ikin bowled him for only 17. He was beaten by 'spin and flight' according to eyewitness accounts, though Denis later maintained that this was the only time he ever batted with a seriously debilitating hangover. He and the others had been out celebrating their championship win and the effects had not really worn off by the time he went in to bat. Believing that he was seeing the ball as big as a football (false) and that Ikin was not to be treated unduly seriously as a bowler (probably true), he executed one of his celebrated charges down the wicket and was comprehensively bowled. By the second innings he had sobered up and hit 139, thus equalling the record number of centuries in a season hit by Jack Hobbs. Anyone who is deceived into thinking that Denis was ever as carefree as he looked should reflect upon the fact that this free-scoring cavalier lingered for half an hour in the nineties. His knee hurt and he was nervous, and he let both get to him and affect his game.

That was the end of the County Championship but very far from being the end of Denis's 1947. Playing for Middlesex in the championship he hit eleven hundreds and a total of 2033 runs. Actually this was fewer runs than either Edrich or the much underestimated Robertson, but Denis played fewer innings and had more not outs so he topped the averages with 96.80. The bowling was expensive but he took 57 wickets off almost 450 overs at 25.26 apiece.

These and the individual performances which produced them are formidable achievements, but they take no account of such representative matches as the Champion County against the Rest, nor Sir Pelham Warner's XI against the South of England. And you could argue quite persuasively that Denis reserved the best of the 1947 vintage for his friends from South Africa. If Denis was dominant in the County Championship, he was rampant in the Test series.

Reg Hayter, the indomitable sports journalist who founded his own sporting news agency just off Fleet Street and was a lifelong friend and sometimes ghost-writer for Denis, wrote an account of the South Africans' visit in 1947 in which he conceded:

> Any team meeting Compton and Edrich in such tremendous form could be regarded as unfortunate. The influence which these two men bore on the tour was so great that, in the hypothetical case of one being allotted to each country, the rubber might well have gone to South Africa.

As always it was largely the manner in which he made his runs which distinguished Denis from other batsmen. Nevertheless the statistics are compelling. As Hayter remarks, 'So masterful was Compton that he hit six centuries against the South Africans, three of his four in the Tests coming in successive innings.'

The results suggest that the South Africans were greatly inferior to England, but Hayter argued, and others tend to agree, that apart from the Middlesex twins there was little to choose between the sides. It could even be argued that the South African bowling was, if anything, rather stronger than the home team's.

Indeed at the beginning it looked as if they might have the upper hand. They were hampered by vile weather at the beginning of the tour. At Worcester it even snowed and John Arlott, who was there, recalls that 'Spectators wore overcoats and scarves; the players took on unfamiliar shapes in two – sometimes three – sweaters: slip fieldsmen were careful to tuck their hands in their armpits between deliveries.'

The South Africans, not unnaturally, were not happy in conditions like these. Nor were they used to rain-affected wickets. Consequently they struggled, and by the time of the first Test they had lost to both Worcester and MCC as well as suffering the humiliation of being bowled out for only 83 in their first innings against Surrey – though they did come back to win the match. By then, as we have seen, Denis had served notice of intent with 97 against them for MCC and 154 for Middlesex.

The first morning at Trent Bridge was damp, heavy and gloomy, yet England, who had unwisely left out Doug Wright, only got one wicket before lunch and in the end the South Africans went on to make an impressive 533. Denis, coming on as the last of seven bowlers, had just the two overs and took nought for 6.

To general surprise England then put up a distinctly lacklustre batting performance and were all out for 208. It looked at one stage as if Compton and Edrich might pull them round, but at 65 Denis played what was described as a 'casual' shot and was caught at first slip. The South African captain, Melville, had just taken the new ball but the delivery was only a loosener.

Following on, England slumped to 170 for 4, but then Yardley joined Denis and the two of them added 237 together. Denis hit 19 fours and made 163 out of 291 before falling, once more, to a catch in the slips. It was not one of his quicker efforts for he was in for four and three-quarter hours. Nevertheless the *Wisden* writer judged it 'one of the best innings of his career for his side'. It was executed 'without relaxing vigilance and without noticeable error. At no time did he offer the hitherto dominating attack the slightest hope.'

When England were finally all out for 551 the South Africans were left 227 to win in 140 minutes and the game petered out into a draw. This lack of ambition does make one think about Reg Hayter's suggestion. Surely in a similar situation Compton and Edrich would have gone for those runs? And, equally surely, in 1947 they would have got them.

Lord's was a lovely match, with 'the twins' at their matchless best. Bill and Denis put on 370 for the third wicket and in doing so established a new world record, Denis making 208 out of a total of 554 for 8 declared. Twenty-five minutes were lost on the first day due to rain and at least one eyewitness account draws attention to the 'swift and sure running' between the wickets. Otherwise everything was much as the legend has it. The ground was packed out and thousands were turned away; the South Africans fielded tigerishly and did not bowl as badly as the scoreline suggests. Denis played every stroke in his book, including a number of successful sweeps off the spinners. He also took wickets, two in each innings. His first was crucial, for the South African openers, Melville and Mitchell, were making almost as much hay in the sunshine as he and Bill and crashed out 95 runs in no time. Then Denis came on and had Mitchell stumped by Godfrey Evans and the rot set in.

An interesting little cameo was played out between this and the next Test. Going through the records I noticed that at the beginning of July Denis played for MCC against Cambridge University at Lord's and did remarkably badly. Cambridge won the match and Denis made a miserable 3 in the first innings and 1 in the second.

In his second innings he was caught by one M.R.G. Earls-Davis, later to become a schoolmaster, first at Downside and later Sherborne, where I remembered him cutting a dashing figure in Irish Guards uniforms when commanding the Combined Cadet Force.

It was such an odd failure at a time when Denis was really getting into his stride that I wrote to Earls-Davis to ask if he could remember what went wrong. It turned out to be a strange incident and not as uncharacteristic as all that. Among other things it demonstrated once again that it was the big occasions and the challenges that brought out the best in him.

Earls-Davis remembered the game well.

Denis was playing just to get some batting practice before the Test, but, for about the only time in that glorious summer, the weather was unsettled. [As we have seen it wasn't the only bad weather of the summer, but it seems to be an almost universal mistake!]

There was thundery rain about and the pitch was fairly lively. Drama occurred early. Hugh Griffiths, I think, got one to lift sharply and Denis was hit in the face. Panic! All at once Gubby Allen, Ronnie Aird and physio were all out in the middle inspecting the damage to the Great Man.

It was indeed the Cambridge opening bowler, Hugh Griffiths, who did the damage. In later life he became a distinguished judge, a peer and President, in 1990, of MCC. The incident became a little joke between the two of them, particularly when, as often happened, the two of them were teamed up to speak after a cricketing dinner.

Denis went off for a bit, and when he returned he didn't seem awfully interested, fairly naturally. A tame shot to our left-arm spinner ended his innings quickly. In his second knock, avoidance of injury seemed the main concern. When he had scored a single, Dick Pearsall moved one away, Denis snicked it and I had a comfortable catch to my right at second slip.

As Earls-Davis said, this little blip did Denis no discernible harm. He added that he 'must have watched Denis score thousands of runs in that graceful style that was all his own and with that dazzling range of strokes. Even at the time I was conscious of the fact that I was probably watching a genius, and memories I have of him even now can light up a dark day.'

The following year, as he was pretty broke on his £300 salary from Downside (the same amount that Middlesex paid Denis for a season of cricket), Earls-Davis took a summer holiday job as Jim Swanton's secretary and met Denis quite often. 'A wonderfully laid-back character, friendly and unassuming, equally at home with the great and the lowly. A cricketing genius, a delightful person.'

Looking back on 1947 one day in El Vino, over a bottle of their house champagne, Denis said that another little nightmare took place in Swansea. It is a long way from the pavilion to ground level at St Helen's. Denis thought there were eighty-four steps. The ground was full and the crowd ecstatic. He was cheered all the way during a longer than usual walk to the wicket. Once there he had to face the threat of J.C. Clay, greatest of all Welsh bowlers, but now an elderly gent, fast approaching fifty. Denis, being Denis, realised that it would be proper to show Clay a measure of respect. 'No immediate fours through the covers!' he said. So, thinking this, he took guard and shaped up to Clay's first delivery. It pitched well outside the off stump and Denis performed an exceedingly sedate, not to say respectful, forward defensive. Unfortunately for him the ball spun prodigiously, evaded the bat, and found the middle stump. So within seconds Denis was walking back to the pavilion, up the eighty-four steps, with the crowd once more on its feet cheering again for all it was worth. 'Bowled J.C. Clay, nought.' He shook his head and laughed. 'Wasn't that arrogant of me?'

The only trouble with the story is that when I looked it up in *Wisden* I found that Middlesex didn't play Glamorgan at Swansea in 1947. My friend Tony Winlaw, a connoisseur of Clay and Glamorgan cricket, put me right. It was the previous year, 1946, and in fact Denis got a run. He was bowled Clay, 1.

But perhaps that's not the point. The point is that when talking about his triumphs Denis tended to become a little embarrassed. He was anxious to make you understand that he had his failures too.

The weather at Old Trafford, following the not very good performance against Cambridge, was again particularly nasty. The north-westerly wind was so strong on the Saturday that it kept blowing the bails off the stumps and on one occasion even bowled over a sightscreen. In these conditions the South Africans did not bat well and were all out for 339. Denis bowled without much success but he did take a spectacular catch at slip, left-handed, high and wide, to get rid of the dangerous Viljoen on 93. An added treat was that the bowler was Bill Edrich.

When England batted he and Edrich shared in a tremendous stand of 228 in 3 hours and 10 minutes. Denis made 115 and it was described by Reg Hayter as 'a chanceless innings full of delightful and impudent strokes'. The best example of their complete dominance is that when South Africa took the second new ball the two batsmen hit it for 38 runs off the first three overs. In the second South African innings Denis bowled 17 overs on a helpful pitch which caused some of his deliveries to rise to shoulder height. However he was not at his best and only took 1 for 58. Then in his second innings he hit his wicket when on only 6.

Between now and the Headingley Test the South Africans not only played several counties but three games against the Gentlemen of Ireland and one against Scotland. Such charming frivolity is yet more evidence of change. One half expects Denis's name to feature as a guest of the Irish Gents. He did attend Irish cricket dinners at least once. There was an occasion when John Arlott, intentionally or not, gave Bill

Edrich a black eye on the flight to Dublin. And it may have been that occasion, as recalled by Joe Hardstaff, when Edrich rose to speak, managed the first two lines of 'Molly Malone' and then passed out.

Headingley was never a very happy ground for Denis and the Yorkshire crowd were never as charmed by him as elsewhere. Perhaps this had something to do with the Hutton–Compton rivalry. Perhaps they thought the Compton style too frivolous.

In any event this was very much Hutton's match, the Yorkshireman hitting a winning six in the second innings after scoring a century in the first. Once again Reg Hayter had to report that 'Heavy rain during the night and leaden skies all day caused unpleasant conditions.' On Monday there was a fierce thunderstorm which transformed the pitch into a spinner's paradise. On this tricky surface Denis made a 'valuable' thirty but it was not, for him, a memorable match.

It did, however, clinch the series for England, so that the final Test was a 'dead' one. As it happened it was one of the most fluctuating and evenly contested of the series, ending with South Africa, at 423 for 7, just 28 runs short of a famous victory. *Wisden*'s editor, Hubert Preston, was able, unlike poor Hayter, to report four days of 'extreme heat'. Denis made 53 and 113 and bowled expensively and unsuccessfully. The wretched knee was beginning to cause him serious trouble after so many busy hours at the crease and in the slips. He had also done more bowling than was perhaps quite sensible. Preston thought England's second innings provided much the most attractive cricket and wrote that Denis, 'after an hour of his best and most versatile stroke-play, went on with such freedom that, when caught from an off-drive, he claimed 113 out of 178 put on during an hour and three-quarters; his drives, cuts and forcing strokes brought 15 fours. His fourteenth century of the season was brilliant in every way.'

It was mid-August and yet, amazing though it seems, there were four more hundreds still to come. There were the ones for Middlesex against Surrey and Lancashire; 101 for the South of England against the long-suffering South Africans; and, finally, a massive 246 with a heavily bandaged knee for the Champion County against the Rest of England.

And that was it.

Denis was never much of a one for records but this one was surely going to last. Innings: 50. Not outs: 8. Runs: 3816. Highest innings: 246. Average: 90.85. In all he made 18 hundreds. And he bowled 635.4 overs and took 73 wickets at a cost of 28.12 each.

Yet, as always with Compton, the way he achieved those statistics is worth even more than the statistics themselves. So much was about style and joy and cheekiness and confidence and pride, all etched into a national consciousness bleak with deprivation.

John Arlott was particularly eloquent in assessing the Compton achievement of 1947, echoing the thought about it not being the breaking of records which was important but the manner of their breaking.

For most record-breakers, argued Arlott, the feat is a 'stolid, machine-like, quantitative triumph of soullessness attained by complete elimination of risk and beauty in execution.'

Not so Denis. He never made any concessions to statistics. 'Never,' wrote Arlott, 'was any trace to be observed of Compton doing anything other than playing just as Denis Compton always plays.'

Arlott went on to make the point that Denis always seemed to be playing for fun, adding that 'rarely has a man made runs so negligently'. My own view is that Denis worked on his game and thought about it just as much as any hard-nosed, slow-scoring grafter. But he didn't like to let it show. Arlott also claimed that Denis rarely played the ball between 'widish mid-off and widish mid-on'. I would be interested to see statistical support for this. It may well be true, but all the written evidence suggests that when he felt like it he could drive as hard and true as anyone. People noticed the sweep and the feathery cuts and glances because they were so rare. He will be for ever associated with the sweep, not because it was his best shot but because no one else employed it the way he did.

On the other hand Arlott is surely right when he said that Denis had

an almost inhuman capacity for knowing, as he plays the ball, just where the field is. It has been observed of some great badminton players that they can take their eye off the fastest shuttle for a split second as it comes to them, or, colloquially, look out of the corner of the eye, to see, or feel, exactly where the opposition is stationed. This gift Compton possesses to an amazing degree: his strokes seem, time and again, to pass between the fielders with uncanny accuracy. He has a perfect eye and his sense of the behaviour of a ball is born in him, so that timing is to him like breathing. He must, being partly unconscious of the rarity of his own gifts, and never having known the lack of them, sometimes wonder why people make so much fuss about batting.

Writing just after the miraculous summer of 1947, Arlott also presciently wondered what Denis would be like when his eyes dimmed and his fitness diminished. Then, he thought,

we shall know that this glorious phase of Compton was only possible in one summer, the sun's summer of a century and the summer of a man's life. And that will help to adjust perspective; then facts will confirm our impression, that we have seen, in this year of 1947, a rare fire of batsmanship that can never burn again because it was unique – the rose that once has blown. Never again, surely, shall we watch even Denis Compton make all the runs in the world in a few weeks, yet, so far from tiring of watching him, wish that he might go on for ever. To close the eyes is to see again that easy happy figure at the wicket, pushing an unruly forelock out of his eyes and then, as it falls down again, playing, off the wrong foot, a stroke which passes deep point like a bullet. Never again will cold, hard figures be smashed so light-heartedly, never again will the boyish delight in hitting a ball with a piece of wood flower directly into charm and gaiety and all the wealth of achievement.

Arlott concluded that a future generation would never quite believe the joy of Denis that summer, that they – us, in other words – would ridicule these stories so that ultimately his feats would 'become a dream that passed across English cricket in a summer of amazing sun and lit the farthest corner of every field in the land'.

Those of us who never experienced it can never quite understand the magic of that summer of Compton's life, but there's no question that in some mysterious way he managed through his cricket to make the whole of England feel that suddenly once more life was worth living. It was a rare gift and a rare moment.

1947 was the year when Denis could truly be said to have attained the status of a superstar. Television and more recently the internet have transformed the nature of celebrity and Compton's status was not the same as that of a modern star such as David Beckham or Andrew Flintoff. On the other hand he was, in 1947, as famous and glamorous as it was possible for an Englishman to be. That fame was communicated through newspapers, the wireless and Pathé News, as well, of course, as personal appearances witnessed by crowds of spectators unimaginable today save at international Test matches.

Two final glimpses of that irrepressible character in that extraordinary summer.

In the final match for his champion county, the knee strapped heavily in extreme heat, suffering quite badly on his way to the double century, he tried to dance down the wicket to Tom Goddard – who took more than 250 wickets that season. Something went wrong. One Compton boot became entangled with another Compton boot, he tripped and fell.

But in falling he managed still to swing the bat, to engage the ball and to send it crisply and with perfect timing to the square-leg boundary. He ended flat on his face as the umpire signalled four. The only other modern sportsman that I can think of who could manage to get something so perfectly right while getting it perfectly wrong is George Best.

The ultimate crowning moment of the season had come at the Hastings Festival when he made his seventeenth hundred and beat the record established by the great Jack Hobbs in 1925. This was a match the South Africans did well to win by nine wickets but no one noticed much, they were much more interested in Denis's achievement. John Young, a reporter on *The Times*, was at Hastings that day and remembers crowds of people lining the clifftops above the town and watching with binoculars to see history in the making.

Down in the natural amphitheatre – now alas destroyed in the name of progress – the South Africans forced Denis to fight for every run, though even so he only took 108 minutes over his century and, in *Wisden's* words, 'offered nothing like a chance'.

The sixteen-year-old Robin Marlar watched, enthralled. His description, forty years later, makes a perfect epitaph to the most memorable summer of the Compton career.

When he reached the magic three figures the crowd erupted.

What was remarkable, even from eight rows back, was that everyone leapt to his feet and stayed there while, from the green and white pavilion far across the ground from the old Southdown bus depot, came two tiny figures with a tray: Walter Robins, who had captained Compton's county, Middlesex, to the championship, and Bill Edrich, one of the world's great celebrants and himself approaching the end of a record-breaking season. The South Africans had fought Compton for every run because festival matches were played hard. Now they crowded round to congratulate and forgive their tormentor.

Wisden says the stoppage lasted for five minutes. For those of us in the crowd, they were moments of eternity.

His celebrity status was enhanced by new commercial interests and exploitation of an unprecedented kind. The original catalyst was Denis's friend and lookalike, Reg Hayter, the sports journalist, whose agency just off Fleet Street became the most famous news agency in sport – a sort of sporting equivalent of Reuters or PA.

Reg told me that Denis came to him with a suitcase full of letters. 'Like most cricketers,' said Reg, 'he hadn't opened them. He assumed they were just requests for autographs.' Reg started to look through them and opened one from the *News of the World* which offered Denis £2000 a year for writing a column. Further down the pile was another letter from the *News of the World* written six months later. This one said that in view of Denis's failure to reply the paper was withdrawing its offer.

'Denis,' said Reg, 'you want looking after.'

So Denis, typically, asked Reg if he'd look after him, but Reg was a writer and, therefore, 'I in my pristine purity said "I'm a writer. So I have to be unbiased. I can't do it."'

However Reg compiled a Cyril Washbrook annual for a company that made cardboard boxes in Wales. A director of the box company was a man called Bagenal Harvey who occasionally freelanced for the *Star* newspaper.

Reg told Harvey the story of the unopened envelopes and Harvey replied, 'The time has come for sportsmen to have agents.'

So Reg introduced the two men with this in mind. Denis and Reg were going to the Albert Hall for boxing that evening. 'Harvey put up his proposition,' said Reg, 'and Denis, being Denis, said "yes" immediately.'

However, after Harvey had left, the other two stopped off at a pub. They never got to the boxing. After his initial certainty Denis was in a terrible dither and kept asking Reg whether or not Harvey was all right. He found it exceedingly difficult to make up his mind, but in the end he agreed to accept as agreed.

Neither Denis's son Brian nor his widow Christine, who later worked for Bagenal Harvey, could remember the details of how Denis and Harvey first met. 'I tend to think the car load of letters version was right,' says Christine, 'whatever Reg said. Somehow I just can't picture Denis with a briefcase stuffed with the great unopened. I do know that when we first got married I had to empty a chest of drawers that was stuffed with letters so that I had somewhere to put my clothes. There was also a cupboard that I opened and out fell yet another load of them!'

The quietly spoken, unflashy Bagenal Harvey was a genuine pioneer and the first man to see the commercial potential of sporting stars such as Denis. On Reg's advice Denis signed up with Harvey and continued to be represented by him for the rest of his life.

The greatest Harvey coup was introducing Denis to the Royds advertising agency, one of whose accounts was Brylcreem, a men's hair cream invented in 1929 by County Chemicals of Birmingham who were the manufacturers of a popular kitchen cleaner called Chemico. For years a flat shiny look had been the standard appearance for the smooth male. This had been achieved by applying such dressings as macassar oil or petroleum jelly and was most obviously exploited by Rudolf Valentino, the black-and-white silent screen star.

Basically Brylcreem was a mixture of water and mineral oil stabilised with beeswax. For the scientifically minded it contained propylene glycol, magnesium sulphate and stearic acid. In Britain it was a white goo which came in a pot though in the States where it was also popular it was sold in a tube and advertised on early TV with a jingle, unknown in the UK, which went 'Brylcreem – a little dab'll do ya!'

During the Second World War the dashing pilots of the Battle of Britain were nicknamed 'The Brylcreem Boys' because their abundant locks were slicked back with dollops of the white stuff. After his sensational success with the bat in 1947 Denis was the nation's sweetheart and blessed with exactly the sort of luxuriant black locks which would suit Brylcreem. Bagenal Harvey, Royds and Brylcreem latched on to the fact, and as a result Denis became the first commercial 'Brylcreem Boy', earning an annual sponsorship fee of £1000 a year which continued for nine years until his retirement from full-time professional cricket.

The main medium for exploiting Compton's gleaming black locks was print advertising and particularly the huge advertisement hoardings along main roads. For almost a decade the Compton face stared down, under a Bryclcreemed mop of hair. Such was his fame that his name never had to be mentioned. Everyone knew who he was. So successful was the campaign that he was followed by other sportsmen such as his friend, the Kent and England wicketkeeper Godfrey Evans, the Fulham and England footballer Johnny Haynes, and the actor Richard Greene who starred as Robin Hood in a movie in 1955.

Later, in the Sixties, Brylcreem declined; there was an effort at reviving its popularity when David Beckham was signed up to do a Compton though he lost the contract after a while when he shaved all his hair off. More recently still *The Times* revealed of the youngish leader of the Conservative Party, David Cameron, 'The young pretender to the Tory throne sported an immaculate glistening coiffure yesterday, courtesy of a slap of Brylcreem.'

Nick Royds eventually took over the family advertising agency from his father and soon sold the business, complete with Denis, to Extel. Royds stayed there for an agreed five years but then left and before long Extel sold the agency to McCann Erickson. McCann's absorbed the business into its own but, as far as Royds can remember ('and it's a very long time ago', he said, speaking in 2006), it wasn't that long before Denis was allowed to depart.

> We employed a lot of cricketers in those days. More than anyone else. Clients liked meeting them in a box at Lord's but I don't think Denis actually spent much time with us in the office. He shared a room with my secretary and I remember once the papers decided to run a story about what exactly people like Denis Compton *did*. They got on to our office and, of course, Denis wasn't in so they spoke to my secretary who said that Denis was a very important part of our organisation and that she herself played a very important role in his life. 'Oh,' they said, 'and what's that?' 'Oh,' she said, 'I pay his parking fines for him.'

CHAPTER NINE

In the Oval Test of 1948 the Australians annihilated a batting side which included Denis, Bill Edrich and Len Hutton – all supposedly in their prime – for a mere 52 runs. Lindwall took 6 for 20; Miller 2 for 5.

Of England's 52 at the Oval in 1948 Len Hutton made 30. Denis was caught Morris bowled Lindwall 4. This is interesting because Denis was, in effect, suckered by the Don. He'd had an escape after edging one over the slips and then got involved in a muddled run with Hutton when he was hit on the thumb and dropped his bat. Seeing him fumble for it, Hassett, the fielder, chivalrously forbore to throw.

Then Lindwall dropped one short and Denis went for the hook. He hit it clean and hard but straight to Morris, who took a brilliant catch somewhere in the region of square leg. Afterwards Bradman told Denis that he remembered a similar stroke ten years earlier. He had instructed Lindwall to tempt him to hook and had positioned Morris accordingly. The ploy worked.

Who knows? Sometimes these things are true and sometimes false. Whether or not it was as carefully planned as he made out, it sounds entirely in character for the Don to talk to Denis in this manner. Bradman was a total cricketer. And ruthless with it. To have explained the ploy to the unsuccessful Compton was a typical example of Bradman gamesmanship.

In some ways, the Oval apart, 1948 saw Denis at his absolute best. There is still, even after the invincibility of the sides captained by Alan Border and Steve Waugh, a school of thought that thinks Bradman's 1948 'Invincibles' the best Australian team ever. They played 31, won 23 and drew 8. Of 23 wins, 15 were by an innings. And time and time again what stood between respectability and humiliation was Compton.

The situation was regarded in England as hopeless from the outset. Denzil Batchelor, the writer who followed the tour and recorded it in his book *Days without Sunset*, went so far as to say that the experts were even gloomier than they had been eight years earlier after the fall of France. In 1948 the pundits were right. The Australians were strong, and although in Hutton, Washbrook, Edrich and Denis the home team clearly had four genuine Test match batsmen, Alec Bedser was the only bowler of truly international class. As for the batting, it seemed impossible for the four stars to succeed simultaneously and the burden of sustaining his side eventually started to grind down even a buoyant personality such as Denis. Batchelor said that he began the season as 'a jaunty genius' but ended looking stale and out of touch. The truth was that in Lindwall and Miller Australia had a pace spearhead to match any in the history of the game, and in Bradman, a captain prepared to use them as unrelentingly – some would say cynically – as Douglas Jardine had deployed Larwood and Voce in the 'Bodyline' tour two decades earlier.

The first Test, at Trent Bridge, was lost by eight wickets after a fairly dismal England first innings and an Australian score of over five hundred which put the issue firmly beyond doubt. Denis, not for the last time, was diddled by Miller in the first innings, bowled leg stump while trying to force. Eyewitnesses say that he gave the pitch a meaningful glare after this dismissal but that it was actually a very good hostile ball. Even though he only made 19 the innings was, in Jack

Fingleton's estimation, 'splendidly defiant' and also wonderfully combative. Denis cracked Miller through the covers for four; Miller, who responded to such treatment less favourably than almost anyone (even though he always played down his ability as a bowler), came back with a bouncer which Denis ducked. And battle was joined. It was ever thus – cut and thrust and intensely, though joyously, competitive.

This was my opinion after talking to both Compton and Miller but I'm now marginally less sure. In what must surely be the definitive account of 'Bodyline', written by David Frith and published in 2002, he reminded us that in 1948 at Trent Bridge Miller had been roundly booed when he unleashed a stream of bouncers at Hutton and Compton in the gloom. Here was a visitor doing just what their Nottinghamshire heroes had done – and been punished for by the authorities – in the 1930s. Miller, naturally, paid not the slightest attention. Hutton and Compton reacted stoically and Denis, later, insisted that it was all part of the game, you had to accept the rough with the smooth. Frith seems to wonder, however, whether beneath that smiling façade Denis was actually thinking such charitable thoughts.

From the first however these two men, Compton and Miller, of very similar character and taste, were the best of friends and adversaries, like two musketeers, duelling or jousting with each other, before throwing away their weapons and joining together for wine, women or a day at the races.

Miller confirmed that despite being the best of friends the competition between them was intense. 'I think,' said Miller, 'that I bowled harder at Denis than some of the others. I didn't bowl the bouncer at him very often because he was such a good hooker. I bowled more at Len because he didn't hook very well, but I didn't dare bowl them at Denis when he was in full flight. Maybe when he'd quietened down a bit . . .'

'He had every shot in the book,' said Miller. I talked to him over the phone after Denis had been in hospital for a hip operation. Miller was as competitive as ever. *He*, he said, with a chuckle, had had *four* hip operations. 'He could play every damn thing, but more than that he contrived shots that weren't in the book so you never knew what he was going to do next.'

Of course it was the exuberance and the flair and the sheer sense of fun that Miller empathised with from the first. 'Salaam, sahib,' they would say to each other, frequently on the field, remembering their early encounter in wartime India.

'Denis was like Gary Sobers,' said Miller. 'He played because he loved playing. And if he didn't do well, if he got out, he'd just say "Well, tomorrow's another day." The thing about Denis is he'd never go off and mope.'

The England second innings at Trent Bridge was perforce a rearguard action. Denis and Len Hutton had a sturdy stand together, with Denis playing a strangely subdued second fiddle and the crowd still booing the bumpers from Lindwall and Miller until dissuaded by a sermon from the Nottinghamshire secretary. There was much badinage between Miller and the spectators. On this occasion he was frequently abused and 'roundly hooted'. Like Denis, Miller seemed to encourage reaction from those who watched. Both of them regarded the crowd as part of the game, not just a backdrop. No one, however, enjoys real hostility and the Nottingham crowd sounds as if they meant their booing.

Eventually Hutton, looking as if he might bat on till close of play, was bamboozled in the flight by Miller's slower ball. He and Compton put on 111 together. Rain had fallen, turning the pitch, in Denzil Batchelor's words, from 'khaki to chocolate', while the light was 'Stygian'. By lunch on Monday Denis was still there and past his fifty but it was an uncharacteristically muted performance. For once he had set few hearts racing, but all who watched knew that they were seeing vintage Test match competition.

'Bitter, calculating', thought Jack Fingleton, but lightened every now and then by 'a stroke of the utmost beauty'.

At 4.30 p.m. Denis reached his century. It was much interrupted by rain and bad light and it took three and a half hours. Occasionally he unleashed something characteristically lethal but on the whole this was an innings of deflections – glides and cuts. 'As slow as a chess match between Grandmasters played by correspondence,' thought Denzil Batchelor, 'and as absorbingly interesting. In a word we were watching real Test cricket.'

Lindwall was injured and didn't bowl in this innings, so Miller had to take on the donkey work, a task for which he was ill suited. On the whole that day Denis got the better of him. At close of play England were 345 for 6, just one run ahead of the enemy. Denis was not out 154 and Godfrey Evans was in with him. It had been Compton's day.

'His the rallying bugle call, his the four-square defence of the iron bastion, and his the first gallant foray in an hour when the rigours of the siege should have exhausted the tiny garrison to the point of surrender.'

The end, however, was pathetic. Just when it seemed that Denis might actually have saved the match as well as the day, Miller bowled him another bumper, our hero ducked and stumbled, falling onto his wicket without even lifting his bat. Out hit wicket – a sad end to a defiant 184. Denis said that he found the ball difficult to see against the murk of the pavilion end. Don Tallon, the Australian wicketkeeper, thought it the fastest ball Miller bowled on the entire tour.

Thereafter England swiftly collapsed to a still respectable 441 leaving Australia only 98 to win. They won at twenty past four, the only consolation being that Bradman, caught Hutton, bowled Bedser for the second time in the match, was out for a duck, the first time such a thing had happened in a Test match in England.

The Lord's Test was worse. England were defeated by over four hundred runs. Batchelor, with his distinctive knack of exaggeration, described this as the 'most deplorable failure of an English team since the nineteen-twenties'. Australia made 350 and 460 for 7, England 215 and 186. Denis was the only Englishman to pass fifty.

Once again Batchelor's prose went into overdrive. At the other end poor Dollery, making his debut, was having a torrid time. Denis, however, 'towered undisturbed in his Churchillian part. Once again the artist, endowed with all the airs and graces, put in long stints of laborious and dangerous overtime to rescue the family from bankruptcy.' When Yardley joined him the two seemed to see the ball as big as a 'bright toy balloon', but the recovery was illusory and at 53 Miller brilliantly scooped a catch off his toes and Denis was gone. 'It was clear,' said Batchelor. 'We lost heart, hope and backbone as soon as we lost Compton.' In the second innings Denis was caught by Miller, 'leaping, juggling and almost – but not quite – spilling the catch.'

And so to Manchester. His greatest moment of the year, I think, was at Old Trafford. This was possibly his best and certainly one of his most courageous innings. Hutton, controversially, had been dropped, so England opened with Washbrook and Emmett. It didn't work. They were out early and Denis was left on the bridge playing Lindwall and Miller in full, bouncing flow. The crowd didn't like it and were barracking. 'Play the game,' shouted someone as Denis smothered Lindwall's second ball off his shoulder and down to earth.

At 32 for 2 Lindwall bowled a no-ball. Denis, typically, attacked it, but the ball flew off his bat and onto his forehead. Down he went and was escorted from the field, vowing to be back as soon as possible. Lindwall had already hit him on the elbow and he was in poor shape. Not out, but certainly down.

The Australians helped the stricken hero from the field, 'his head flung back like the head of Harold at Hastings in the picture in one's first history book'.

Two stitches were inserted in the wound; he was bandaged; then went off for a restorative period in the nets plus a large medicinal brandy. The call to return came sooner than he would have wished. At 119 Edrich was caught, and then at 141 skipper Yardley went too. Fingleton thought Yardley had played the pace attack particularly well, not least because he did so off the back foot. This, thought Fingleton, was an object lesson 'to those innumerable Englishmen who are obsessed with the conviction that the way to play pace is to push up the pitch'.

Denis, head in bandages, marched out to do battle.

Jack Fingleton, poacher turned gamekeeper, a first-class opening bat who became an equally first-rate writer, has written that on Denis's bloody bandaged return the game became 'dull, apathetic, and pathetic, strangely unlike a Test'. Denis remembered it very differently. His recollection was that Ray Lindwall bowled demonically, as if determined to hit him again and knock him out of the game once and for all.

David Frith judged that the middle-aged Bradman had, since 'Bodyline', 'subtly amended his view on certain matters'. When Denis was being assaulted by his pacemen the Don said affably, 'I can't understand why you fellows don't step inside them and hit them to the leg fence.' It would have been pertinent to ask Bradman why the Australians hadn't done that against Larwood and Voce, back home down under, in the days of his youth.

Frith wrote:

When Compton returned to the crease at Old Trafford with plaster over a stitched cut inflicted by a Lindwall no-ball which the bat of England's most popular player diverted close to his eyes – an injury not all that dissimilar to Oldfield's – there was no great outburst of protest when the bowler greeted him with further bumpers. The mild and affable Lindwall kidded the batsman that he was going to knock the plaster off. The humour behind the remark was lost on Compton.

Forty years on Denis seemed to have regained his sense of humour and talked about the incident with a grin, albeit a rueful one. He was beaten several times and gave chance after chance. He also ran Alec Bedser out with a bad call after Bradman and Loxton collided in the field. But he battled on and on. The indefatigable Batchelor thought he was like 'Samson at the Temple of Gaza'. In the end he made 145 not out and England advanced from 141 for 6 to 363 all out. Fingleton was moved to wonder 'what would have happened had he not been hurt and made his runs at second wicket down instead of much lower down when he came to bat after being injured'. But the point was that after the debacle of Lord's Denis restored some pride. Or as Batchelor put it, 'While Compton lived the lion had wings.'

Denis thinks that this was the innings, more than any other, which won the north of England over to his side. Hitherto they had seen him as a dilettante – all style and no substance. Now they had no alternative but to admit that the cavalier had grit and backbone too.

In the middle of this epic Old Trafford encounter there was another odd incident that went unreported, but which, many years later, Denis told me about. He had been a keen and proficient golfer since those early days with Arsenal, and felt he would like to join a club. At first he considered Beaconsfield, which was the nearest to his home in Gerrards Cross, but a friend of his, a Cambridge man and, in Denis's phrase, 'out of the top drawer', told him he couldn't possibly join Beaconsfield and he ought to go to Denham which was an altogether better class of club.

Denis wasn't sure. Denham was very snobby and Denis was a professional. To the unpaid, amateur Hon. Sec. of the Denham Club this looked like 'trade'. Famous though he might be, Compton was really only qualified for the Artisans. He wasn't really a gent. Not officer class.

His friend, the Cambridge man, told him not to be ridiculous and that he should certainly not be deterred.

Denis recalled being one of the not-out batsmen at close of play on the Saturday evening of that Old Trafford Test in 1948. Once back in the dressing room, he put his feet up and began to drink the usual pint of beer brought for him by the steward.

Halfway through it a message came to say that someone wished to speak to him on the telephone. It was urgent. Denis went to the phone and heard a plummy voice say 'Compton. It's the Honorary Secretary of the Denham Golf Club here. The Committee would like you to lunch with them tomorrow. They have something important to say to you.'

Denis asked, a little feebly, if the message couldn't be conveyed over the telephone. After all, even though Sunday was a rest day he was in the middle of a Test match and he was halfway through his innings.

'Certainly not, Compton,' said the Hon. Sec. 'This is something which has to be said personally man to man.'

So Denis went along to his skipper, Norman Yardley, and asked for permission to go to lunch in Denham on Sunday. Yardley acquiesced and next morning Denis drove down to Denham in his 'old jalopy'.

'It really was a jalopy,' he said with feeling, 'and there were no motorways in those days. It took me five hours.'

At the club he was shown into the committee room and given a gin and tonic. Then the Hon. Sec. spoke.

'Compton,' he said, 'I have very good news for you. Your name has been proposed for membership of this club and it is my pleasant duty to tell you that not a single one of the committee voted against you. So I have great pleasure in telling you that you have been elected a member of the Denham Golf Club. Congratulations. Now let's finish our drinks and we'll go and have some luncheon.'

Afterwards Denis got back in his jalopy and drove the five hours back to Manchester, went in again on the Monday morning and knocked off another fifty or so runs. He was delighted by his new membership and continued to delight in it to the end of his days. Even so, he, quite reasonably under the circumstances, always believed that he could have been told over the telephone.

In the Test series that year Denis made over two hundred runs more than any other England batsman and averaged 12 runs an innings more than the next-best man.

His most tantalising moment that summer, however, came at Leeds. They never warmed to him at Leeds. Once when he dropped a catch there they reacted as if Pavarotti had gone flat: a cat-call from the crowd, demonstrating their derision for the King of the South. As a batsman he made 23 and 66. Not for him anything at all special, though the bowling was lethal and as hostile as Larwood on the 'Bodyline' tour. Fingleton recalls a nettled Lindwall almost taking Denis's chin off with one bouncer. Denis in turn retaliated with 'one of the loveliest strokes ever seen – a full-blooded pull off a bouncer from Lindwall'. At another point, however, Denis scored only two runs in half an hour and was seen to be hitting his pads in disgust.

On the final day Australia were left with 404 to win in 344 minutes. Before long Norman Yardley called on Compton to bowl. 'The arrival of Denis Compton to wheedle spin out of the wicket gave the subfusc game a blush of colour,' wrote Batchelor.

At 55 Godfrey Evans had an easy stumping chance but

missed. If he had taken it, Morris would have gone for 32. As it was, Morris went on to 182. Then Denis had Lindsay Hassett caught and bowled. The ball spun sharply and Denis caught him following through fast, inches off the ground.

And now Bradman. Immediately he pulled Denis for a single. Hutton was bowling at the other end, and bowling poorly. Then came another Compton over which Fingleton, no less, describes as 'most incredible' and 'Bradman's most uncomfortable in his whole Test career'. First the Don failed to detect the 'bosie' (which we now call a googly). He got an edge past the luckless Crapp at slip. Denis rated it an easy chance. Yardley put in another slip. Bradman glanced the next ball for four. Denis then bowled another 'bosie', and Bradman once more misread it and snicked an even easier chance to Crapp. Crapp was normally a consummate slip fielder but once again he dropped it. Alas poor Crapp! The final ball of Denis's over completely deceived the great Australian on the pads. Not out. 'Phew!' exclaimed Fingleton. 'What an over of excitement this was!'

Keith Miller at this point thought the game was up and was packing his bags. Fingleton too was in no doubt: 'Had chances been taken in this pre-lunch session, England, of a surety, would have had this game won before tea. Hassett, Morris and Bradman out would have left the Australians gasping, because this pitch was a very different proposition to the plumb one of the first innings.'

But, alas, from an English and a Compton point of view, it was not to be. To Denis this remained his greatest lost opportunity. To have Bradman dropped twice in a single over! To have Morris unstumped by Godfrey Evans of all people! And the record book shows that in the end Bradman advanced to 173 not out and that the match was won with 15 minutes to spare.

Fingleton, with matching disdain, describes Hutton and

Compton as 'two very St Swithin's Day bowlers trying to do the job of a Test match-winning bowler'.

And yet, and yet . . . twice in an over he made Bradman give a catch and once he might have had him lbw. Generous in old age, Denis just shook his head and smiled, but he rued the day like none other. Jack Walsh would have been proud of him.

The final Test at the Oval was, from the English point of view, the worst of the lot, and by now Denis seemed mentally and physically exhausted. 'As usual,' wrote Denzil Batchelor, he was 'entrusted with the role of the Dutch youth who kept out the North Sea by putting his thumb in the hole of the dyke'.

For once the thumb wasn't big enough, and in any case it was injured by Lindwall.

1948 was not the statistically record-breaking year of 1947. Australia won the series easily. In the championship, won for the first time by Glamorgan with the fifty-year-old J.C. Clay who had dismissed Denis so cheaply but memorably at Swansea a year or so earlier, Middlesex managed third place.

One final point. The rule in 1948 was that the new ball came round every 55 overs. And Australia had Lindwall and Miller, England only Alec Bedser. Denis's recollection was that Lindwall and Miller seemed always to have a dangerous, shiny swinging ball in their hands. The dice that year were always loaded, but this particular fact loaded it still further.

This wasn't England's year, nor Middlesex's. It belonged to Bradman more than anyone. Yet, in adversity, Denis was Denis at his bravest and most British. Literally bloody and bloody-minded too, he was consistently the saviour of our national cricketing pride.

CHAPTER TEN

R onald Harwood, the Oscar-winning South African-born playwright, was fourteen years old when Denis first visited his country. Fourteen was just about the perfect age at which to see Denis in his prime and Ronnie was smitten from the very beginning. He tried to take his photograph as Denis trotted up the back steps of the pavilion at Newlands in Cape Town and Denis obligingly posed for him, his finger pointing like a gun at Ronnie's camera. It would have been a fine photograph if it had come out, but it never did. Ronnie must have put a finger over the lens in his excitement.

Ronnie has written:

Compton D. C. S., Middlesex and England, had for the previous eighteen months, invaded my imagination and taken possession of that inner world to which young boys escape and where fantasy runs riot. It is the world of gods and heroes where the mythology allows for Harwood R. and Compton D. C. S. to bat together, to break records and be enshrined together in the Pantheon. Heroes it seems to me, are the expression of ourselves in faultless form. Jonathan Swift wrote: 'Whoe'er excels in what we prize/Appears a hero in our eyes'. Compton D. C. S. was my first hero: he represented ability, flair, talent, brilliance, courage and daring, the very qualities I lacked but to which I aspired when I took a cricket bat in my hand and asked for middle-and-leg.

It wasn't only fourteen-year-old boys who idolised Denis during the 1948–49 tour of South Africa. Denis's friend and sometime ghost-writer Reg Hayter was a reporter on the trip and though he was some five years older than Denis he had a more than passing resemblance to him. People didn't often mistake Denis for him, but they did quite often mistake him for Denis.

One evening, Reg told me, many years later, there was a knock on the door of his hotel room and when he opened it there was a man standing there who said: 'Hello, Denis, we're having a party in my room just over the corridor and we'd be very pleased if you'd join us.'

Reg said he was sorry but he wasn't Denis, he was Reg.

'Oh come on, Denis,' said the man, who had clearly had a beer or two, 'I know you're Denis; you know you're Denis; so why not just come over for a beer or two?'

Reg grinned rather shamefacedly and said, 'Oh all right, thank you very much, don't mind if I do.'

A few beers later he returned to his room and, opening the door, was surprised to see a very attractive naked woman getting into his bed.

'Hello, Denis darling,' she said, 'I just came to say good-night.' Before Reg could compose an appropriate reply there was the sound of running footsteps and a very angry, fully clothed man came through the door, grabbed his wife (for it was she) by the hair and yanked her out of Reg's room.

Perhaps there was some justice in the decision not to send Denis on tour before the war on the grounds that he was 'too young and too good-looking'.

By the time of the South African tour Denis was well past

this boyish vulnerability but, despite the dodgy knee and the extra weight, emphatically in his prime of life. He was just thirty. 'That's the Style,' said the Brylcreem advertisement of that year. 'Men who hit the headlines know that smartness counts – and count on Brylcreem for perfect grooming.' The accompanying picture showed an immaculately coiffed Denis, bat aloft, eyes glinting into the distance where, somewhere in the region of long-on, he has clearly driven the ball effortlessly to the boundary. Looking at him you can understand that he was someone men – and more obviously women – might die for.

Harwood had seen film of his hero and remembers the Gaumont-British commentator telling the cricketing world 'Watch out! Compton's bang on form!' In anticipation of his hero's visit he even started using Brylcreem himself.

English bowling in this period was still not good. In the first match against Western Province MCC's bowlers were Bedser, Gladwin, Wright, Young and Denis himself. Denis was smashed for 41 runs off only seven overs and the provincial team made an ominous 386 for 4. MCC won this opener by nine wickets but only because of an overgenerous declaration. It was insane at this moment in cricket history to set a side with Denis in it only 118 to win in 55 minutes. They did it with nine minutes to spare. All that was missing was Bill Edrich.

Edrich had been omitted from the tour and Denis thought it was a crass decision. In cricketing terms it was manifestly ludicrous, for he had enjoyed a thoroughly successful summer season and was beyond dispute one of the best half-dozen batsmen in England. Alas, during a crucial Test match, he had spent a long and merry night out, only returning to his hotel room in the small hours of the morning. Unfortunately his room was next to that of Gubby Allen. Allen heard Edrich lurch in at some ungodly hour, knowing that he was a not-out batsman with a mission to accomplish later that morning against Lindwall and Miller. Another version of the story is that Edrich was entertaining female company in his room and Allen heard everything that went on through the thin hotel wall. In any event he was unamused and Edrich missed the tour.

Denis made a duck next time out, then hit a century with a lot of swept fours against Cape Province, sharing a rare stand of 191 with Hutton. Then he made 150 against Griqualand West in just over an hour and a half as well as taking five wickets in tandem with his old adversary Roly Jenkins. Against Natal in his next innings he took slightly longer to make 106. The ground fielding, according to Reg Hayter, was superb, the light bad and the outfield slow. Hutton took three hours to make 61. 'In contrast,' wrote Hayter, 'Compton could not be subdued.'

Then came Benoni.

This was, in some ways, the most extraordinary innings of his career – the fastest triple century in history.

Ronnie Harwood recalled congratulating him on the innings and said that Denis just smiled and said, 'Yes, that was fun.' He took 66 minutes for the first hundred, 78 for the second and an incredible 37 for the third. His strokes included five sixes and 42 fours and the great challenge was the stand behind long-on which housed the black spectators. After Denis had cleared this with the first six they kept clamouring for more. 'Another six, Massah Compton. Another six, Massah Compton!' He did his best to oblige and Harwood, who wasn't there but saw it on film, remembers one six 'hit holding the bat in one hand, using it like a tennis racket'.

'Often,' recorded Reg Hayter, 'he walked down the pitch before the bowler released the ball and he mixed orthodoxy with a bewildering assortment of unclassified strokes which went from the middle of the bat at lightning speed. He whipped balls pitched outside his off stump to the mid-wicket boundary and he stepped away in order to cut leg-breaks pitched outside the wicket.'

It is sometimes forgotten that Reg Simpson, at the other end, made 130 not out in a stand of 399. Simpson was modestly self-effacing in giving the maestro the strike at every opportunity.

A tour de force, certainly, but everyone has subsequently admitted that the North-Eastern Transvaal bowling was exceptionally mediocre. It sounds mildly ridiculous, but Denis was almost shamefaced about Benoni. As a result he was given the freedom of the town and on occasion when he returned to South Africa the mayor would call him and ask him to visit. This was gratifying. So too was the record. And no matter how trundling and ordinary the bowling it is still a prodigious feat. Yet there are many smaller scores that he regarded with greater pride. Many of his fans still writhe in pleasure at the thought of majestic mammoths in the midday sun but Denis, despite the canards to the contrary, always relished adversity and what he liked most was the situation evoked by Sir Henry Newbolt in his famous poem 'Vitaï Lampada': 'Ten to make and the match to win – a bumping pitch and a blinding light, an hour to play and the last man in.'

Benoni wasn't like that.

The first Test at Durban was, though. Denzil Batchelor, in his book *The Match I Remember*, sets this down as Compton's match, though the truth is that Denis was so overcome by the tension of the final moments that he couldn't bear to watch. Batchelor described it as 'the hardest-fought Test match in the saga of the game'.

All through this game the rain threatened from the Umgeni Hills and the wicket was treacherous. South Africa were all out for 161. At the end of the second day England were struggling and Denis had made only 17 in just under an hour. 'Tufty' Mann put a brake on Denis and, as Batchelor wrote, 'To render Denis unrecognizable in a time of crisis is a solid achievement for any bowler.'

On the third day the light was dire and rain threatened. Hutton was out early and Denis was left 'grimly defiant, paying off the mortgage by thrift and hard work . . . a miserable destiny for the young cavalier'. Batchelor, extravagantly over the top, described the ensuing conflict as similar to the battle of Minden, with Denis in the role of the gallant British infantry against the French cavalry. Denis made 72 in three and a half hours and in doing so 'he made victory possible; and without him defeat would have been inevitable'.

On the last day, according to Batchelor, the light 'gave a positively *Götterdämmerung* setting for the most exciting – not to say the most hellishly unnerving – cricket ever known in the long saga of Test matches. If the sky had forked flames from its dusky cloud-wrack it would hardly have added to the Wagnerian awfulness of the scene.'

Denis himself bowled 16 overs and had the remarkable figures of 11 maidens, one wicket for 11 runs. South Africa were finally all out for 219 which left England with 128 to win in two and a quarter hours.

Despite the conditions they decided to go for the runs. Drama piled on drama. There were injuries to kneecaps, violent rainstorms, dropped catches. When the captain, George Mann, came to the wicket, he entered running, was dropped in the deep, then caught at slip. Now the young Cuan McCarthy began to bowl frighteningly fast and out, in short order, went Watkins, Evans and Simpson.

With an hour left there were 58 runs still needed and only four wickets left – one of them belonging to Denis. The light was bad, so bad according to Batchelor that 'it might have been the last hour before the world sank like a bubble'. They did remarkably well. Denis made 28 before being bowled by McCarthy and Jenkins reached 22. *Wisden* described Denis as being 'in grimly determined mood' and added that his innings 'contained no sparkle, but was worth more than many a double century on turf favourable to batting'. Nevertheless when Gladwin, the Derbyshire fast bowler, came in at No. 10 there were still eight runs needed with an ashen-faced Alec Bedser at the other end and only Doug Wright to follow.

'Coometh the hour, coometh the man,' said Gladwin defiantly to Dudley Nourse, the South African captain. Denis did a passable imitation of Gladwin's thick Midland accent and grandiloquent gesture. Despite this confidence, however, he sent a catch to mid-on off his very first ball. It was duly dropped.

One over to go and still eight needed. A leg-bye; an explosive and improbable four from Gladwin; two more leg-byes. The match is tied. The last ball of the match. Gladwin jumps down the wicket like Denis, swings and misses. The ball misses the wicket too and the keeper is, incomprehensibly, standing back. More than forty years on Denis could not understand why. Bedser charges down the pitch; the keeper flings the ball and breaks the wicket, but Bedser is in by inches and England have won.

'And where,' asked Denzil Batchelor, 'is Denis Compton, the man who made victory possible with his superb first innings and his brave partnership with Jenkins which brought us within sight of the haven? Well, if you want to know, he couldn't bear to see the end – this modest hero blames himself for not having stayed on to make the winning hit. He's locked himself into the lavatory. It's some little time before he ventures out – to read the result in the faces of his team-mates. That was the Test match Denis will never forget. He still has nightmares about it sometimes.'

Certainly more than forty years after the match its memory still had the ability to make him shake his head and suck his teeth.

Hostilities resumed a day after Boxing Day and were a stark contrast to the dramatic first Test. Neither the wicket nor the atmosphere at the new Ellis Park ground in Johannesburg did anything to help the bowlers, and in all 1193 runs were scored for the loss of only 22 wickets. Denis, sweeping prodigiously, made an inevitable fifth century of the tour and took his average to 116, but it was a hollow triumph in a dull drawn match.

The next Test was Ronnie Harwood's first chance to see his hero in person. The fourteen-year-old was not greatly interested in anything except seeing Denis bat. He was therefore irritated when Hutton and Washbrook put on 88, and pleased when Hutton tripped and fell flat on his face to be run out. Then there was Crapp, whom Ronnie couldn't take seriously because of his name but who made a maddening 35.

So it was just before tea when Denis was finally cheered to the crease. Harwood found him smaller than expected and his hair more wayward. 'But he had a wonderfully eccentric walk, as though double-jointed, which added to the aura of pleasure he brought with him.' Shades of Swanton's first impression of Denis at Folkestone in 1936.

Ronnie could hardly breathe. In no time at all Denis was bowled by Athol Rowan. 'Compton walked eccentrically back to the pavilion,' recalled Harwood. 'The partisans cheered. Compton was out for one.'

Harwood's memory of the rest is blurred. However, his hero performed in an unexpected way and bowled successfully, taking five wickets including a spectacular caught and bowled to get rid of Dudley Nourse. He did remember, in those restrained, pre-TV-camera days, how George Mann patted Compton on the back and 'Compton grinning with pleasure. It was his sense of pleasure, I think, which compensated for my disappointment of the previous day and which allowed me to look forward to what remained of the game with hopefulness.'

A tame draw ensued despite a 'sparkling' 51 not out from Compton. And sadly that was the most Harwood ever saw his hero score.

A few days later he made 108 against Eastern Province. The pyrotechnics seem almost commonplace: two sixes, 13 fours. What else would one expect? There were some modest scores before the next Test, which consisted of two 'brisk' cameos. Then 141 against a Natal XI and a couple of forties against South Africa in the final Test, won, memorably, by a tense three wickets.

As a final *bonne bouche* Denis signed off with his eighth century of the tour against Combined Universities as well as taking eight wickets in the match, six of them for 62 in the second innings. *Wisden* wrote that the students were 'puzzled by the wiles of Wright and Compton'.

It was an apt finishing touch, and it meant that as a batsman he had surpassed all the records for high scoring in a South African season, just as he had done with the English records in 1947. In all matches he scored 1781 at an average of 84.80. His bowling was expensive but he sent down 275 overs and took 30 wickets. Reg Hayter's opinion was that he was never quite at his brilliant best in the Test matches, where he was excelled by Hutton.

That, essentially, is a technical opinion. I am more moved by that of Ronald Harwood, who looked back on his first glimpses of Denis and said that 'his love and joy were, in my case, infectious and long-lasting. His participation in a match guaranteed excitement and he bestowed on cricket a rare dash which kindled one's own delight and pleasure in the game.'

It was on this tour that he met Valerie, who was to become the second Mrs Compton. The member of a wealthy and prominent South African family, Valerie was one of the team's chauffeuses and evidently made a determined set at Denis. They had an affair and after the team departed she wrote to Denis at his home address where Doris apparently intercepted her letters before Denis returned. Doris was prepared to be tolerant of her husband's adventures on tour, well aware of the temptations on offer and of Denis's susceptibility to feminine charms. Valerie, however, was determined. It took more than a year for her to persuade him but he did finally succumb. According to Denis and Doris's son Brian, Denis treated Doris very unpleasantly, and, although very reluctant to divorce him, she finally gave in because of worry about the effect of the rows on Brian. She forced Denis to pay Brian's school fees by threatening to tell the press about his affairs if he didn't.

Valerie apparently never took to England, particularly the English climate, and for her South Africa was always home. Eventually at the end of the 1950s she finally did go home, leaving Denis to a decade or so of middle-aged bachelordom in the Buckinghamshire village of Fulmer.

His divorces caused Denis sadness, despite the pleasure he took in his three sons – one with Doris and two with Valerie. For all his generosity of spirit – perhaps because of it – Denis could be careless in his private life, and in moments of introspection he would concede that perhaps he didn't work as hard at marriage as he might. He would admit ruefully that in this respect he failed to live up to the example of his own parents.

The truth is, I think, that Denis was always temperamentally one of the boys. He said he had not been one for nightclubs, which he could never stand, but he was fundamentally gregarious, seldom happier than in the company of friends whether on or off the field of play.

He came to regard South Africa as a second home. 'I liked South Africa during my first visit and have liked it ever since,' he wrote in his memoirs. 'Of all the countries that I have played cricket against I have always liked South Africa and

South Africans best. Perhaps it's something in my temperament or in theirs, but that is the way it worked out from the beginning'. He added with what subsequently looked sad and possibly ingenuous, 'Of course, my wife is South African.' He could have added later that all three of his sons ended up living in South Africa and that the grandchildren of his first two marriages were all South African. The emotional ties to the country ran deep.

After the heady moments of that first South African tour, Denis's benefit year in the summer of 1949, despite some excitements and achievements, was something of an anti-climax. Nevertheless the benefit yielded £12,200, a sum which easily beat the Middlesex record.

One cricketer who remembered the year well was Colin Cowdrey, then captain of Tonbridge School, who presided over a disastrous defeat by Clifton College at Lord's but nevertheless topped their batting averages and made 85 not out for Southern Schools against the Rest. Shades of the fourteen-year-old Denis being watched by Plum Warner.

One day in July an SOS went out to Tonbridge saying that Denis was bringing a side to play in a game next to a local pub and he was a man short. Could Cowdrey pack his bag and help out?

Cowdrey duly presented himself and found that the Compton side was batting first and that Denis was going in at No. 4, with Cowdrey at No. 5. Denis came in with just one over to play before lunch and found himself confronted by the off-spin of the local captain's fourteen-year-old son. Denis treated the boy's bowling with enormous respect and played out a maiden, thus making the boy's summer and quite possibly giving him a 'how I bowled a maiden over to Denis Compton' story which would last the whole of the rest of his life.

Soon after lunch another wicket fell and Cowdrey came in. It was a particularly daunting occasion, not just because the incomparable Compton was at the other end but because this was hop-picking time and in all the adjacent fields hop-pickers from the East End of London had been toiling in the summer sun. The pattern of their day's work was to start very early and end in time for a picnic lunch, leaving the afternoon free for fun. That meant that this match was watched by a crowd that Cowdrey later thought must have been in excess of a thousand – far larger than anything he was used to. That afternoon Cowdrey and Compton put on 130 runs together, and of these Cowdrey scored just 7.

Denis farmed the bowling brilliantly, but what Cowdrey remembered, apart from the generous way he treated the boy's bowling in the morning, was how 'terribly nervous' he was. Even though this was a village match, it still evidently mattered that he did not let the crowd down and played attractive cricket. He was constantly asking Cowdrey such questions as how many overs he thought were left before tea. The impression was some way removed from the popular image of the laid-back cavalier. Later when the two played Test cricket together Cowdrey thought much the same. He was not relaxed.

The visiting Test side were New Zealand, generally thought to be the weakest of the countries then playing Test cricket. After the success against South Africa on their own turf it was assumed that England would be much too strong for the Kiwis, but England failed to win a single one of the four Tests.

This was mainly due to the weak bowling and strong batting of both sides. Indeed Denis came top of the English bowling averages with 5 for 126, and even though his unorthodox style could be very tricky he would be the first to admit that in a serious attack he should not be averaging better than everyone else. Nor did it help that the matches were confined to a mere three days each. Denis thought this Test series the most boring he ever played in. He never did enjoy draws.

At Leeds in the first Test he made 114 and shared a rare century stand with Len Hutton, but it was not one of his better innings for he was pegged down by nagging New Zealand bowling and, like Hutton, took over four hours to make his century. At Lord's after a sticky start he was more like his dashing self, scoring a second century and sharing a stand of 189 for the sixth wicket with Trevor Bailey. At Old Trafford he was bowled while trying to force the pace. At the Oval he made only 13 in a big total of which Hutton made 206 and Bill Edrich 100.

So by his own standards his was no more than an average Test performance against an only modest attack. Simpson, Washbrook, Hutton, Bailey and Edrich all had better averages and the two New Zealand batting stars, Donnelly and Sutcliffe, both scored over a hundred runs more.

The County Championship that year was enthralling and ended in the first tie since 1889, with Middlesex sharing first place with Yorkshire. Their form was topsy-turvy and though *Wisden* conceded that Denis played some 'glorious innings' he also experienced some 'lean patches'. Overall he made more than 1700 runs and headed the batting averages. His bowling average was an expensive 33.38, but he sent down over six hundred overs and took 60 wickets. This was the weak spot in the Middlesex attack: they were forced to rely far too much on their spin bowlers, Denis, Young and Sims, who took 299 wickets between them; whereas the new ball men, Allen, Warr, Gray and Edrich, took only 130. It is difficult, in an age so dominated by fast or fastish bowling, to imagine any team having such a balance in their bowling, let alone sharing the championship with it.

Denis's benefit was against his favourite opponents, luckless Sussex, in the traditional Whit weekend fixture which he enjoyed so much and with which he had opened his account in the last-wicket stand with Gubby Allen. Although rain washed out much of the first day the crowds flocked in and almost fifty thousand went through the turnstiles. Denis started slowly – for him – but after reaching his century in two and three-quarter hours he let rip and hit 13 more fours, scoring 79 in 44 minutes, mainly with ferocious driving. He finished on 182. It is sometimes suggested that Denis was all cut and sweep, but the records suggest otherwise.

There was more magic to come in his career, but that benefit year marks the end of the consistent glory days. He was now the wrong side of thirty and his body was beginning to rebel. To be sure there was drama left, and heroics, particularly towards the very end of his career when life really did become a struggle, but over the next few years there seems to be sometimes a sense of déjà vu and world-weariness. You feel, to an extent at least, that much of the time Denis had been here before – indeed been before and done better. He never equalled the figures of 1947, for instance, nor the derring-do of the battle against Lindwall, Miller and all the odds in 1948.

That love affair with South Africa subsequently got him into a lot of trouble. He himself was keen to set the record straight. It is a complex and in many ways unsatisfactory story, recently illuminated by Peter Oborne's prize-winning book on what became known as 'The D'Oliveira affair', from which few if any members of the English cricketing establishment emerged with their reputations unscathed.

Over the years South Africa paradoxically caused him more pain and more pleasure than any other country in the world. His first and thoroughly enjoyable visit was, as we have seen, in the winter of 1948–49, when he made a great many runs and met his second wife, Valerie. Ever since then he enjoyed going back as a cricketer, as a journalist and as a family man.

Years later, after his retirement, the Queen presented him with a CBE. The night before, or perhaps more accurately earlier that morning, Denis had been out partying. As she pinned the medal to his chest Her Majesty smiled sym-pathetically and asked 'How is your poor head?' She was recalling the moment at Old Trafford when Lindwall had hit him on the head and he had retired hurt. Denis, nursing a hangover, didn't realise this. Instead his reaction was 'How did she know I'd been up till all hours at the Bag O'Nails?'

CHAPTER ELEVEN

In 1950 Denis, at thirty-one, was widely regarded as a spent force in all terms. Even he, incorrigibly optimistic as ever, doubted whether he would ever play first-team football for Arsenal again. Brian Glanville, who had so admired him in the war years, recalls unkindly that he returned from India 'fat as a hog' and never really got rid of the weight. In fact Denis spent hours pounding the streets of Highbury wrapped up in layers of heavy sweaters and he did manage to shed 'the best part of a stone'. Nevertheless he was not the slim youth of the Thirties.

And then again there was the wretched knee. It was giving serious trouble now, so much so that by summer he would be back in hospital for surgery. Bernard Joy judged that 'he could no longer beat the back up the wing and he had "bellows to mend" in the last few minutes'.

In fact Denis was so pessimistic about his prospects that on his return from the 1948–49 cricket tour of South Africa he had asked Tom Whittaker if he might retire gracefully from soccer. Whittaker wouldn't hear of it, and so eventually Denis returned to Highbury and, once back to something like full fitness, began to play for the reserves. He didn't tell anyone, but his right knee was giving him pain. He knew he was a yard or two slower than before. He knew it better than anyone, and in January 1950 he was close to going back to Whittaker and throwing in the towel for good.

However Arsenal were far from convincing in the early rounds of the Cup and only just defeated second-division Sheffield Wednesday who were reduced to ten men for most of the game. Swansea, another second-division side, also ran them close and had a late equaliser disallowed for handball. Both these matches were at home at Highbury.

One of several problems was on the left wing, where neither Roper nor McPherson was performing satisfactorily. Whittaker called Denis in and told him that if he could win back his old form the outside-left position was his. 'It's up to you,' he said. 'See what you can do.'

That Saturday Whittaker didn't watch the first team but went to the reserve game to run a rule over Denis. Denis rose to the occasion, played a blinder and scored two goals.

Whittaker decided to take a risk and play him. He would bring maturity to the side, he was a man for the big occasion, the left foot was still lethal and even if he did run out of puff it was better to have a real menace on the left for an hour than mediocrity for the full hour and a half.

He warmed up against Bolton at the end of January – only his twenty-third League match since the war – and was then picked for the fifth-round cup match against Burnley at Highbury. 'This,' said Whittaker, 'is the game that needs the Denis Compton dash.' Denis wasn't sure. 'I was almost a "crock",' he said.

More *Boy's Own Paper* stuff. It was rainy and the surface was slippery, the atmosphere predictably electric and, in Bernard Joy's words, 'Arsenal found their best form, and the inspiration came from Denis Compton.'

Denis, with characteristic modesty, said afterwards that the match had belonged to his colleague Alex Forbes. One commentator, Robert Findlay, remarked that if that were so,

'Denis was certainly number two. His duels with Arthur Woodruff, the Burnley captain and right-back, made the crowd roar. I never knew he had so much real football in him. He dribbled Woodruff, who gave him too much room, out of the game.'

Cliff Bastin said that Denis did exactly what Whittaker wanted. His contribution meant 'more dash, fire and finishing power'.

Arsenal won 2–0, and Denis set up the first goal, giving a pass to Lewis which he shot in from twenty yards, and then scored the second with a classic Compton left-foot blast into the top corner of the net. Denis conceded that it was probably one of the best half-dozen games he ever played. 'Nearly all my tricks came off,' he said.

Bernard Joy wrote:

His form made one regret that Compton the cricketer had interfered with the career of Compton the footballer, because on this display it was easy to see why he was an automatic choice for England during the war. His left-foot shot was more powerful than Cliff Bastin's and if he did not have Bastin's cleverness for making an opening, the manner in which he kept his volleys down made him more dangerous when the centre was dropping lazily over from the other wing.

As predicted, he had 'bellows to mend' towards the end and was not exactly conspicuous for the last twenty minutes. That scarcely mattered, for by then he had done all that Tom Whittaker wanted.

In the next round Arsenal drew Leeds United. Again they were lucky and entertained them at home. Leeds, managed by the legendary former Wolves player Major Frank Buckley, were tough, rugged and durable, but even though they were playing the young Welsh genius John Charles they lacked finesse. It was simple lack of class that did for them when Forbes beat no fewer than four men before slipping a deft pass to Roper who gave it to Lewis who had the ball in the net before young Charles could intercept. That was the Bernard Joy version, though others saw it differently. The *Sunday Times* gave Compton the credit. According to their correspondent, Roland Allen, it was Denis who 'flicked the ball on to Lewis much in the manner of a late cut'.

The superior Leeds fitness gave them the edge in the last few minutes, but Arsenal held on to their lead thanks to the determination of Scott, Barnes and big brother Leslie, who spent the last quarter of the game with a sponge in his hand to stem the flow of blood from a nasty head wound.

Next came Chelsea. As it was a semi-final they met on neutral ground at White Hart Lane, the home of Tottenham Hotspur. This was a real hammer and tongs affair. Arsenal went all out for an early lead but this left them exposed at the back. Chelsea took full advantage and were two goals up within 25 minutes.

On the bench Tom Whittaker was far from downhearted. He actually turned to his colleague Bob Wall and said, 'We're going to win this match.'

The turning point came 35 seconds before half-time when Freddie Cox scored from the most extraordinary corner-kick. He hit it with the outside of his right foot in order to make it an in-swinger. The defence seemed to have it well covered until, as the ball reached the goalmouth, it suddenly veered inwards as if magnetised or 'attached by elastic to the iron stanchion'. Subsequently every 'expert' in the world tried to produce an explanation, but it seems to have been a pure fluke. Cox, credited with every conceivable sort of wizardry, said only 'I just hit it.'

Arsenal came back in the second half but were still a goal down with thirteen minutes left. Then Denis forced a corner on the left and shouted at his brother to run up ready to head a goal. An angry Joe Mercer shouted at Leslie to stay exactly where he was. Leslie hesitated. He was never one to question the captain's orders and yet instinctively he felt Denis was right.

After a moment of indecision he set off at the charge, leaving Mercer to fume impotently behind him. Denis hit the ball hard and true with his left foot. Just as it soared into the goalmouth, Leslie arrived at a gallop. He never saw what happened next but he hit the ball a tremendous whack with his head and in doing so somersaulted to the ground. The ball shot between Winter and Medhurst and slapped into the back of the net. Two all.

Joe Mercer was one of the first to help him to his feet. 'Sorry,' said Leslie. Characteristically Mercer beamed and also apologised. 'Made a mistake,' he said.

Near time Denis almost went one better. The writer John Moynihan, then a young Chelsea fan, was standing behind the goal when Denis hit the crossbar with a stunning header. 'I remember the D. Compton header,' Moynihan told me, 'whizzing over our schoolboy heads packed behind the goal. The tumble winded Denis – it would have been a glorious finale for him and a tragedy for us. Apart from the corner he had hardly touched the ball before then. Then came his streak of "Pele" genius and the clang of the ball hitting the top of the crossbar as it went over! I gulped!'

In his book *The Chelsea Story*, Moynihan remembered sitting, years later, in El Vino in Fleet Street, sharing a bottle of hock with Denis and reminding him of the near-miss. 'That was an amazing one,' said Denis. 'I actually dived and caught the ball perfectly – a novel act for me . . . it would have been a wonderful winner.'

The replay was four days later and Arsenal won 1–0 on a grey greasy day with another Freddie Cox goal. It was so dark that the Chelsea defence almost literally lost their way. This was the first time that Arsenal had beaten Chelsea in the cup for twenty years.

Arsenal were in the final against Liverpool, who beat Everton in another local derby semi-final. Apparently George Swindin, the Arsenal goalkeeper, had predicted an Arsenal–Liverpool final way back in November when staying in the same hotel as the Liverpool team. He told the Liverpool players, but otherwise kept quiet. Arsenal already had a reputation for being 'lucky', and he didn't want to be called 'cocky' as well.

It was a strong Arsenal side and despite his flashes of genius Denis was by no means the best player in it: Swindin, Scott, Barnes, Forbes, Leslie Compton, Mercer, Cox, Logie, Goring, Lewis and Denis himself. Nevertheless, because of his legendary cricketing feats and because of his occasionally spectacular football past Denis was a star, if not *the* star. The personality and the debonair appearance both helped. Brylcreem tailored a special cup campaign round their Brylcreem boy – 'When up for the Cup make smartness your goal – Brylcreem your hair.' That was the advertisement which appeared to coincide with the semi-final. For the final, the slogan alongside a smiling Denis with super-sleek hair was simplicity itself. It just said, 'The Final Touch'.

The weather dimmed the final but probably helped Arsenal win. There was a dank drizzle all day and the effect of this on the Wembley turf was to make the ball come off with what Bernard Joy described as 'a wicked zip'. Arsenal had six men, including Denis, who had played at Wembley before. With an average age of over thirty, they were the oldest side ever to play in a Wembley final. By contrast, Liverpool chose to axe their veteran striker, Jack Balmer, and bring in a much younger man, Kevin Baron, to lead their attack. In the event Baron simply lacked the maturity and experience to cope, and it probably cost Liverpool the cup.

In the dressing room immediately before kick-off Whittaker revised the original plan. They had intended to play an open game, but the surface was so tricky that they elected instead to play a close, short-passing game. It wasn't particularly pretty but it was devastatingly effective, and Arsenal were in complete control from the start.

By his own standards Denis did not have a great game. Lewis, who scored twice, was probably man of the match. Leslie was leonine in defence and helped set up the first goal. Mercer was heroic.

An odd thing happened at half-time and I only have Denis's memory to rely on. He came off knowing he had not performed well. His knee hurt and the tension was such that he was hardly thinking straight. His old mentor Alex James was in the crowd and apparently waylaid Denis before he got to the dressing room. James thought Denis had played poorly and told him so. What he needed was a pick-me-up. He produced a hip flask and poured a generous measure of brandy. Denis knocked it back and went out to play an infinitely better second half. He promised that this was one of only two occasions on which he played first-class sport after a drink – the other being the innings at Manchester in 1948 after being hit by Lindwall's no-ball. The only doubt about this story is that the brandy might have been administered by Tom Whittaker in the dressing room. According to Laurie Scott it's the sort of thing Whittaker might have done. His men worshipped him, not least because if the situation demanded it he was prepared to bend the rules. Scott thought that maybe Whittaker slipped Denis the Micky Finn.

Anyway they won. Mercer was in tears, though he didn't realise until Scott told him. He could barely hold the cup and was so close to dropping it that the King told him to give the base to someone else. The confusion was compounded by the Queen giving the first two or three Arsenal players losers' medals by mistake. The Comptons came last in the presentation line and Leslie, as always, pushed his little brother forward, taking last place for himself. 'There he was,' said Denis, 'backing me up, as he has been all my life.'

I am too young to remember that final, but I did manage to get hold of the cinema news clip of the occasion. It was much as I would have expected: grey and grainy pictures, lots of phlegmatic policemen, the Queen in feathers, the King hatted and austere, the commentator remarking with surprise that many people had come to Wembley by car. 'Well here we are!' he began, sounding just like Harry Enfield in the Mercury advertisements.

The film only lasted three or four minutes but Denis featured prominently. There were a couple of booming corners with the famous left foot and one dazzling double-feint to go round an opponent. 'Compton's working like a Trojan,' the commentator told us. What struck me most was the players' boots and the ball. As they came out onto the pitch you saw that they were wearing really serious footwear, heavy reinforced toe-cap numbers, quite unlike the light-weight boot of today. And that leather ball on a wet day quickly became heavy. Every time a player put in a long pass it was a real hoof, and even on the ancient soundtrack you got a real smack of leather on leather. Of all the players on the field it certainly looked to me as if Denis's left-foot kick was the genuine article.

There was just one more footballing moment to savour before he hung up his boots. That night the team celebrated with dinner at a Piccadilly hotel – the name of which no one seems able to remember, but it wasn't the Ritz. Their guests were Portsmouth, the League champions, and after dinner the two chairmen tossed to see who would host their challenge match the following Wednesday. Once again Arsenal were lucky. They won the toss and played at home. In the whole of their victorious cup campaign they had travelled no more than 32 miles in all.

The FA Cup stood on a table at Highbury that evening in May, glistening in the sunlight 'stolen from midsummer'. The crowd gave Denis a splendid ovation. Arsenal won 4–1 and he scored a goal.

'So I finished on a high note.'

Despite this high note he knew that he could not sustain classy performances at the highest level. He knew that a man in his thirties would, inevitably, struggle to compete against players a decade or more younger. He knew that by the highest standards of professional football he was overweight and also – which the public were unaware of – that his joints and in particular his damaged knee were bound to let him down even if they could be patched up for the relatively less athletic game of cricket. He thought he could continue his cricket for a few years and football could only jeopardise that. Above all he had an unusual sense of timing. The cup-winner's medal was an unexpected bonus and a high point which would almost certainly be unrepeated. For all these reasons it was time to bow out gracefully.

In his *Denis Compton Annual* the following year there is an article under his byline entitled 'Farewell to Soccer'. Denis on his own admission was never as accomplished on paper as he was on grass, and I suspect the influence of A.N. Other, probably Reg Hayter, on the words that follow. Nevertheless they are a fond farewell with just the right note of self-deprecating regret.

Unknown to many thousands who poured from the exit gates the referee's signal sent a shiver down the spine of Arsenal's outside-left, a portly individual named Denis Compton. What an occasion that was for me to remember.

I doubt whether at that moment more than two or three people other than myself realized that I had just finished my last game of big football. No more would I wear the Arsenal colours; or for that matter, those of any leading soccer club.

I knew, and the knowledge carried little pleasure.

As he himself said, it's unlikely that any man has played so little first-class football and yet played on the winning side in an FA Cup Final. At that moment his great contemporary Stanley Matthews had not yet won a cup-winner's medal, and when Denis thought of that he admitted, 'I almost (though not quite) blush for shame.'

CHAPTER TWELVE

The writer and broadcaster Peter West, who wrote a biography of Compton with characteristic understatement, described the rest of 1950 as 'difficult days'. Denis was disparaging about the book, written without his cooperation, but on this occasion at least West was quite right.

The immediate aftermath of the Cup Final was heady enough and Denis scored fluently and freely in cricket during May. At Whitsun in his much-loved jamboree against Sussex, however, he met his nemesis. Batting with his usual success against the county, he notched up fifty but ended the day feeling crippled and was admitted to the London Clinic next day. His injured knee was beginning to become seriously debilitating. As a result he missed a large chunk of the season, including the first four Tests against the West Indies.

One of his comeback games, paradoxically against Sussex although this time at Hove, fuelled the Compton legend for casualness and unpunctuality. He overslept, was late for the game, arrived in plimsolls, jumping over the boundary fence, and was promptly put on to bowl by Robins as a punishment. Denis, predictably, atoned immediately by taking two cheap wickets.

The Test series, against the West Indians, was dominated by the 'three Ws' – Worrell, Weekes and Walcott – and 'those two little pals of mine, Ramadhin and Valentine'. The latter pair wrought havoc at Lord's, where England, comprehensively bamboozled, lost by 326 runs. When Denis finally locked horns with them at the Oval, Len Hutton ran him out after he had scored 44. The run looked safe but Hutton sent him back and he was unable to regain his ground. There's no question that this was more Hutton's fault than his, though he bore no grudge. Contrary to popular legend he admired Hutton hugely both as a player and a person. In the second innings he was caught off Valentine for 11 and England were ignominiously defeated by an innings and 56 runs.

Denis had seen the West Indians on TV, and although the picture was rather fuzzier and greyer than what we are used to now, he could see that Ramadhin, in particular, was a tricky and novel proposition. He remained so when Denis played against him for real and was unable to tell, from either wrist or hand, whether he was about to deliver his leg-break or off spinner. In other words he couldn't read him. Bill Edrich had a similar problem. He said that having Ramadhin bowl at you was like being showered with confetti.

In all first-class matches that year Denis made fewer than a thousand runs, the first time in his career that he had sunk so low. This was a nadir in his cricketing fortunes and doubly sad because it came in the wake of that unexpected triumph at Wembley.

Nevertheless, Denis was selected for the Australian tour and, moreover, as vice-captain. This elevation later prompted the same sort of derisive snort that accompanies the notion of his being a sergeant-major. A picture taken on board ship at what appears to be a press conference shows him looking every inch the part, self-assured, smiling, smartly suited, definitely chunkier than before and with a lighted cigarette dangling nonchalantly from one hand. He looks as if he was having fun.

He shared a cabin and subsequently a room with Trevor Bailey, the Essex all-rounder, who told me that although they had played together before this was their first tour and therefore the first time he had really got to know Denis well. He thought that Denis was almost as chaotic as he was except in the matter of clothing where it was just about a dead heat.

Bailey, like others, also confided that he had never ever come across anyone who was so attractive to women. He said this a shade guiltily and *sotto voce* because Denis's widow, Christine, was with us at the time. 'Bill Edrich,' said Trevor, 'was different. He was predatory when it came to women – a hunter who made a great deal of effort. Denis wasn't like that. He didn't have to do anything. They just flocked to him.' Denis was similarly blessed when it came to cards. He actually preferred poker which was a chancier, less cerebral game but there was a lot of bridge played on board. Bailey rather fancied himself as a bridge player but it didn't make any difference. Denis always seemed to have a perfect hand. The cards just fell into his lap. It was the same with the horses. Such was his luck that his team-mates christened him 'Golden'.

He was not, however, to enjoy this tour. Far from it. The knee was in dreadful shape. It became severely swollen and was causing him almost constant pain. On the voyage out, observers at various ports of call reported that Denis was limping heavily. To make matters worse there was publicity on tour about his acrimonious divorce from Doris. It also seemed that responsibility was getting him down. His friend the wicketkeeper Godfrey Evans wrote of his appointment as vice-captain. 'When he captained the side his strategy was sometimes successful, sometimes it was not; when it was not, he seemed to have a tendency to lose grip on the game. This was certainly due to his inexperience as a captain.'

He made some big scores in the state and country games but the statistics, for once, tell their own gloomy tale. In eight Test innings he scored 53 runs at an average of 7.57, with a highest score of 23.

It was not all over yet, not by any means, but the true gaiety, song and dance, had necessarily gone out of his game. From now on he would almost always be in some pain; the knee would be, at best, stiff.

Denzil Batchelor, writing shortly after the disaster down under, suggested that if Denis's batting form in the two Australian series had been reversed then we would have lost even more easily to Bradman's team in 1948, while actually regaining the Ashes in Australia under Freddie Brown.

Batchelor is probably right and he certainly has a point. What is almost as significant is the way that his panegyric is phrased. Even though there was no hint of Denis giving up, Batchelor seems to know that the best had already been. He believed that there were some Australian bowlers in that dreadful winter who were so upset by Denis's predicament that they 'really wanted him not to get out for ducks – who really tried to offer him, burdened with the handicap of his injured knee, a chance to produce scoring strokes early in his innings. But Compton could never get into top gear; indeed he could never get out of neutral.' Trevor Bailey confirmed this. 'The Australians would never do anything like deliberately drop catches or present him with free runs but they wanted him to do well. They liked and admired him and it upset them to see him having such a bad trot.'

More importantly, Denis seemed already to sense that the career was entering its twilight years.

Ranging over that career Batchelor felt that, as a cricketer, Denis achieved real greatness against the 1948 Australians with his 184 at Trent Bridge, 'the finest I ever saw in my life', though he concedes that others would prefer the 145 not out after being knocked down by Lindwall.

Perceptively Batchelor continued,

Whichever innings you pick, you pick it for the same reason: it exhibited not only all the technical graces but also a spirit of indomitable courage which was then almost entirely lacking in British cricket. All through that sad season, Compton was set the unnatural task that falls to a carefree younger son who inherits the heavy mortgage with which his elders have encumbered the family honour. He renounced a career that was meant to be gloriously cavalier and set himself to pay off that mortgage.

I like to think of Compton in lighter vein: sweeping the short ball first bounce over the leg boundary; cracking it through the fuddled covers. Or bowling his subtle left-hand spinners; or fielding in the deep like the great runner he is, and breaking off when a wicket falls to sign autographs for any pink-faced school-boy who can produce a toffee-paper. He was meant to be the Happy Warrior of Cricket.

After the tour was complete Denis and most of the team visited Fiji where Philip Snow, brother of C.P. Snow, the novelist and sometime Labour minister, was British High Commissioner. At the time he was also President of the Fiji Cricket Association. Michael Green, the manager, and Freddie Brown, the captain of the MCC touring party in Australia, had returned by the opposite route, leaving Denis, as vice-captain, in charge of the party.

Mr Snow, in a letter to me in 1994, reported that he thought it appropriate to organise 'a chiefly reception' which took the form of an elaborate 'kava' ceremony, at which Denis was the guest of honour.

The ceremony is a most solemn one carried out with great dignity. I advised Denis that, after receiving a whale's tooth, their most precious gift, carrying in former times the power of life and death (it was given to Lord's by Denis on his return) and being required to drink in one quaff the first bowl of kava (not to everyone's liking on first taste: he drank it with sang-froid) followed by others in the front row which included Len Hutton, Cyril Washbrook and Alec Bedser as well as myself, sitting next to Denis, he would be expected to make a speech of thanks. He had only about half an hour while the whale's tooth and bowls of kava were being presented in which to compose something to say in a totally strange setting. What he did say was most graciously worded, but what did impress outstandingly was the splendidly cultured accent with which he delivered his speech. It had been my first meeting with him (I had been appointed to Fiji as Commissioner in 1938) when I introduced myself at the airport and he introduced each member of the team in turn. Knowing of his start as a scorecard seller on the groundstaff at Lord's I had expected a London accent. I was therefore surprised when he made his speech in impeccable style and cultured voice.

Herbert Sutcliffe once told Snow that he had lost his Yorkshire accent by mixing with so many fancy-hat amateurs on foreign tours. Denis had had relatively few such opportunities. Snow adds, by way of a PS, 'I knew Freddie Brown well, and he could not have passed the formidable test better.'

I thought this interesting on a number of counts, not least that I suspect Denis had greater leadership qualities than most people allowed. However, as his experience with the wartime commandos at Mhow demonstrated, he lacked the qualities of a martinet. He might have been an effective captain in the style of a Lionel Tennyson or a Colin Ingleby-Mackenzie, but I have a feeling that the times were not right and in any case that sort of laid-back style would have been considered inappropriate for a professional.

It is true that Denis did speak with a mellifluous voice almost without trace of regional accent. I'm told that his brother Leslie, whom sadly I never met, always retained a strong north London accent and had a much higher-pitched voice than Denis, who had a chocolatey timbre to his which was not so far removed, in pitch, from that of his old sparring partner John Arlott.

I put Snow's remarks to Denis and he was thoughtful. He had certainly never had elocution lessons. His parents always made a point of emphasising the importance of speaking correctly and grammatically so he would never have been, as he put it, 'a bovver boy'. He thinks that, actually, the same process applied to him as to Herbert Sutcliffe. Although he hadn't made so many long foreign tours in the company of public-schoolboy amateurs, he was one of those young men who were taken up and almost made a pet of. In adolescence he was often in the company of 'Plum' Warner, Gubby Allen, Walter Robins and Jim Swanton. Something of their speech and mannerisms must have rubbed off, and some close observers believe the first Mrs Compton had an effect too, but it was never a conscious process.

I told Philip Snow what Denis said, and he remarked that 'the accents of professional cricketers would almost make up a Ph.D. thesis'.

The curious kava ceremony sounds rather jolly and came as a welcome break. 'It tasted like muddy water,' he remembered. The comment is apt, for life had been a bit like muddy water since the heady euphoria of the Cup Final.

It would be preposterous to say that from now on it was downhill all the way and yet there is no denying that what had hitherto seemed effortless superiority was now transformed into a constant struggle against anno domini and creaking limbs. Only Denis would ever know how much the effort cost. The touch was there; the timing; the class; the will to run. But in physical terms he was suffering.

One top-class opponent of these latter years was the spinner, later commentator, Richie Benaud. Benaud first saw him play on that glum 1950–51 tour, in Sydney, when he was out for 5. At the time young Benaud had just made his debut in the Central Cumberland first-grade team. A little later Benaud was due to play against him for the Australian XI at Sydney but broke a thumb fielding the last ball of the day before and had to withdraw. They finally came up against each other in the opening Test at Trent Bridge in 1953. Benaud had first become aware of Denis in 1938 when he was a boy of eight at Jugiong, 250 miles south-west of Sydney in New South Wales. His father was the local teacher in a school which numbered just 23.

It is some measure of Denis's achievement that his doings should be followed, however sketchily, by an eight-year-old in so remote a spot.

'He was the best exponent of the sweep shot I ever bowled against,' says Benaud, 'probably the best I ever saw. I once saw Bradman sweep every ball of a Compton over at the SCG [in 1946] and I am sure Denis could have done the same thing. He swept finer than anyone else I knew and this made him very difficult to bowl against.'

Benaud says, as do so many, that it was 'flair' that characterised Denis. Miller had the same. So did Sobers. It led to unpredictability, and therefore 'he was very awkward to bowl at. A great sweeper, he was also an excellent cutter of the ball, but it was his footwork that was the most memorable aspect of his batting. He seemed instinctively to be in the right position for the shot or, if not, he had a great ability to adjust to the stroke.'

Tragic, in view of what Benaud says, that the nimble agility of his footwork should be so profoundly affected by the damage to his knee. Benaud was a class act, but it is interesting to wonder how Denis would have dealt with him on two good legs. A more leaden-footed player might not have suffered quite as much, but for Denis, a dancer at the crease, the stiffness in the joint was literally a crippling handicap.

Reg Hayter, writing in *Wisden* at the beginning of the 1950s, noted that Denis refused to offer his game knee as an excuse for any shortcomings, but added: 'Medical experts who knew the full history and state of his knee did not lightly tolerate disparagement of Compton. They preferred to praise his courage against adversity. They should be allowed the final word.'

It was obvious to anyone who knew him well that he was in trouble. In 1951, however, he was appointed joint captain of Middlesex together with Bill Edrich. Denis was a touch sensitive on the issue of captaincy. In Australia when he stood in as skipper for Freddie Brown he did not particularly impress. Trevor Bailey told me that he was made vice-captain on that tour because he was obviously the outstanding player. As other careers have demonstrated, ability as a player does not always translate into shrewd or inspiring captaincy. Denis was much liked and admired but he did not always inspire others. He sometimes fell out with less talented players, particularly if they came from Yorkshire. There was a famous incident in the Lord's dressing room when the Yorkshire fast bowler Coxon played his only Test and Denis abused him. Much the same, according to Freddie Trueman, happened with Brian Close. His attitude, as exemplified by his style as a sergeant in the East, was relaxed and laissez-faire. He obviously had the genius to get away with this but it seldom extended to others. Despite his manifest talents Denis simply wasn't a natural leader.

Under Compton and Edrich the county only finished seventh. In mitigation, Denis was only with them for about half the season, and in all first-class matches he scored over 2000 runs at an average of over 60. For almost anyone else this would have been a triumph, but for Denis even this was an anticlimax. By the standards of '47 and '48, '51 was a dullish summer.

Paradoxically it was the best May of his career and he almost made a thousand in the month. In the end he fell 91 runs short but looked in fine fettle. As Peter West has said, there was 'not the slightest doubt about his form or confidence'.

Despite a classic century in the first Test against South Africa, his fourth in succession at Trent Bridge, things slightly fell apart thereafter. For instance in two overs he dropped three catches off Alec Bedser at Headingley, his least favourite ground, and was booed horribly by the crowd. I suppose the Yorkshire failure to appreciate him was rooted in that old north–south, Hutton–Compton rivalry, yet the Leeds crowd's reaction to him does slightly give the lie to the popular notion that this is a place where the average spectator understands cricket like no one else. Not to have appreciated Compton is, surely, not to appreciate cricket. The Yorkshire problem was exacerbated when he was caught at the wicket in the county match when Bob Appleyard, the Yorkshire Test bowler, wholly unexpectedly and uncharacteristically bowled one straight at his head. Yorkshire thought this wildly amusing but Denis, for once, failed to see the joke.

He missed three weeks of the season with a septic toe, had a brilliant Gentlemen v. Players match in which he captained the Players and made 150 in the first innings and 74 not out in the second. In the final Test he was the top scorer with 73.

All in all he couldn't reasonably complain but, statistics apart, I detect a loss of urgency at this stage in his life. There were no more hills to climb. Besides, he was newly married to Valerie, he was comfortably off, he was a celebrity, owning a comfortable house in Gerrards Cross, Bucks., then as now one of the most affluent and expensive towns in England. Now that he was retired from the Arsenal he had no football to occupy him, so he did something that winter which was quite without precedent. He took time off. He went racing, played golf, stayed home and generally enjoyed himself. Confronted with this, Denis in later years looked a shade rueful but agreed. 'Backpedalling' was the word he used. The rest of his life was going too well. He had, for a moment, lost his combative edge for sport.

In 1952 he once more led the Middlesex batting averages but it was not quite the same – 1880 runs at an average of 39.16, though as a bowler he took 77 wickets, his best ever. The tourists were the Indians, who were a dullish side, but even so Denis did not do well against them, scoring only 59 runs in four innings. He was so depressed about his form that he wrote to the selectors asking not to be considered for the remainder of the series. Somehow he seemed to have run out of steam.

In 1953, his appetite came back, at least a little. This was partly because the visitors were the Australians, and in those days there was absolutely no question that they were the great opponents. Those baggy green caps they wore symbolised one of the all-time sporting rivalries. Besides it was Coronation Year. John Hunt's team conquered Everest. There was a general mood of jingoism and euphoria in which everyone wanted to share. Denis did so by helping regain the Ashes and actually scoring the winning runs at the Oval. This was a fine moment, with an enthusiastic Oval crowd surrounding Denis and Bill as they left the field, but it still didn't really see Denis at his vintage best. Many like Ronnie Harwood felt, morosely, that they would never see the real Compton again. Luckily, however, he had an Indian summer in store for the doubters – among whom he would definitely have counted himself.

There followed a tour of the Caribbean, epitomised by the explosive performance of 'Fiery Fred' Trueman and a memorable party on board Errol Flynn's yacht. The Flynn yacht was moored off Port Antonio on the north coast of Jamaica, home berth of the MCC banana boat. Flynn, an avid cricketer, sent a note across asking MCC on board for cocktails. Denis remembered a slightly dishevelled film star, clearly unwell, but eminently hospitable and with a gorgeous wife. This moment slightly made up for the failure to visit Hollywood a few years earlier.

Looking back on that tour, Denis remembered more than just the cricket. 'In the first three Tests,' he said ruminatively, 'we had the bottle throwing in Guyana, then they burnt down a stand in Trinidad and there was a riot in Jamaica.'

It was, in truth, a disastrous tour apart from the cricket. We shared the rubber with two wins apiece and a draw but as Jim Swanton wrote, 'Incident and misunderstanding followed steadily atop of one another until the original fabric of goodwill, despite much good and exciting cricket, had been ripped more or less to ribbons.'

Part of this was down to Denis. In the fourth Test at Port-of-Spain, Hutton, the captain, brought him on to bowl before lunch and he immediately had a dangerous-looking Stollmeyer caught and bowled. He then had a go at Holt, who made a lot of runs on that tour but was never comfortable against Denis's unorthodox and unpredictable spin. Sure enough, Holt failed to read Denis's googly and chopped a comfortable catch to Tom Graveney at slip. Holt turned to leave, then hesitated and stood his ground. Denis, in the middle of being congratulated by his colleagues, looked at umpire Achong, a former West Indian Test player, and appealed. Achong said 'Not out'.

The story becomes slightly confusing after this and everyone has a slightly different version. What seems beyond dispute is that Graveney, usually phlegmatic, threw the ball to the ground and swore. The 'f' word seems to have been used. Alex Bannister, writing for the *Daily Mail*, described Denis as gesticulating and waving his arms. Denis's own version was rather cooler. He said that in very sarcastic tones he said to Achong, 'What an interesting decision. In English cricket the rules are that if a batsman hits a ball to a fielder and he catches it before it hits the ground then the batsman is out. Obviously you have different rules.'

The story has an uncharacteristic air to it. On the one hand one can't help wondering if he would have spoken quite so cuttingly to a Caucasian umpire. On the other, from a man who had such a reputation for sang-froid and nonchalance his overexcitement is unexpected.

In any event the umpire was unamused and filed a formal complaint. He said it was a bump ball. Everton Weekes, batting at the other end, appears to have thought it a clean catch but changed his mind. The crowd booed. Not that it mattered a great deal because Holt was out shortly after lunch when Denis, fielding at backward short leg, pulled off a very neat catch off Fred Trueman's bowling. Finally the match, the only one Denis played on a matting wicket, was drawn.

He averaged almost fifty in the Tests without being quite at his best. Swanton wrote: 'Compton nowadays is usually at his best when he is taking the bull by the horns. Strangely enough as he gets older his judgement and patience, once among his paramount virtues, have tended sometimes to slip, whereas the brilliance of his stroke-play when the mood seizes him is as remarkable as ever.'

Valerie accompanied him on this tour. Once when he was hit painfully on the foot she made him soak the afflicted limb in very hot salt water for two hours. There was something to be said for having a wife on tour.

In the 1954 season Denis really did seem to be back on song. Against a Pakistan side playing their first full Test series in England he averaged over 90. He himself rated the 53 he made in the final Test as one of the most satisfying innings of his life. It was a very low-scoring match which Pakistan won by 24 runs. The wicket was difficult and Fazal Mahmood took twelve cheap wickets bowling medium-paced cutters. Denis's fifty took over two hours and he was dropped several times. But it was a stout resistance in difficult circumstances, and it is intriguing that this relatively low score, in a lost Test, battling against a largely forgotten Pakistani medium pacer, should have rated so high in his memory.

This year he also made his top Test score, 278 at Trent Bridge. Typically he hadn't realised that he was in sight of a record. David Sheppard was captaining the side in Hutton's absence, and at one point when Denis was past 200 and blazing away he took him to one side and said, 'I can give you just one more hour to do it, but then I'll have to declare.' Denis remembered looking at 'the bishop', as he called him, and not knowing what he was talking about. When Sheppard explained that he was within sight of the highest score ever made in Test cricket he still didn't care and, playing in his own sweet way, was soon bowled by a sixteen-year-old leg-spinner called Khalid Hassan. He had hit a six and 33 fours and *Wisden* described the best of his innings as 'a torrent of strokes, orthodox and improvised, crashing and delicate, against which Kardar could not set a field and the bowlers knew not where to pitch'. Kardar, a former Cambridge blue, was the unfortunate Pakistan captain. However he had few days as bad as this one, and with their narrow victory at the Oval Pakistan unexpectedly squared the series. Denis shared a stand with Tom Graveney which was the only time that Graveney felt he almost matched the master's explosive style. Normally Graveney found himself standing at the bowler's end marvelling at the execution of shots he knew he could not play himself. This was an exception but it was somehow typical, thought Graveney, that even so he was out in his eighties while Denis went on to make over three times as many.

The now infamous knee curtailed Denis's '54 season and delayed his departure for the 1954–55 tour to Australia. His belated journey out by air was marked by a scary crash landing at Karachi. The general opinion was that he had been back to very nearly his best against Pakistan and that, if his knee held up, he and Hutton should tilt the balance of the series in England's favour.

In the event he averaged 38 in the Tests, coming third behind May and Graveney. Both were much younger men and this was essentially a tour won by a new generation of England cricketers. Len Hutton only averaged 24 in the Tests and Alec Bedser was bottom of the bowling averages. The star, of course, was 'Typhoon' Tyson, who ripped out 28 Australians at just over twenty a head.

It wasn't just the knee that caused problems. On the first morning of the first Test in Brisbane he collided with the boundary fence while trying to save a boundary and fractured a finger in his left hand. He missed a whole month of cricket because of this and was only really fit during the two final Tests. He managed 84 in the very last, though his finest innings of the tour was probably his 184 against South Australia, made in just under five hours. Not as speedy perhaps as the grand scores of his prime, but still something like the old maestro. The final innings, however, was a touch pawky. He was involved in a long slow stand with Trevor Bailey; Alan Ross, reporting for the *Observer*, wrote hurtfully that 'generally he has seldom timed the ball worse'.

One telling vignette of this tour also suggests, to me at least, that he was missing some of his old enthusiasm and braggadocio. It was conjured up by Colin Cowdrey, who by now was an international cricketer. Cowdrey remembered one day watching Ray Lindwall from the dressing room. Lindwall was past his best and there did not seem a lot in the wicket, but Cowdrey recalled Denis getting really quite fidgety as he watched his old adversary. He kept muttering about how quick he was looking and the wicket being dangerous. It was not that he was scared, he just seemed a tad twitchy. The remedy, mind you, was typically Compton. He suddenly reached across to Godfrey Evans's bag and, despite the wicket-keeper's protest, stuffed a pair of socks into a trouser pocket as an improvised thigh pad. He must have been getting old.

Jack Fingleton was sad to see the last of him and penned a graceful and perceptive tribute in the *Sunday Times* at the end of the tour as he contemplated Denis walking from the Sydney ground for the last time. Fingleton remembered him, curiously, 'surrounded, as he always was in Australia when play ended, by a doting band of the British merchant service who unfailingly convoyed him from the field and then, after depositing him at the dressing-room door, just as unfailingly convoyed themselves in the general surge to the members' bar'.

Fingleton lamented the fact that no Australian ground would ever again see Hutton, Compton or Evans. Fingleton was suitably laudatory about the other two, but it is obvious that it is Denis who had a special place in his affections:

Compton, like the majestic Hammond before him, has known some of his greatest and some of his poorest days in Australia. The latter are soon forgotten. Those who know genius will always carry the mental picture of Compton smacking the ball fine to leg as only Compton could; of the sheer beauty and thrill of his cover-drive and hook; of his impish run-out before the ball was bowled and, sometimes, his scamper back like a schoolboy caught helping himself to jam.

In Melbourne, once, when that weird bowler 'Wrong Grip' Iverson (who flicked off-breaks off his second finger with a leg-break action) was befuddling the Englishmen at their first meeting, Sheppard, who had been doing best of all, walked down the pitch and asked skipper Compton whether he (Sheppard) shouldn't change from defence to attack. 'Go on as you are, David,' said Compton, who had been in the most abject bother. 'Leave the antics to me.'

South Africa is the country outside England which he loved the most, but there is something in the Australian psyche which Denis might have relished even more. Like his mate Keith Miller he had much of the larrikin in him.

The following year, 1955, he achieved what for him was a miserable return for Middlesex with only 590 runs all season, yet in Tests against the South Africans he made almost as many, 492, at an average of well over 50. In his seventies he still talked about the summer of '55 with tremendous enthusiasm. He loved playing against the South Africans and he rated the Test series that year as one of the most evenly and fiercely contested he had ever played in. Tayfield, the spinner, was an adversary who always put him on his mettle, and he always rated the fast bowlers, Heine and Adcock, as two of the most dangerous he ever played against – not far short of Lindwall and Miller in their prime.

The Old Trafford Test has become something of a legend in the Compton life, not just because of his cricketing performance but also because of an extramural incident to do with punctuality. Gubby Allen, chairman of selectors, and Peter May, the captain, were adamant that every member of the team should turn up at 3 p.m. for net practice. Denis cut things rather fine and was still on the beach in Sussex with Valerie and their little boys, Patrick and Richard, when there was only an hour or so left before nets. Skidding home, he realised that he was never going to make it to Manchester in time. Never mind. He had a friend and neighbour who owned a light aircraft. By great good fortune both man and plane were available.

Denis persuaded him to provide a lift up north, though unfortunately the plane was too small to accommodate his gear and this had to be left behind. The next problem was weather. Over the Midlands they ran into heavy turbulence and had to make an emergency landing at Derby.

Meanwhile in Manchester Allen and May were not amused. Net practice had been and gone and the players were at dinner when Denis finally put in an appearance. Colin Cowdrey told me he remembered the moment of Denis's arrival as if it were yesterday. The second he put his head round the door Allen and May were on their feet, taking him out of the room in order to issue a stern wigging. Characteristically the three of them were back in the dining room ten minutes later, all apparently forgiven. Denis said that this was the only time that May, with whom he had a very affectionate relationship, was really cross with him.

Although England lost at Old Trafford, Denis himself had a splendid match. Batting at No. 4 with a bat borrowed from a reluctant Fred Titmus (he had paid for it out of his own money and was afraid Denis would break it), he went in at 22 for 2 and hit 158 off the always dangerous Heine and Adcock. In the second innings he made 71, and many observers considered this an even better innings than the earlier century. It was to no avail, however, for South Africa, set to make 145 in two and a quarter hours, achieved a thrilling victory with three wickets and nine balls to go. It was one of the great Test matches and Denis played an eventful and thrilling part in it.

But this was all at a cost. The knee was agony and sooner or later something had to be done.

CHAPTER THIRTEEN

I n November 1955 he had his right kneecap removed.

The specialist, Osmond Clarke, said it was his only chance. If the patella came off there was a possibility, a slim one, that he might be able to play cricket again. If it didn't there was no chance at all. Without the operation he would be condemned to continual pain and at best a heavy limp. That was the specialist's opinion. Today's advice might have been different. Surgery has become more sophisticated, and modern doctors are less keen on reaching for the knife as a weapon of first resort. In a later age Denis would have been in hospital for just a few days, subjected to some painless minimalist micro-surgery, and emerged as right as rain after a fortnight.

Denis was not enthusiastic about discussing the knee in later life. It was obvious that his knee had dogged much of his career, had given him severe pain and ultimately precipitated a premature retirement. At seventy-five it was still – in every sense – a sore subject. In particular he was well aware that had he been born later medicine would have become more sophisticated and he would not have had to suffer as he did. He also suspected that even by the standards of the day he had been unlucky.

The kneecap is still with us. Bill Tucker, the orthopaedic surgeon who dealt with the knee before calling in Osmond

Clarke – who was one of the great orthopaedic surgeons of the day – kept it as a souvenir and would occasionally produce it as a sort of family heirloom to be shown off to visitors to his consulting rooms.

Before he died Tucker sent the kneecap to Gubby Allen so that he could place it where it belonged – in the MCC archive. Stephen Green, the Lord's librarian until his retirement in 2003, confirmed that the kneecap was indeed at cricket HQ but he, like Denis, was too squeamish to look at it. However, he arranged a viewing. It was still in what appeared to be an old biscuit tin. It also still had the Bermuda customs clearance label from Tucker's retirement home on it: 'Contents – One knee-cap'. On opening the biscuit tin I found a transparent bag containing an object which looked very like a Dorset knob biscuit. It was about the size and shape of a medium-sized mushroom, honey-coloured and honeycombed. Compton's knee.

Stephen Green, who flinched at even the idea of examining it, refused to let the patella go to a modern hospital for examination on the grounds that it was part of the Lord's archive. The plastic bag, and the biscuit tin, had allowed it to dehydrate so that it was unlikely to be of serious interest to medical science. Yet there it sat at Lord's, one of the most crucial pieces of human anatomy in the history of cricket. A macabre memento of physical frailty which played havoc with the career of one of the few authentic sporting geniuses of the twentieth century. It is not on public display.

Denis was a rotten patient in 1956 and his convalescence was prolonged and difficult. The long-suffering Valerie grinned and bore him, but he was, on his own admission, 'bad-tempered, wretched and without much hope'. The knee bent just so far but no further. There was endless physiotherapy week in, week out, but still the protesting joint refused to go beyond a certain point.

Glum and bothery, he somehow got through the winter, but at the beginning of the 1956 season there was no real improvement. He was still hobbling, and the idea of playing cricket of any kind was completely out of the question.

It was an Australian year, which made his disability even more depressing. He longed to have a crack at the old enemy and a final tilt at Keith Miller and Ray Lindwall. But when the Australians arrived in April 1956 the prospects seemed bleak indeed.

Shortly after the tourists came Denis was invited to a dinner given by the cricket writers in their honour. Another guest was the man who took away his kneecap, the consultant, Osmond Clarke. Clarke had been thinking about Compton's knee, and he and Denis's other orthopaedic surgeon, Bill Tucker, had a new idea. They wanted to get him back into the operating theatre and manipulate the knee under a general anaesthetic. A good wrench, they thought, might just do the trick.

It did. After three sessions the joint was back to 75 per cent flexibility. It was not perfect but, in the doctors' estimation, it was good enough for first-class cricket. The treatment was painful and the knee was weak but, by early summer, he was feeling reasonably confident for the first time in months.

He took it gingerly stage by stage. First he went to the nets. The early sessions were gentle and short but gradually he extended them until he was confident enough to try some one-day games for MCC and others. In one of these, for the XL Club, he made 72 against Eton on Agars Plough. The XL Club, captained by Walter Robins, included the Australian opener Arthur Morris as well as Denis's brother Leslie and several other Middlesex players. Sir William Becher, the long-serving secretary of I Zingari, made a sound 29. He remembered that 'Denis batted very carefully in order not to damage the famous knee. He took his bowling carefully as well.'

The bowling was not as successful as the batting, for he

allowed the boys to hit him for 51 runs off eight overs without a wicket. Eton scored 257, including 43 from one of their opening batsmen, H.C. (Henry) Blofeld, subsequently a highly individual broadcaster, and then bowled out the Club for 253, thus winning by four runs. Denis, with 72, was the top scorer. The *Eton College Chronicle* wrote, 'It was a good sight to see D. Compton back in action and to watch him play many of his favourite shots again.'

One man who spent a lot of time watching Denis that summer was the actor, and later novelist, Douglas Hayes. Hayes was so enthralled by the experience that he wrote an entire book about it. The manuscript is charming, elegant and scrupulously observed but still, alas, unpublished.

There are a number of telling glimpses of Denis in his text; sometimes batting, almost more often bowling and causing ripples of laughter whenever he does, and catching some unorthodox catches. One particular picture sticks in my mind because I don't recall anyone else painting it. This is Compton in the nets:

> Those behind me, at the nets, can be standing in the rain to watch one man only. Compton drives with power, limping. He wants six more. They bowl him seven for luck and he leaves the net. A photographer asks him to pose. Boys present autograph books, scorecards, scraps of paper. He signs them all. The woman with daisies in her navy blue hat wishes Compton a quick return. He thanks her. A shadow of weariness or old pain is on him. In the gloom of the afternoon the greatest player of his time limps along behind the Grandstand, on his way to the Pavilion.

By the end of June he felt well enough to turn out for Middlesex and took the field at Lord's against a strong Lancashire side which included Washbrook and Statham. Denis's memory was again slightly at fault and his own account, in his book, does not quite tally with that of *Wisden*. The Almanack, as so often, is wonderfully laconic. 'He limped slightly,' says the report, 'and found difficulty in moving sharply but on the first day before about 17,000 people he started dramatically by helping to dismiss the first four batsmen. He took a wicket with his fifth ball and caught three at slip.' Denis himself wrote 'I wasn't any good in the field'. But if not, how come he caught three at slip?

Perhaps he overdid it. The day was hot, Lancashire batted throughout it, and by close of play at 6.30 Denis was, by his own admission, 'just about all in and limping badly'. He was discouraged. His fans and fellow players buoyed him up as best they could, and his reception from the crowd was genuinely affecting. But Denis sensed that everyone was thinking that he was too handicapped to be able to play, and although he was loath to admit it he was not nearly as confident as he was trying to appear. In his heart of hearts he himself didn't think he'd make it either. When it was Middlesex's turn to bat it rained and the wicket became difficult. The whole side struggled and had to follow on, when they struggled again and only just avoided an innings defeat. No one, alas, struggled more than Denis. In the first innings Wharton – whom he had dismissed himself, caught by Bill Edrich – bowled him for 4, and in the second he went for a single, caught by Bill Edrich's cousin, Geoff, off the spin of Hilton, who finished with 5 for 19 off 24 overs, 15 of them maidens. No wonder Denis was glum.

The next game was at Westcliff-on-Sea against Essex, but Denis didn't play and the team won comfortably without him, which, though he was obviously pleased for them, made him even more despondent.

From there, however, Middlesex went down to Somerset for Maurice Tremlett's benefit at Glastonbury. This was a terrific game and Denis played a crucial role, although in the end Somerset almost won. Edrich set them 208 to win in two and a half hours, and they got to within five runs with three wickets still standing.

Before this excitement, however, there had been some Middlesex batting which even reminded the *Wisden* correspondent of 'their great days of 1947'. 'They', of course, were Bill and Denis, Edrich and Compton. Edrich made 89, Denis 110. He hit 15 fours and a six before coming down the wicket to Colin McCool, one of a long line of successful Somerset Australians, and being stumped by Stephenson. In the second innings he made 40 after Lobb, the Somerset fast bowler, took the first two wickets for no runs at all. He also bowled 16 overs, taking the first Somerset wicket with an lbw, and he caught a catch off the bowling of his old friend John Warr.

The knee was still stiff, but he was back in business with a vengeance.

In the following match they thrashed Gloucester despite a stylish 156 from the young Tom Graveney. Denis made 47 in his only innings and bowled 24 rather expensive overs which included another lbw.

He missed the game against Kent, which was sad because it was at Maidstone, a ground of which he was particularly fond and where he felt lucky. He was missed too because his colleagues were skittled out for 64 in the first innings. Doug Wright, who had entered first-class cricket 24 years earlier, did for them with his 'whipping leg breaks and googlies'. Kent went on to win by nine wickets.

The next game was the one he really wanted to play in, for it was the visit of Ian Johnson's Australian team to Lord's. This was not one of the great Australian sides, and they had just come from the Headingley Test, where they were beaten by an innings. They had already developed an aversion to the spin of Jim Laker and Tony Lock, though the debacle at Old Trafford, where Laker got 19 wickets, was yet to come.

Nevertheless the team included Lindwall and Miller, Harvey and Benaud, all of whom were world-class, and there were others not far behind. By Australian standards theirs was not a successful tour, but Australia is Australia, and for a cricketer of Denis's generation they were always the ultimate challenge.

In the event his great mate Keith Miller did not play in the Middlesex match, which turned out, however, to be one of the better Australian performances of the summer. It rained again – the wet weather was one reason for the tourists' below-par performance that year – and batting first the Australians slumped to 114 for 7 before Benaud and Lindwall shared a hard-hitting stand of 87.

It seemed all Australia when they took the first two Middlesex wickets for only two runs. Denis came in at 14 for 3 and left an hour and three-quarters later having made 61 runs. A strangely muted Bill Edrich hardly contributed, since their stand together was worth 77. This was a sparkling Compton innings, ended only by a brilliant run-out from that most excellent cover-point, Neil Harvey. In the end the match was drawn, with the home team on 108 for 5 and both Edrich and Compton having been unaccountably held in reserve.

He was looking good. Stiff and in some pain, but playing his shots and timing them immaculately. He missed the next two matches, then scored a 'flawless' (*Wisden*) half-century against Hampshire when his team won by twelve runs. Against Sussex at Hove he was run out for 3, and against Surrey on a green wicket against a tigerish Loader he made a defiant 14 in an hour and twenty minutes. The defence was not reassembled as effectively as the attack.

Next day he embarked on a thoroughly enjoyable game against Kent which Middlesex won by an innings and 73 runs. Denis made 101 in 3 hours and 10 minutes with 16 fours. Part of the fun of this innings was that his old friend and partner

Godfrey Evans was behind the stumps, laughing and chatting in his usual chirpy style even as the bowler was running in. Denis couldn't help feeling buoyant when Evans was jollying him along. His effervescence was contagious.

In the next match, the return against Surrey, he made only 2 and 17, but the selectors still felt that he had done enough to play in the final Test. Gubby Allen, their chairman, approached him. Was he fit to play? Denis was in a quandary. If he was scrupulously honest with himself he did not really think he was well enough to play in a Test against Australia. On the other hand he had made a couple of hundreds and he had made runs against Lindwall and company. Besides, the Ashes had been retained at Old Trafford, so even if he performed badly the most important prize could not be lost.

So he said yes.

Cricket in general, and the return of Denis in particular, was a welcome escape from the troubles of the times. It was the era of Mintoff in Malta, Makarios in Cyprus and above all Nasser and the Suez Canal. At the beginning of August, *The Times* thundered, 'if Nasser is allowed to get away with this coup all the British and other interests in the Middle East will crumble.' Everywhere, it seemed, the British lion's tail was being tweaked. To have won the Ashes was a recompense, but the return of Compton would make a good cricket season even better. Everyone knew that he was not a hundred per cent. At the same time everyone wanted him to do well. It really was a matter of national concern. 'Finally,' wrote Norman Preston, editor of *Wisden* and son of Hubert, 'came Compton to the Oval, emphasizing that cricket is a game to be enjoyed and he reaped the reward for his indomitable courage after so many operations on his troublesome knee.'

Jim Swanton thought that though Denis was 'struggling bravely' he was 'scarcely half the cricketer he was in those golden years before it beset him'.

He was still assailed by doubts as he walked out to bat at the Oval. If he failed it would be the end of his career, and he would be sad about that on several counts. He loved the game and did not feel ready to give it up, and he very much wanted to go out on a high note with the sort of buccaneering performance for which he had become famous. He was particularly anxious not to let down Peter May, who was a relatively young and new captain. And finally there was the bait of South Africa. England were touring his favourite foreign country that winter, and there were still places left. A good performance in the final Test might just clinch it for him. In retrospect he said that it was the prospect of one last tour of South Africa which finally made up his mind for him.

So it was a peculiarly apprehensive Denis who came in to join his captain at twenty past two on the opening day. The score was 66 for 3. Richardson, Cowdrey and the Reverend David Sheppard had all gone. Rain had taken the shine off the ball and Johnson was keeping the batsmen on their toes by making frequent changes.

Keith Miller, of all people, was bowling. He had just had Richardson caught behind while trying for a cut, and although the wicket was not particularly quick he was in full flow. The crowd gave Denis a huge ovation, he took guard, said a superstitious under-the-breath prayer to his bat and faced up to the man *Wisden* described as his 'old friend and foe'.

There was no fear nor favour between these two. The first ball was an absolute fizzer, one of the fastest of the day but luckily not straight, so that Denis was able to let it go through on the leg side to Langley behind the stumps. Years later I asked Denis if he didn't think this opener was a slightly unfriendly act, but he just smiled that rueful smile of his and said no, that was the way you played – hard, competitive, fair and a pint or two after close of play. He didn't expect charity, least of all from Keith.

The relationship between Compton and Miller was as close as possible between two men living on opposite sides of the world. They talked on the phone every week right up to Denis's death. Miller's third son – he was blessed with four – was named Denis Charles in his honour; they shared a past which has provided some of the most riveting duels in twentieth-century cricket.

They had first met in 1943 at Lord's when Denis ran himself out for 60. Miller recalled that he turned for a second run, saw he couldn't make it, 'grinned and gasped', and charged on home to the pavilion. Had he turned, the other batsman would have been out, but that was not Denis's style. 'The whole incident was typical of Compton,' said Miller, 'and it made a deep impression on me. I have never had cause to change that first impression.'

For Miller 1956 and the comeback was Compton's greatest hour. At the time Miller thought he was a fool to try it. Having been the 'Golden Boy', why take such a hideous risk, knowing that he could never again scale the earlier heights? In the event Miller reckoned he was wrong and that Compton's return that summer was a triumph which underlined his 'true greatness'.

Miller never held anything back on the field of play. Indeed he was Denis's soulmate in that respect. 'When I bowled against Denis I tried everything in the book,' he said. 'He has a style of his own. You never know what he is going to do next. So you try and get him working along the same lines; but whereas other batsmen instinctively block an unusual type of delivery Denis will try and hit it.'

The first quarter of an hour was pretty agonising for Denis, for May and for the crowd. He did not score a single run in those fifteen minutes and he seemed well pinned down both by Miller's ferocious speed and the spin of Benaud from the other end. But then, gradually the confidence began to ebb back. The perspicacious *Times* correspondent (John

Woodcock) remarked, 'Presently he was twiddling his bat, with his hair out of place in much the old way.'

Looking back on this innings, one of the most crucial in his career, Denis described it as 'cruel and painful', and yet to some onlookers it evoked a glorious past and seemed as charmed and exhilarating as ever. Bradman himself told him later that it was the best innings of the series, and *Wisden* was ecstatic.

'Gradually Compton unfolded all the familiar strokes of his golden days. The special leg sweeps of his own brand and the most delicate of late cuts, as well as peerless cover drives took him and England to prosperity. In less than an hour the partnership went to 50, and at 33 Compton overtook his captain.'

Others were more doubtful. Len Hutton himself came up to him at a black tie dinner that night and asked bluntly if he'd enjoyed it. 'Didn't you find it ruddy hard work?' he wanted to know. And the sharp *Times* man wrote that when he was finally out, 'his passing was not altogether surprising for he was by then lame and tired. Compton's performance came straight out of a story book. One wonders if he has ever experienced anything much more nerve wracking.'

By 6.15 p.m. the two of them had put on 156, of which Denis had made 94, but just as a memorable century seemed to be within his grasp he was out, caught off Archer. 'It was a triumph as much of character as skill, and when eventually he was out everyone must have shed a silent tear,' said one onlooker.

England then suffered a collapse in fading light, eventually being all out the following day for only 247, with the captain carrying his bat. Australia, by now thoroughly alarmed by the mere sight of Lock and Laker, were all out for 202, and in the second England innings Denis made 35 not out in another stand with May which was noticeably more careful than the first. By now heavy rain had seriously affected the wicket and the match. May, anxious not to lose the match and square the rubber, did not declare until tea, which left the Australians the impossible task of scoring 228 in only two hours 'on a soft pitch and a dead outfield'. Even so at close of play they were 27 for 5, with Laker having taken 3 for 8.

For Denis it was a triumph, albeit a painful one. And it was crowned by the news, shortly afterwards, that he had been selected for South Africa.

There was one revealing private moment after Denis's first-innings 94. His surgeons Bill Tucker and Osmond Clarke showed an X-ray of the famous knee to a third expert ortho-paedic surgeon without telling him whose it was. After some thoughtful study the great man said sagely, 'This man will never walk again.'

'This man,' he was told, 'made 94 yesterday for England against Australia.'

The South African tour of 1956–57 was an appropriate overseas swansong. There was an idyllic domestic element, for during the trip one of his sons was christened. His captain Peter May was roped in as godfather. The family album shows the happy group, wreathed in beams and sunshine. In only a year or so Denis's marriage to Valerie ended but at the time, at least to a casual cricketing visitor South Africa still seemed relatively safe and sunny.

Alan Ross, who covered the tour for the *Observer*, has some poetic descriptions of the country which make you understand just why it was so seductive. On 6 December, for instance, when England would have been shivering, the tour party made the twenty-seven-hour journey to Pretoria on the Blue Train. Gin was a shilling a glass, the six-course meals included Cape lobster and sweet fresh succulent melon. Outside beyond the air-conditioning was an ever-changing landscape with fleeting glimpses of paradise, or as Ross put it, you exchanged 'the golden Hesperides of peach, apricot and grape for the red plains and grey scrub of Karoo'. Ross was a published poet of some distinction, later editor of the *London Magazine*.

Denis had a good time but not a particularly good tour. In earlier years he would surely have tripped nimbly down the wicket to the South African spinner 'Toey' Tayfield or the medium pace of Goddard, but the knee simply wasn't up to it and he found himself rooted to the spot like some old bear being baited by the dogs.

He started well enough against lesser opposition and was 'masterly' against Transvaal, but when it came to the first Test, Ross, assessing the surprisingly fragile-looking English batting, said succinctly of Denis, 'For Compton one must keep one's fingers crossed.'

Indeed. In Johannesburg Denis mustered 5 and 32. It sounds rather awful. First time round Denis kept playing and missing balls on his leg stump, got frustrated and was caught off an inside edge. In the second innings he clearly played some exquisite shots but was frequently hit on the fingers and the bottom. Even his dismissal was dodgy. Tayfield had him caught and bowled but many present, including Denis himself, thought it was a bump-ball.

It was nearly Christmas. Ross, like Arlott before him, was aware that despite the limpid loveliness on the surface all was not well in the Dominion. 'It is easier far,' he wrote, 'in this easy country, to remember a Christmas Day with old, good friends, the swimming and tennis and cocktail parties and laden, decorated tree.' That was Denis's South Africa, but Ross, unlike Denis, was troubled. 'It is all part of the same life,' he continued, 'lived by a similar kind of human beings – or is thinking that, in Nationalist South Africa, the greatest heresy of all?'

The second Test began on New Year's Day in Cape Town, just as it had eight years before when Ronnie Harwood first clapped eyes on his hero. England won by more than three hundred runs. Denis made 58 and 64, and only Colin Cowdrey of the English batsmen did better. Wardle, with twelve wickets for under a hundred, was the main destroyer.

Compton's first innings had moments of charm and happiness interspersed with 'the familiar struggle and constraints of recent weeks'. In the second he played some lovely strokes but again seemed constrained. He looked out of sorts and tired. Ross said it was 'application rather than genius', which doesn't sound like the true Denis.

He got 16 and 19 in the third Test at Durban, which was drawn. On the Saturday however, Valerie and he gave a magnificent party at Isipingo, Valerie's family home. Years later Denis rolled the name Isipingo round his tongue as if it were the name of a particularly intoxicating cocktail. Both the South African and English teams were there, all dancing in a variety of eclectic styles. I get the impression that Denis, for once, enjoyed the party more than the cricket. There were still flashes of genius but, in truth, he was a shadow of the cricketer he was.

Nevertheless he made a hundred against Transvaal. However in the fourth Test at Johannesburg it was 41 and 1, with Heine and Tayfield defeating him once more. There was even one hour when, facing Tayfield, he made no scoring strokes at all and Ross, characteristically, wondered if 'Port had been poured into the Coca-Cola'. He took two and a half hours over his first 13 runs, then made 20 in no time at all. Even reading about it is sad stuff.

South Africa won that match, and the next too, when England were all out for 110 and 130 and Denis made 0 and 5. It was his last Test for England and he looked singularly out of sorts. Alan Ross penned a sad little epitaph:

He played not one innings in character: simply he struggled, patient as Job, a plain man in a world of riddles. Where he used to charm and invent and delight, he was now silent; a gay, daring conversationalist who, having said all he had to say still remained on at table, handsome, legendary, but mute . . . a more charming, agreeable, human cricketer there has never been; one would have preferred, infinitely, that he had lost his wicket each time in daring rather than in the humble submissive role he felt somehow called on to play.

There was no more Test cricket for Denis and, in 1957, just one more full season for Middlesex. This was illuminated by flashes of brilliance and he once more headed the Middlesex averages. I was watching him by now, a thirteen-year-old, sitting usually in the Mound Stand. Once, outside the Tavern, I even got his autograph. He was talking to another man, and as I walked away well satisfied, a third party asked if my book had been signed by Denis's friend. I said 'No'. He told me that the other man was the film director David Lean but it meant nothing to me. I had Denis's signature and that was more than enough.

I remember his last match as a professional at Lord's in 1957. He managed a wonderful valedictory century in the first innings against Worcestershire. Then in the second innings he was on 48 and made a big hit to the long-on boundary where a man called Outschoorn made a juggling catch, and that was it. My hero limped off and we all stood, lump in throat and tear in eye, watching the end of a legend.

CHAPTER FOURTEEN

Denis played his final match as a professional at the end of 1957. Half of his life was yet to come and almost forty years is a long time to spend in anticlimax.

By most conventional standards his life as a Sunday newspaper columnist, radio and TV pundit, after-dinner speaker and advertising agency consultant was full and rewarding. However, after a life of sporting stardom such as that enjoyed by Denis it was small-time stuff. There was never any suggestion that in his later years he would disappear into the sort of obscurity or even penury experienced by some of his less famous colleagues but the fact remains that by the exalted standards of the first half of his life, the second was relatively mundane. In a very real sense the second was a shadow of the first.

As far as playing cricket was concerned he continued to make occasional first-class appearances as an amateur. In 1964 on a carefree trip to Jamaica with the Cavaliers he scored his 123rd first-class hundred and at the end of that season played his absolutely final first-class match when he hit a fifty for MCC versus Lancashire.

For some years after that he went on playing charity matches and social cricket in the same bonhomous vein as he had played in his prime.

Graham Lord told me about one of these games, some time in the Sixties or Seventies, when Denis turned out for his employer, the *Sunday Express*. Lord was then Literary Editor of the *Express*.

In the late sixties and seventies I used to play Sunday cricket regularly for the *Sunday Express* against other Sunday papers (not to mention our annual fixture against the Oxfordshire Vicars and Gravediggers) with Denis and he was fantastic with my two small daughters. One, Kate, who was then aged three or four, was mentally handicapped and Denis would sit her on his lap and play with her for ages and make her laugh. Lovely man. In one match against the *Sunday Mirror* (whose fearsome bowlers were Ted Dexter and Alf Gover) I came in as usual at number 11 with 60-plus to make to win. This looked impossible since I rarely scored more than single figures and in our previous match against them Dexter had bowled me first ball, the bastard, because he was on a hat-trick, but Denis was at the other end on 55, met me as I walked trembling to the wicket, and told me just to keep the ball out of the stumps and he would farm the bowling and do the rest. For half an hour or so I poked, prodded, snicked and missed the ball completely time and time again while Denis was carving fours in all directions except for the last ball of each over, when we'd sneak a single. He got the 60-plus runs and we won by one wicket, with Denis on 106 not out and me on 4. And as we reached the pavilion he stood back, made me go up first and applauded me all the way. What a gent.

Denis's social and charitable cricket appearances were not always as successful. Rachel Heyhoe-Flint, best known of all England women cricketers, remembered another occasion, on an unspecified date in an unnamed place. It was apparently a charity match between a team of 'Gentlemen' and another of 'Ladies'. And Heyhoe-Flint thought it probably one of his last outings as an active player. 'Denis,' she said, 'spent too much time in the hospitality tent, and when it came to his turn to bat I think he may have been seeing two balls. Anyway he chose the wrong one to hit, and the ball trickled past his bat and gently dislodged his bails. Denis laughed all the way back to the hospitality tent, saying, "Would you believe it, bowled first ball by a woman!"'

Rachel Heyhoe-Flint made much of the laughter, believing that this was an appropriate way to remember him. Spectators who turned up in the hope of seeing the maestro recapture a few moments of glorious youth might have been forgiven for being less amused.

In later years his doctor did warn him about drinking too much. Denis did not usually pay a great deal of attention though he did cut back on the spirits, insisting, perversely, that the medics had told him he could drink as much wine as he liked because it didn't count. When his third wife, Christine, remonstrated and checked up with the doctor she was told that he had said nothing of the kind, only that a little wine in moderation would do him no harm.

Generally speaking Denis, and his friends, made light of the booze question. Denis had a favourite story about being invited by the Tory Cabinet Minister Willie Whitelaw to speak at a dinner in St Andrews, when Whitelaw was President of the Royal and Ancient Golf Club. Before the meal began Whitelaw took Denis to one side and said in an avuncular way, 'Denis, I'd be grateful if you didn't have anything to drink before you speak.' Denis was mildly disappointed but did as he was told and spoke skilfully and amusingly, as he nearly always did. Afterwards Whitelaw congratulated him and then said, 'Now we're going to adjourn to my room where I have particularly good malt whisky and you and I are going to get well and truly sloshed.'

In my own experience Denis was always a convivial drinker.

I remember seeing him from afar at the table inside the front door of El Vino's in Fleet Street. That was the late 1960s and early 1970s. He would sit there every Friday after delivering his copy for the *Sunday Express* and share bottles of Pommery and Greno champagne with Vic Patrick, the paper's deputy editor and Derek Marks, editor of the *Daily*, both generously girthed trenchermen. When I saw a lot of him in the early 1990s he was mainly drinking white wine. Occasionally, however, when asked what he'd like to drink, Denis would reply 'A pink gin please old boy.' After a while I came to recognise that the pink gin was a form of anaesthetic reserved for days when he was in particular pain from his various malfunctioning joints.

My impression was also that the conviviality was as important as the drink. Certainly the two went together but the company was important, as to a lesser extent was the food and also the setting. He enjoyed the Savoy Grill, especially when the maître d' recognised him and addressed him by name. He enjoyed the Cricketers' Club in Marylebone where he was latterly president. He was thoroughly clubbable and I personally saw him have a thoroughly good time at the Garrick, the Groucho and the Travellers' clubs, all occasions enhanced by an element of recognition sometimes edging over the boundary into idolatry.

When Andrew Duncan took him off for a column he wrote in the *Sunday Express* magazine called 'Out to lunch', Denis chose the old-fashioned dining room at a block of flats in St John's Wood called Oslo Court. He described Denis's lunch. 'He ordered oysters,' he reported, 'but changed his mind when he discovered they were French and had scallops with bacon instead, followed by a veal chop with a light Fleurie.' Oslo Court was always Denis's sort of place and the meal was equally typical: all very English/Continental in a formal 1950s manner with flambés and steaks tartare at the table, waiters in black jackets and striped trousers, an elderly clientele with a sense of film producer, faded blonde and cigars.

Other favoured watering holes were various pubs such as the Belgian Arms at Holyport near Bray and the Black Horse at Fulmer where he lived in an apartment at Fulmer Place from the early Sixties to the mid-Seventies. Paul Lott, who ran the Fulmer pub for twenty-five years, recalled that the stables next door once caught fire in the middle of the night. Denis, whose flat was nearby, was woken but on being told that it was 'only' the stables said, 'Thank God, I thought it was the Horse – now we can go back to bed.'

Lott continued,

Denis always had a word with anyone who came into the pub. I can remember people coming into the Middle Bar asking him to sign a copy of his book which he always did with a message. He would nearly always drop in on his way home from London, sometimes quite late. On one occasion we were clearing up after closing; there were a few customers still hanging on chatting when the police arrived, clipboards in hand to take names. Denis walked in, asking the barmaid what all the fuss was about. The sergeant replied, 'No trouble – just a routine check.' 'That's all right then,' said Denis. 'Now, can I buy you a drink, sergeant?'

His friend the actor Trevor Howard was also a Black Horse habitué whenever he was filming at Pinewood Studios a mile or so away. Howard was so keen on cricket that he had a clause in his contracts stipulating that he would never be required to work if England were playing a Test match. He was also sufficiently keen on a drink that the Orange Tree Theatre in Richmond-upon-Thames has a Trevor Howard bar in which benefactors may buy enough space to put their pint of bitter or large gin and tonic. It's the drinking man's equivalent of a debenture. After he died, Howard's ashes were scattered, like Denis's, on the hallowed turf at Lord's.

Howard had a routine of slipping out of Pinewood Studios and going down to the Black Horse in Fulmer where he would order a couple of drinks before phoning Denis at his flat in Fulmer Place with the simple but sufficient words 'I'm here'.

It was said that whenever Denis was driving past the Horse his car would invariably develop some minor technical fault which would make it essential to pull into the pub car park. On another occasion Edward Guinness, scion of the brewing family and President of the Fulmer Village Cricket Club, saw Denis pushing a pram. This was in itself an unusual occurrence. The pram must have contained one of his infant daughters, Victoria or Charlotte, which places the incident some time in the early 1980s. Guinness watched as Denis, by then in his sixties, pushed the pram along the pavement until alongside the front door. There Compton paused, thought for a moment, seemed on the verge of pushing towards the pub, thought better of it and walked on. Guinness said that not only was this the only time he saw Denis pushing a pram, it was also the only time he saw Denis going *past* the Black Horse.

Despite the pram and the two daughters Denis could never, I think, be described as uxorious. Devoted, yes; but domesticated, not really. Valerie, the second Mrs Compton, became homesick for her native South Africa. She hated the English climate and was determined that their two sons, Patrick and Richard, should grow up with a South African sun on their backs. With Denis retired she saw no reason for either of them to stay in England. Denis loved South Africa and later professed to have still loved Valerie but he opted to stay in England.

In 1960 Valerie returned to South Africa, taking eight-year-old Patrick and four-year-old Richard with her to Everton, a leafy suburb 15 miles west of Durban. Patrick spent the best part of a year at Kloof Primary School before returning to live with Denis in England. He remembers:

> Mum always told me that she didn't want to divorce Dad because the press publicity would be terrible for me, particularly the details of the divorce. I never questioned that and didn't reflect on it a great deal until many years later. It's one of my great regrets that I never properly discussed this with Mum before she died in 1994 at the age of sixty-six.
>
> Whatever the real truth of the matter, it seems that some deal was struck so she could get the divorce, and that part of the arrangement was that I would return to England and live with Dad for the rest of my schooldays, while Richard stayed with her.
>
> Incidentally, I truly believe that Mum divorced Dad because he was never at home. Not, as you might expect, conducting affairs, but forever chatting with friends and fans about cricket and horse-racing in the pub!

More than forty years after he began living with his newly single father, Patrick, now a successful journalist in South Africa, remembers the experience vividly. Before his parents' separation he had attended Gayhurst Preparatory School, not far from the family home in Buckinghamshire. There, aged nine, he returned as a weekly boarder in 1960. His weekends were spent alone with Denis who, by now, was living in a mansion flat in the pretty village of Fulmer, halfway between Gerrards Cross and Slough. He recalls:

> In the winter, Dad would pick me up on Saturday morning, when I was allowed out, and we would go to the nearby Bull Hotel for lunch. I used to (typically) have the most enormous plate of spaghetti while dad used to engage most intensely with the waiters on the racing card that afternoon – if there was a sport that he was genuinely passionate about, it was horse-racing. One

of his favourite dishes, by the way, was jellied eels, a very English dish that looked absolutely disgusting to me.

After lunch, it was on to the football match that he invariably covered for the *Sunday Express* at that time. Obviously these would vary, but I remember particularly vividly the matches he covered at Highbury. We would walk through the press entrance, where the man on duty would always say, 'Hello-Denis-how-are-you', whereupon Dad would invariably reply, not knowing the man's name, 'Hello old boy', and in we would go. He never ever had to pay for me to go to Highbury, or for that matter Lord's, if I wanted to go with him to a game. Always, the 'man at the gate' would let me in, sometimes with a whispered 'Go on son'.

I would sit with dad in the press box, goggle-eyed of course as I saw the magical pitch, the goals and the terraces, shortly to be populated by the fans and my footballing gods. How could I fail to immediately become a fanatical supporter of my dad's old team, despite the fact that they didn't set the world alight in those days. After the match was over, dad, who'd been making a few notes, would send me back to the car while he composed his story and telephoned his match report back to the newspaper (no laptops in those days!).

I would sit in the car for perhaps an hour, listening to the sports round-up on the radio, before Dad joined me again. We'd then pop in at a nearby fish-and-chip shop (one of the highlights of my weekend) before we drove home.

Sunday was like a three-act play, always the same. First a huge breakfast, courtesy of chef Denis: fried eggs, fried bread and sausages. I eventually came to the party when he taught me how to make a good pot of tea, swilling hot water in the pot first before letting the tea brew. After early-morning tea, which I brought into his bedroom, and breakfast, it was the Sunday newspapers where of course I used to read the sport, never missing Dad's report on the match the day before. (I'm sure it was during this period that my attraction to journalism was fostered).

Dad's flat at Fulmer was in a large and beautiful white building that had a picturesque lake at the end of the grounds. We'd often go for a walk around the lake as well as feed the horses that frolicked on a farm that adjoined the property. Fulmer comprised a little shop, a church (not attended!) and the Black Horse (frequently attended), a lovely traditional pub where dad would be quickly engulfed by well-wishers. Later in life, when I was allowed to drink, I often went with him there.

Act two was, of course, Dad's round of golf at nearby Denham Golf Club. This was his only exercise of the week (he wasn't a good exerciser in general because of his troublesome knee) and it was a very important ritual for him that he rarely missed throughout the year.

We would drive to the course where Dad and I and many others would eat roast beef and Yorkshire pud in the majestic dining room at the club. After that I would either caddy for him or go home. Funnily enough, he wasn't a huge hitter on the golf course, in that sense his sensible, almost utilitarian game was rather unlike his flamboyant cricket. He was moderate in length off the tee and with his irons, but very straight. His real strength lay in his accurate chipping and putting. As far as I remember, he managed to get down to a handicap of six, but was more usually hovering around the eight or nine mark when I was living with him. He always got home in time for our favourite TV programme on Sunday night: *The Saint,* starring Roger Moore.

Early on Monday morning, the newspapers and my eagerly awaited comics (*Lion, Tiger, Beano* etc.) would arrive. Then a quick read, my routine cuppa for Dad, breakfast and into the car to school for another week.

In 1966 I moved on to Marlborough College. There I was a full-boarder and so, in many ways, my life with Dad effectively ended. He'd attend the odd game of cricket, including one or two at Lord's where Marlborough traditionally played rugby every year, and even, on one occasion, a rugby match, but I suppose that he had to work on most Saturdays and so it was difficult.

Denis Silk, Patrick's housemaster at Marlborough, remembered Denis phoning him around noon each Sunday to enquire how Patrick was getting on. Silk told me that Denis rang then because it was just after school chapel and he knew that he'd catch him. Silk imagined him sitting in the golf club at Denham wearing a polo-neck sweater and dying to get out on the course while knowing that, somehow, this weekly phone call was the sort of fatherly duty he should be performing. Silk, who later became Warden of Radley as well as President of MCC, said, 'he was chaotic. Unlike anyone I've ever known. The lovely thing about Denis was that he never grew up.'

Unsurprisingly many of his attitudes were conditioned by the Forties and Fifties when he acquired celebrity and prosperity. In a sense men like Silk – Oxbridge-educated public schoolmasters – became role models. The world in which Denis achieved success was masculine, traditional, deferential and dramatically undermined by the social revolution of the 1960s. Denis was comfortable with it and less so with the more casual, egalitarian and sexually emancipated times that followed.

Jeffrey Hill in his interesting Nottingham Trent University paper on 'The Legend of Denis Compton' wrote:

Having a drink, or thinking about having a drink, figures prominently in the many stories about Compton, and comes across strongly in *End of an Innings* (one of several autobiographical books by Denis). It is the ritual that seals friendships and resolves antagonisms.

Compton, the drinker, was perfectly captured in a television advertisement for Watneys Red Barrel beer in the early 1960s.

He appeared fleetingly in the final scene, in a crowded bar into which the viewer was drawn by the camera, to be greeted by a welcoming but wordless gesture from Denis which clearly signified: 'come in – what are you having?' Here was no lounge lizard, but a convivial chap in his element which was essentially, male company. There was therefore reproduced throughout the Compton legend a particular strain of British masculinity. And, moreover, in the context of gender relations and male hegemonies of 1940s and 1950s Britain, who is to say that this representation of manhood was necessarily rejected by women?

Bachelor life, which he led for a decade or so in the Sixties, seemed to suit him and it surprised many when aged fifty-four he married Christine, a young and dynamic PA in Bagenal Harvey's office. Later Christine said ruefully that she tried to organise his life from the office but finally decided that the only way she could do the job was to marry him. Denis was devoted to her and they stayed together till the end though on Denis's own admission, 'I am not the easiest person to live with because the problems I am having with my hips make me quite moody at times.'

It was the masculine alcohol-fuelled conviviality of pre-Murdoch journalism that so appealed to him about Fleet Street where he spent much of his later years. Norman Giller, who was a sports writer on the *Daily Express* in the 1960s and 1970s, remembered a man who 'was everything you hope for in a hero: entertaining, modest and always approachable'.

Giller, in the introduction to his anthology of Compton stories and anecdotes, recalled that the opening line of a session with Denis was invariably 'I'll have a large G and T, old boy.' There then followed a long, largely liquid hour or so in which various old Fleet Street hands exchanged gossip, badinage and anecdote. As Giller recalled, 'Keith Miller, his greatest friend and rival from Down Under, was also on the *Express* staff, and my sportsroom colleagues and I used to have wonderful sessions in Fleet Street watering holes such as El Vino and the Cheshire Cheese listening to them swapping summertime yarns about their Test battles and off-the-pitch escapades.'

The culture of Fleet Street in those days is difficult to convey to those who have only experienced journalism in its Murdoch-dominated era of Canary Wharf, Wapping and Kensington with its designer bottled water and sandwiches at the desk. There was at that time an *Express* leader-writer whose most important task seemed to be to hurry up the road after morning conference to bag the editor's favourite table just inside the front door of El Vino. It was here that Denis did much of his Fleet Street socialising. After several rounds of champagne the editor would walk down the street to the Press Club where he would lunch off kippers and Scotch whisky and water. Eventually he would go back to the office but not without stopping at the paper's nearest pub and having a port and brandy or two. This was not considered particularly excessive or unusual.

Colleagues recall that Denis was seldom if ever late with his copy but there were times when he was economical with the truth. 'On one occasion,' remembered Paul Lott, the landlord of the Fulmer Black Horse, 'he watched the whole of one Cup Final in which Arsenal was involved on the TV in the Bottom Bar, going home afterwards to phone in his report. Next morning his *Sunday Express* column started "Sitting in the Directors' Box watching this great Final".' It was somehow typical that Lott's only comment on this was 'We smiled to ourselves.' It was somehow characteristic of Denis that he was so often indulged as if he were a naughty schoolboy.

His friend Graham Lord told me that John Junor, arguably the best-known editor of the *Sunday Express*, never mentioned Denis once in his memoirs even though Denis worked for the paper all the time Junor was in charge and never missed a deadline.

In many ways, however, he fitted perfectly into the rackety, convivial village which was Fleet Street in the Fifties and Sixties. As in his sporting life, he became one of the lads. Norman Giller, in his anthology of Denis anecdotes and memories, recalled the days when he himself was a football writer on the *Daily Express*.

> He was a regular visitor to our sportsroom during my days reporting football for the paper. He used to give a pretty poor performance at pretending he had come down to see what was happening in the football world when it was transparently obvious that what he really wanted to do was pick the brains of the Holy Trinity of racing who occupied the adjoining desks. Peter O'Sullevan, Clive Graham and Charles Benson were all close chums of Compo, and did their best to satisfy his thirst for winners.

O'Sullevan himself commented affectionately to Giller, 'Denis had a deep knowledge of racing after many years as an enthusiastic punter. It was a joy to talk racing with him, but I'm not sure he always took the right advice. Denis was an impulsive, instinctive gambler, just as he was an impulsive, instinctive batsman who did things off the cuff.'

This goes some of the way to explaining why money simply didn't seem to stick to Denis's fingers. The thousand pounds a year he earned for almost a decade from his Brylcreem sponsorship was a lot of money in those days. The average farm labourer was earning £4.10 for a forty-eight-hour week so Denis's thousand was about five times what a man like his father would have received for a year's hard manual graft. Despite this Denis never seemed financially secure and gave the impression of living a relatively hand-to-mouth existence in which most of his security came from the independent money of his second and third wives. Lucky in almost every other respect, he was unlucky with money. Even when

Middlesex stepped in to help him with the money he earned from his benefit they invested it in the ill-fated 'groundnut scheme', which involved a disastrous attempt to revive the economy by planting groundnuts in West Africa, and Denis ended up losing every penny. As he commented, he'd have been just as well off blowing the lot on the 2.30 at Sandown.

It's very difficult to say with certainty or precision how good he was as a newspaper or broadcast commentator or pundit. I remember once sitting at his much-loved Denham Golf Club with him and my son Alexander who had been helping research the Compton football career. Denis suddenly patted Alexander on the knee and said, 'Wish I could write like your dad.'

The obvious rejoinder was 'Wish I could bat like you, Denis' but, joking apart, I knew what he meant. He had spent much of the latter part of his life as a sort of sporting journalist. For this he was, in one way, supremely well qualified. In another however he was a man who had left elementary school at fourteen and was profoundly un-bookish. He never really read anything except the *Sporting Life*.

It's therefore very difficult to evaluate his journalism. He liked the hacks of his generation and they liked him. They shared his raffish, swashbuckling qualities and he theirs. But I don't know how much of his stuff he really wrote himself; how much was actually written by 'ghosts' or 'assisted' by creative sub-editors.

In some ways the journalistic success of Denis and colleagues such as Keith Miller and Len Hutton who were among those who made the transition from playing to 'writing' was a disaster. The great cricket writers of the golden age were writers before they were cricketers. Men such as Neville Cardus or John Arlott were past masters of the English language but not much known for their cricket. Cardus was an accomplished coach; Arlott, whom Denis cordially disliked, was alleged by him to scarcely know one end of a bat from the other. Denis left school early and was on his own admission desultory in his academic studies. He had no journalistic training or background.

Denis always maintained that he wrote most if not all his own copy but there is still some dispute about this. His wife Christine once or twice intercepted drafts of his pieces which had been written in Reg Hayter's office but Denis always said these were exceptional. When he was eventually dismissed by the *Express* the justification was not that the paper could no longer afford Denis but that they couldn't afford his ghost-writer.

As time passed he, unsurprisingly, acquired a reputation for being something of an old curmudgeon forever banging on about how much better things were in his day. This is not entirely fair for many of his judgements were spot on and he seldom seemed to allow his personal feelings to get in the way. Of Colin Cowdrey, for instance, he wrote:

I just don't know what to make of him. In all my years around the game I have seldom seen a player more gifted. His timing is the envy of every other player in the game, his range of strokes wider than that of any other player in the world.

It seems that the only person who needs convincing of Cowdrey's ability is Cowdrey himself. He sometimes appears so uncertain of himself at the crease that he makes the game a torture. This thing called confidence seems to have been dished out very lop-sidedly. I have known players with less than half Cowdrey's talents carry on like the Cassius Clays of the game.

Not only does this still strike me as a shrewd judgement, it also required an element of personal courage, for he had not only played with Cowdrey, he regarded him as a friend – a friendship which was always reciprocated.

His technical analysis – something his detractors thought he was incapable of – could also be impressive. Of Ken Barrington, for instance, he wrote:

> Barrington's problems, I felt, were more technical. His mental outlook adds up all right – he simply wants runs. Unfortunately at this stage he wasn't getting them. I felt that his stance had become so open, 'two-tyed' as they say, that he was almost bound to hit across the line of the ball. He had adopted this method of batting to counter the movement towards slips of Australia's Alan Davidson, bowling left arm over the wicket, but with Davidson's retirement, it looked to me as if Barrington had become more open than ever.
>
> In addition, he had become almost solely a back-foot player.
>
> Ability to play off the back foot has been the hall-mark of all great players, yet Barrington seemed to be finding it hard to get on to the front foot at all. Even the half-volley found him going back or only half forward. On overseas wickets where there is little or no movement of the ball, he could get away with it, but it is not a worthwhile method in England.

Intriguingly he not only analysed the failings of these two fine established cricketers, he also hailed the arrival of Geoffrey Boycott when he suddenly erupted on the international scene in 1964.

> This chap is something English cricket has been hunting for a long time. He is sound technically with a range of neat strokes. That hardly makes him outstanding. There are two or three other players with the same qualifications. It is his ambition, his appetite for runs that makes him different from the others. He wants runs every time he goes to the crease. If he fails, no matter how good his preceding scores, he will spend up to an hour in the nets next morning. It was typical of him that while everyone was congratulating him on his partnership with Bolus against the

Australians, he was disappointed with himself. He had got in and reckoned he should have had a century.

Ultimately Denis became disillusioned with the young tyro but only because in giving way to that voracious appetite for runs he became over-concerned with his own statistics and averages to the detriment of his naturally fluent stroke-making. He became, in other words, negative in the same way as Barrington and Cowdrey who, in Denis's estimation, 'devote their great gifts to placid survival. They do themselves less than justice.'

In 1994 I spoke to Denis about the moment in Trinidad when England were bowled out for 46 all by the West Indies pace attack led by Walsh and Ambrose. Geoff Boycott, commenting on Sky TV, kept saying that the reason for the disaster was that England were always playing off the back foot. They should get on the front foot. That was the only way to play fast bowling, according to Boycott. I was surprised by this. A year or so earlier Sir Gary Sobers had told me that the English would never cope with the West Indian quicks until they learned to play off the *back* foot.

Denis, pretty dismayed by events in the Caribbean, shook his head and said that despite the menace of Ambrose and Walsh, 'We weren't awfully good.' But as far as Boycott was concerned, Denis said witheringly, 'If I owed five million pounds and wanted to commit suicide I'd play Curtley Ambrose off the front foot.'

He continued his association with the *Express* until the early 1990s. It was a strange paper which under two legendary Beaverbrook editors, John Gordon and John Junor, made few obvious concessions to the changing times but continued to serve up a tried and tested formula to an ever-diminishing body of veteran readers. Battles of the Second World War, familiar to this dwindling constituency, but of little or no interest to younger generations, were refought in traditional manner every Sunday. Denis's column appealed to these older readers in much the same way, reminding them of the days when they were young and ruled their worlds much as Denis, in those days, had ruled his.

One of his bosses was Robin Esser who had seen and worshipped him as a child in the 1940s when he saw him and Len Hutton, another more local hero, at Headingley. Esser edited the *Sunday Express* from 1986 to 1989. Esser was in charge at the time of Denis's seventieth birthday in 1988. 'His old friend Keith Miller came over from Australia for the occasion,' he told me. 'I took them both to Green's – the St James's restaurant run by Simon Parker Bowles – for lunch.' Compton and Miller were clearly still objects of awe and affection to the sort of people who went to Green's, for Esser remembers 'Everybody who came into the restaurant that day came over to shake hands with my two guests.'

Later in the day Esser gave Denis a birthday present on behalf of the paper. Knowing that his correspondent was almost as keen on golf as he was on cricket, Esser sent him to cover the Masters in Augusta alongside the *Express*'s regular golf writer.

'He had a ball,' recalled Esser. 'And his dispatches gave an enthusiastic tone to our coverage. But then Denis's commentaries on cricket gave the sports pages of the *Sunday Express* a huge distinction – as was fitting for what was once a great newspaper.'

An uncritical love of white South Africa and white South Africans was not wholly fashionable in the years of Denis's maturity. In England it split the world of cricket and there was much bitterness. Denis believed – though he could never prove it – that he lost his job with BBC television because he was 'soft' on South Africa at a time when the BBC was strongly opposed to the regime there.

Certainly it soured relations between men like Denis and Brian Johnston, both of a naturally Conservative and pro-South African disposition, and others like the Liberal, John Arlott, and Denis's sometime team-mate, The Reverend – later Right Reverend – David Sheppard. Words and opinions were said and expressed in the heat of the moment which were later regretted. Feelings ran high. On one occasion during a Scarborough Festival the journalist and broadcaster Michael Parkinson heard that a very angry Denis was anxious for a word.

Parkinson, writing in the then left-of-centre *Sunday Times*, had apparently called Denis a racist because of pro-South African sentiments expressed by Denis in the decidedly right-of-centre *Sunday Express*. Finally Denis ran Parkinson to earth and proceeded to deliver himself of a few choice words involving Parkie's ancestry. Unsurprisingly, Denis, the southerner in a pub full of Yorkshiremen, had no regard for his personal safety even though it was obvious that his audience was a hundred per cent hostile. Parkinson thought, with unchivalrous hindsight, that this was not the first pub Denis had visited that day.

Eventually Denis drew breath and Parkinson said, 'I must say, Denis, I admire your balls. I wouldn't do what you've just done in a pub in Pinner.'

At least that is how Parkinson remembered it. When I asked Denis he frowned thoughtfully and conceded that something along those lines might have taken place but he couldn't be sure of the details. Interestingly when Michael Parkinson wrote a generous eulogy after my earlier book appeared he never mentioned South Africa nor the incident in the pub in Scarborough.

On the day of Denis's famous record-breaking triple

hundred John Arlott, despite being the BBC cricket correspondent, did not go to Benoni but stayed in Johannesburg.
There, walking down Commissioner Street, he witnessed
something which had a profound effect on his attitude to South
Africa. A black man was walking towards him on the outside of
the pavement minding his own business in a perfectly ordinary
way. Then, Arlott recalled, writing as was his habit in the third
person, 'Suddenly a white man walking in the opposite
direction swung his leg and kicked the coloured man into the
gutter. The victim got up and, apparently apologetically,
walked away. J.A.'s stomach turned over.'

In later years Arlott was to become a passionate opponent of
apartheid and supporter of South Africa's oppressed black
majority. His own belief was that this passion was originally
inspired by the incident on Commissioner Street.

Meanwhile in Benoni, Denis was making hay. Not only
that, he was being adored by the black section of the crowd.
Although they were all crammed into a single stand while the
handful of whites were scattered about the whole of the rest of
the boundary, they were hugely enthusiastic, particularly after
Denis hit his first six over their stand at long-on.

Perhaps one can read too much into these two virtually
simultaneous experiences. Certainly Arlott regarded his as
seminal. It was the first of many such incidents and it 'changed
his entire outlook'. Apartheid was already practised
unofficially but during that tour there was an election, General
Smuts was thrown out, the Nationalists were elected for the
first time and apartheid became law.

Arlott was appalled and resolved to speak out against it as
soon as he returned home. 'If he [Arlott] had gone to Benoni
to watch Compton and never seen the Bantu kicked in the
gutter, would his life have been different?' he wondered.
'Would he have been a less disturbed, if more ignorant visitor?'

It was an interesting speculation, and interesting in reverse as well. If Denis had not been breaking all the records with his bat in Benoni and had instead seen the black man being kicked into the gutter, would he have become less ignorant and more disturbed? Impossible to say with certainty.

Denis's attitude was as simple and straightforward as one would expect from the man. His enemies might call it naive, but they would be wrong, I think, to call it malicious. South Africans loved the way he played cricket, and his brand of cricket flourished there. He, like Arlott, was made more than welcome and he was given a wonderful time. There was always plenty of wine, women and song, not to mention spectacular scenery and constant sunshine. Denis was a great believer in doing as he was done by and he therefore believed in repaying the kindness and loyalty shown to him by South Africans with similar kindness and loyalty. And he took the view that when the world turned against them kindness and loyalty was even more important.

Denis never terribly cared for Arlott anyway. He thought he patronised cricketers, and he didn't think he knew that much about cricket. On the only occasion Denis actually saw him play it was evident, according to Denis, that he was a cricketing duffer. This was at a Sunday charity match in Didsbury, Lancashire. Depending on whose account you accept there is some argument about the details but none about the essentials. What is not in dispute is that it was plain to all that Arlott played the game less well than he wrote about it. It was also unfortunate that George Duckworth, the old Lancashire wicketkeeper, was on the Tannoy – and Duckworth had a wicked sense of humour. It wouldn't have been so bad if Arlott had been out first ball, but he stayed in long enough for everyone to see how poor he was.

According to Denis the bowler was old Charlie Hallows. Hallows, quickly seeing that Arlott was unhappy, bowled five innocuous deliveries outside the off stump, all of which Arlott missed. He then bowled a sixth ball which was equally innocuous but straight. Arlott missed, the ball hit the wicket – end of story.

Denis himself added a little postscript. When Arlott came in, Denis, passing him on the way to the wicket, said mischievously, 'That must have been a particularly good ball, John.'

To which Arlott replied, 'Denis, you know that Charlie Hallows still bowls a wonderful Chinaman.'

In any event Denis made an enemy of Arlott and he came to antagonise others over his South African attitudes even if their friendships survived. I spoke to several of those involved, and years after apartheid was dead and buried I encountered an embarrassment and a reluctance to get involved again in a matter which far too often degenerated into a personal feud. I encountered a widespread feeling that Denis himself was 'used' by people more politically sophisticated than he was. One man actually used the word 'betrayed'. Having got to know him, albeit after the event, my own view is that Denis simply didn't have it in him to be a racist or a fascist. On the other hand he was a traditionalist and a conservative and a devout believer in loyalty between friends. In political terms I suppose his views were much the same as most members of the Denham Golf Club, but the real point is that he was just not a political animal. Yet, during the impassioned debate about apartheid and the sporting boycott of racist South Africa, he expressed what were, effectively, political opinions in support of the South African government. Those who knew him well would have expected him to react just as he did, but equally they probably would not have taken him very seriously. Those who knew him less well might have listened because of his fame as a cricketer. And it was just this fame, together with his loyalty and his naivety, that was exploited.

However, he argued fiercely that in no way does that make him a racist. He was not a political animal but he points out that on his first visit, in the late Forties, apartheid had not been invented and the Nationalist Afrikaners were only just elected during his visit. Arlott, on the other hand, was profoundly influenced by that election. In a controversial memoir published in 1993 his son Timothy wrote, 'When he stopped outside a National Party campaign headquarters on election night with an English-speaking Unionist supporter who made an exclamation of dismay on hearing the latest results, Afrikaner National Party supporters covered the car windows with spit.'

'If,' commented Timothy Arlott, sadly, 'my father had only been interested in cricket he might have become a fan of South Africa.'

In essence this was at least part of the difference. To be sure Denis had a conservative disposition, but he was not passionately concerned with politics. However, he said that he – unlike some he might name – always went out of his way to encourage black youngsters in the townships. He coached them at their schools and nothing gave him greater pleasure than causing them pleasure, as he did to such effect when hitting those celebrated sixes over long-on at Benoni. His impression of South Africa and South Africans was that black people were treated well. His South African friends treated their servants just as upper-class English people would treat their servants. This might be paternalist or even feudal, but it was not inhuman and it could be genuinely warm and affectionate.

Besides, he maintained, cricket was always a multiracial game and he was perfectly happy to play the Indians and West Indians at home and away. Until the South African row flared up thoroughly in the 1960s and people started to smear him as a racist, he was popular both in the Caribbean and on the subcontinent. In the war, as we have seen, he was more than happy to play in Indian sides. Racist? Not me old boy.

The debate about South Africa really became a row with the

involvement of Basil D'Oliveira, and oddly enough 'Dolly' became the cause of it largely because of John Arlott himself. In 1958 Arlott received a letter in green ink from the then unknown D'Oliveira asking for help in getting a coaching job in England so that he could 'pass on the knowledge to my fellow Cape Coloureds'. In his brief career D'Oliveira had already scored some fifty hundreds, including a 225 in 70 minutes which even Denis would have been pressed to emulate. As an off-break bowler he once took 9 for 2.

He had no luck at all until at the last moment the Middleton Club in the Central Lancashire League failed to sign Wesley Hall in succession to Roy Gilchrist as their overseas professional and, through Arlott, offered the job to D'Oliveira at £450 a year.

He had a disastrous start, managing only 25 runs in his first five matches. Then a former Middleton professional, Eric Price, stepped in with advice and coaching, and by the end of the season he was top of the League averages. He never faltered after this, and while playing in a Commonwealth team one of his fellow players, Tom Graveney, suggested that he might sign for his own county, Worcester. This he duly did, averaging over 60 in his first season and scoring a century for A.E.R. Gilligan's XI against Bobby Simpson's Australians. He went on to play 44 times for England.

The first hint of trouble arose in January 1967 when the South African Minister of the Interior, Pieter le Roux, objected to the inclusion of D'Oliveira in the England team to tour South Africa. Had D'Oliveira stayed in South Africa he could never, as a 'Cape Coloured', have been selected for the all-white South African national side, and the South African Government of the day could not countenance a black or coloured man playing on the same field as whites, no matter who he was representing. Since England weren't touring until 1968, Mr le Roux was jumping the gun. Presumably he intended a pre-emptive strike but the general opinion in England was that the selection of the England team had nothing to do with him or any other foreigner. It was, in fact, a matter for MCC, and Billy Griffith, then the club's secretary, said at the time that the matter would be dealt with 'when it arises'.

Poor Griffith was apparently in a terrible quandary at this time. He had been on the 1948 South African tour and accompanied Arlott on his visits to the townships. As a decent and honourable man he deplored apartheid and, on the basis of what he had seen, he felt strongly about it. Yet in his official capacity he could not side with the South African 'rebels'. There are those who witnessed his dilemma who say that they feared he might become genuinely suicidal.

The left regarded the MCC line as a cowardly evasion but not as bad as the decision, at the end of the following season, to omit D'Oliveira from the team. Few omissions have caused such a furore, though there is a long tradition of selectorial boobs followed by public outcry. This happened as long ago as 1902, when Hirst and Jessop were left out, and it was still happening in the 1990s when David Gower was similarly treated. Selectors can often seem moronic to the rest of us.

Leaving out D'Oliveira was a dubious decision on cricketing grounds, not least because in the final Test that summer he made 158 in a single innings and took the crucial wicket. His century boosted the scoring rate when necessary and his wicket was the vital breakthrough. If his omission had been decided on purely cricketing grounds, a large number of armchair cricketers would have been noisily 'Disgusted of Tunbridge Wells'.

But the widespread sense of outrage that greeted the news was because it was so manifestly, in the words of his champion, Arlott, 'clear evidence of English cricket – and therefore Britain trucking to apartheid'. Arlott continued:

Governments with no interest in cricket – who do not even care what it is – will make capital of what seems so plainly to be racial discrimination on the part of a section of the English Establishment. To the people whose cricket is described in South Africa, where they live, as 'non-European', and to whom D'Oliveira is the unique hero who, by his ability, rose above the barriers of race and was accepted in the free country of England, this must seem the ultimate betrayal.

Jim Swanton thought that despite an otherwise poor season and an indifferent tour of the West Indies the previous winter D'Oliveira had done enough to justify selection. Indeed he said so to one of the selectors, adding that 'if after all the palaver about whether he would be accepted or not in South Africa, he isn't picked, you know what the world will say don't you?'

The selector disagreed and added 'something fairly strong about what the world could do about it'. But Swanton was right, and the omission sparked off what he regarded as 'such an explosion of feeling as no sporting decision surely had ever aroused'.

Poor Swanton! He found himself very much in the middle of the argument. Those involved on both sides were his friends, but he felt that the whole business was botched, and being a journalist of integrity he wrote what he felt. Consequently, 'I hated every minute of the autumn of 1968.'

There were angry letters to the press; MPs protested; members of MCC resigned; a group of dissidents was formed under the leadership of the Rev. David Sheppard; Doug Insole, chairman of selectors, went on TV to try to explain; Tom Cartwright withdrew from the touring party and was replaced by D'Oliveira; Dr Vorster, the South African Prime Minister, complained that the MCC had succumbed to pressure from the anti-apartheid lobby and therefore his country wouldn't accept the team; two of the South African cricket board flew to London in a fruitless attempt to sort things out.

Finally, just a month after their original decision to leave D'Oliveira out, MCC called the tour off.

There was still the Special General Meeting of MCC to come. Feelings ran high. Swanton tried to act as an intermediary between the warring factions but, on his own admission, got less than nowhere. David Sheppard spoke first for the opposition and by all accounts spoke persuasively. Generally however, the level of argument was not high and the tone was acrimonious. Denis, of course, was firmly on the side of the South African government and the Establishment and he, like others, felt passionately. In the event the voting went the MCC committee's way – easily on the postal ballot, less so in the hall at Church House. But in a sense the vote was an irrelevance. The damage had been done, and for years to come the issue of South Africa continued to provoke a nasty civil war within the world of cricket and one in which Denis was seen, rightly, to be a leading protagonist on the South African side.

The South Africans were due in England in 1970 and the issue became a matter of national and international importance. The 'Stop the 70 Tour' group led by Peter Hain, now a Labour MP, threatened direct action, and MCC invested in 300 reels of barbed wire. There was an emergency debate in the House of Commons and finally the President and Secretary of MCC were invited to his office by Jim Callaghan, then Home Secretary, and asked to cancel the tour. The Cricket Council duly complied.

Sport and South Africa remained on the agenda until and beyond the release of Nelson Mandela. For a generation or more South Africa was barred from international sport. In cricket, men such as Denis continued to fight the South African corner and to argue that 'law-jaw' was better than 'war-war'.

In 1983 the issue blew up again with a debate in the same forum as the one on the D'Oliveira affair. This time the motion before a Special General Meeting of MCC was 'that the members of MCC Committee implement the selection of a touring party to tour South Africa in 1983–84'. MCC, traditionally a 'private club with a public function', was no longer synonymous with 'England', and the idea was not that a full-strength England side should go to South Africa but that it should be a club side of average ability.

Once again the debate was acrimonious and split the world of cricket. Hubert Doggart and Colin Cowdrey were of the Committee view and argued against any tour, while Denis and Bill Edrich were on the opposing side. There were some interesting ironies too. Sir Anthony Tuke, for instance, who was President of MCC and therefore committed to opposing the tour, was also a director of RTZ and Barclays Bank, both of which had strong business interests in South Africa.

This allowed John Carlisle, the Conservative MP who led for the rebels, to remark: 'There must be many in this room who have substantial business interests in South Africa and good luck to them. Good luck to the directors of RTZ and Barclays Bank.' This drew a cheer but failed to win the day. In the event the committee won a substantial majority both in the postal vote and the hall itself.

Denis himself spoke, as did David Sheppard, who had by then been elevated to the Bishopric of Liverpool. Denis, reported Matthew Engel, the sprightly *Guardian* correspondent, 'played and missed once or twice but effectively accused the West Indians of omitting a white all-rounder, Steve Farmer, who, he said, was almost as good as Sobers.' More recently Engels remarked in a letter to me that 'the Steve Farmer allegation has never been corroborated by anyone, and West Indians all say it's baloney.

Now, of course, the South African sport argument has been

laid to rest and their cricket team is back in international competition. Its exclusion lost us the chance of watching a generation of their cricketers, yet it may – or may not – have contributed to the abolition of apartheid.

The repercussions in the English cricket world were formidable, and the whole affair led to a miserable rancour and bitterness, most of all perhaps for David Sheppard on the one side and Denis on the other.

Matthew Engel has pointed out that South African hospitality was generous and seductive to a fault when he first encountered it in the 1970s. It is important too to remember that on Denis's first visit he was the Golden Boy fêted wherever he went. He fell in love with Valerie as well as the country; and after the austerity of Britain in the 1940s South Africa seemed bountiful beyond belief. Given the circumstances, it is hardly fair to expect him to be impartial.

A final footnote. It was clear to me, having spoken to both Denis and David Sheppard, that any personal animosity that might have existed between the two was well dead and buried. Sheppard's convictions about apartheid and about the part sportsmen could play in its defeat went back to a meeting with Bishop Trevor Huddleston in 1956. He remembered pacing the terrace at the House of Lords as Huddleston persuaded him that he might have a role in the struggle. And he particularly remembered once refusing to captain the Duke of Norfolk's XI against the South Africans. He had captained the team in previous years and his refusal caused a furore.

At one stage Sheppard headed a 'Fair Cricket' campaign which included Betty Boothroyd, later Speaker of the House of Commons, as its secretary. In cricketing circles he was regarded as rather to the left of Lenin but then, as even Denis would admit, the cricket establishment of the day could be somewhat Neanderthal.

When the row was at its height Stephen Green, then the

Lord's librarian, found himself at dinner next to a particularly boneheaded MCC committee member. 'I'll tell you one thing,' said the committee member. 'That feller Sheppard's finished in the church. I have it on the highest ecclesiastical authority. There's no way he'll ever get promoted now. He'll be a curate the rest of his life.'

Next day it was announced that the Rev. David Sheppard was to be the next Bishop of Woolwich.

Now, most of the protagonists are dead and gone, the dust has settled, and the anecdote made those old team-mates, D.C.S. Compton and D.S. Sheppard, both smile reflectively. It was a shame though that what should have remained a purely political affair should have cast such a long personal shadow.

Everyone has personal likes and dislikes but I can't help feeling that Denis's attitude to Arlott and D'Oliveira had a lot to do with South Africa and Denis's own perhaps misguided loyalties. He was not, in fact, a particularly significant player in the political debate even if he was vociferous and passionate. All in all it was a wretched affair and too many members of the cricketing community allowed matters to become bitter and personal. Denis was no exception but that didn't make him a racist.

Denis's Fleet Street career came to a conclusion with the end of the Aitken family's ownership and the introduction of a dynamic and ruthless new editor, Eve Pollard. Pollard, whose husband Nick had been editor of the *Daily Express* since 1986, came from editing the *Sunday Mirror* in 1991 and immediately set about a wholesale clear-out which in her eyes was long overdue. One early casualty was the literary editor Graham Lord who had shared in that famous last-wicket stand in the cricket match against the Sunday Mirror. Lord took legal action and won.

After I had sued the *Sunday Express* and the dreaded Eve Pollard successfully for constructive dismissal, Denis rang me several times to ask for advice about suing them himself after forty years or more as the paper's cricket correspondent. Pollard had booted him out with just three months (I think) pay and not even a farewell lunch or thank you. Denis was thoroughly pissed off and wanted to know the name of my lawyer, what tactics I had used, etc, but he never did do anything about it.

When I taxed Eve Pollard with this she said that she had no recollection of Denis at all. She had certainly never met him and she didn't think that she personally had ever fired him. She conceded that she wasn't interested in cricket until the miraculous series of 2005 but she found it impossible to believe that a legendary figure such as Denis could have been abandoned in such a peremptory fashion. At the very least there would have been some sort of wake – a lunch or dinner with tears and speeches.

In fact it sounds as if there was an element of misunderstanding over the dismissal which was, apparently, carried out by the sports editor, Peter Watson. Watson admired and liked Denis but was under instruction to modernise and to make cuts. As Denis was by now into his seventies he was an obvious candidate for removal; Watson offered to keep him on but was unable to pay for someone to ghost his copy. Denis took umbrage and only spoke to Watson once again when he rebuked him harshly over the phone. Watson would have liked to offer him a job writing some sort of nostalgia column, which sounds like a feeble sop. In order to appeal to younger readers the *Express* hired David Gower as a replacement. This served to rub salt into the older man's wounds. The lack of financial compensation seemed, to Denis, to add insult to injury but the *Express* was notorious for not financially looking after its own. He was far from being the only one of the old

Beaverbrook stars who ended on hard times because the *Express* had no proper pension schemes and the often-repeated promises to look after the old guard turned out to be effectively empty.

I certainly remember that Denis always felt bitter about the end of his relationship with the *Express*, even though he was employed by the paper for the best part of forty years and survived long after most of its correspondents would have retired.

'I would never have sacked him,' said Robin Esser. But he remembered worshipping Denis as a schoolboy in the 1940s. Eve Pollard did not share the privilege. The fact that more than a decade after his departure she remembered nothing about it tells its own story.

Compton's career as a TV pundit came to a similarly unpleasant end. Christopher Martin-Jenkins has described how Denis became 'the regular "expert"' in 1958. From the first, said C M-J, in a history of cricket broadcasting 'his ready sense of humour made up for an obvious nervousness in his early days whenever he was in front of the camera'. The nerves evinced themselves in the occasional malapropism or Spoonerism as on one occasion when he referred to the fine new-ball bowling of Trayman and Stootham.

Denis's first TV series was the 1958 New Zealand one in which he shared the duties with Brian Johnston and Jim Swanton in the last four Tests – Peter West filled the Swanton slot at Edgbaston. The touring team the following year was India. Denis, Brian and Jim provided the TV commentary for the MCC match near the beginning of the tour and Swanton's behaviour provoked a furious memo from the producer Anthony Craxton to Peter Dimmock, the Head of Outside Broadcasts.

Craxton did not mince his words about Swanton, including his difficulties with Denis Compton, a hero as a player but not, evidently, as a broadcaster: 'Compton has only been in the game for five minutes and his views are not worth hearing. The feeling between Compton and Swanton is so red hot that an explosion is inevitable before the season is out.' There was even, apparently, a 'heated exchange with Brian Johnston' during which Swanton apparently told him that he, Johnston, was 'only there to provide entertainment, implying that Johnston had no standing as an expert'. It took a lot to rile Johnston, who was famously anxious to avoid confrontation, but this clearly got up the famous nose. Craxton even goes so far as to say of Swanton that 'I know of no member of the corporation, Sound included, who would regret his departure.'

Swanton replied to an apparently polite letter from Dimmock at inordinate length but finally got round to expressing a view on Denis. 'I like working with him,' he wrote, 'and think he certainly has something to contribute in the way of first-hand knowledge of the players and great experience of Test cricket.' However, Swanton continues, he is of the opinion that he gets much better material out of Denis than Brian. 'Brian,' he wrote, 'tends to use Denis rather more than me, because he is not often prepared to advance a technical opinion. My own view is that sometimes his commentaries develop into something like a conversation piece with Denis.' The letter concluded in a magnanimous way hoping that all can be settled in a civilised manner and hoping that Dimmock had had a good holiday.

On the same day Craxton wrote to his colleagues in Manchester and Birmingham, addressing the problem of Compton and Swanton.

'Denis Compton,' he wrote, 'is one of Swanton's big bones of contention. Swanton is, I believe, excessively jealous of Compton's position, and feels he has usurped his position as an expert. I believe the public are more interested in Compton's views than Swanton's, and I have told Compton that he is at liberty to comment when and as often as he pleases.' Craxton, who was at school at Gordonstoun, had been with the BBC since 1941 and ended up making more than 200 royal broadcasts, was not a man to be bullied. 'To sum up,' he concluded, 'be as firm as you can with Swanton, and if you have any trouble with him do not hesitate to let us know.'

The row rumbled on throughout the summer and into the next when the visitors were Denis's beloved South Africans. Once more Craxton wrote to Dimmock, again complaining about Swanton who, he wrote, 'has never got on well with Roy Webber the scorer, and even less so with Denis Compton'. Evidently there had been rows with MCC at Lord's and a 'famous contretemps over the feeding arrangements at the Oval'.

Apropos of Denis, Craxton produced an interesting double-edged paragraph in which he wrote,

Denis Compton has, in my view, improved out of all knowledge since I first tried him out a year or two ago. No-one will doubt his great cricketing knowledge as a player, and this is most apparent from his comments. He is not, and never should be considered, an authority on the game as Swanton is, but Compton is still a great name in the game and will always remain a legendary figure as one of the greatest batsmen this country has ever produced. I would like to think that we could retain his services for at least the next series of Tests. I have approached Colin Cowdrey to find out whether he would be interested in doing the kind of thing Compton does. He has expressed very great interest in this, and although he may not be available to us for a few years he would be able to give the time to it and I think would do it with exceptional skill. He is, of course, a far more intelligent person than Compton, with a far stronger personality.

All this seems a little unfair on Denis whose first-hand knowledge of the game was incontestable and whose breezy style, reminiscent of his approach on the field of play, was in strong contrast to Swanton's more portentous one. Denis brought a sense of fun to the commentary box just as he had once done to the cricket field.

As a result of this letter Dimmock proposed ending Swanton's contract but in the end a compromise was reached so that Jim continued to do one TV Test a year till 1967 when he bowed at Lord's during the match against Pakistan. His radio summaries went on without a break until he retired in 1975. Meanwhile Dimmock wrote that Denis should continue as the main summariser. 'Although Swanton's summaries were good he was not prepossessing in vision. There is no doubt that Denis Compton looks better and certainly means more to the marginal and younger viewers.'

According to Christopher Martin-Jenkins in his history of BBC cricket broadcasting, Denis and Brian Johnston were eventually fired by Brian Cowgill, a tough former Marine Commando from Clitheroe in Lancashire, who became Controller of BBC1 in 1974. He had been head of BBC Sport from 1963 to '72 and Johnston and Compton somehow survived. Then in 1970 Johnston transferred from TV to radio for the Rest of the World Series. Denis continued less and less frequently until his final swansong at Lord's for the Ashes Test of 1975. There were, apparently, no 'thank you's and no regrets.

Denis had no time for the new gritty approach, telling Martin-Jenkins that one morning when he began broadcasting with his habitual, cheery 'Good morning, everyone' he heard the producer's voice in his earphone, 'No "good morning"s on television, Denis.' This was definitely not his style.

In fact Denis had a long and, by the standards of the day, adequately rewarded career as a sports commentator. Like such contemporaries as Trevor Bailey and Fred Trueman, effectively past their sell-by dates. In a sense these men were lucky to have enjoyed enough fame to make them sufficiently celebrated to be a celebrity catch for newspapers and broadcasting organisations. But unless they are as unusually gifted as Richie Benaud (and it is hard to think of any other great cricketer who managed to turn himself into an equally celebrated commentator), the time comes when great players are simply not familiar to the majority of sports fans. Also it is inevitable that their nostalgia for the days of their youth begins to grate. By the 1990s cricket had moved on from the 1950s when Denis last played. Many agreed with him that floodlights, 'pyjamas' and protective clothing were not really cricket but every year their numbers diminished and, like the readers of the *Sunday Express*, they simply died off. Sadly but inevitably there came a moment when, in journalistic and broadcasting terms, Denis became a dinosaur. Of course he didn't like it and there's no question that he was brusquely, perhaps shabbily treated, but unless you are the Pope or royalty you aren't allowed to continue at the forefront of the popular imagination until you drop.

I don't mean by any of this to imply that Compton's post-cricket years were a complete anticlimax for him. In many ways I got the impression of someone wondrously at one with life, but after what he accomplished on the playing field how could the rest of life be anything but an anticlimax, however mild?

The degeneration of physical strengths, sad for everyone, is particularly galling for those who have played first-class sports. In the early 1990s he had to have a hip replaced. I hated watching him creaking along on rusting limbs and joints almost as much as he himself must have done. It was obviously tiresome to have such trouble getting out of the car at the golf club or limping up Fleet Street to El Vino after Reg Hayter's funeral in St Bride's. But did he complain? After he was out of hospital and doomed to crutches for several weeks he did allow himself to admit 'Well to tell the truth old boy I'm not awfully patient about not being able to move around.' And that was it. I was worried about him going under the knife, not least because I had watched him and the Bedser twins and Godfrey Evans in church, a pew or two in front of me, and a few feet away was Reg in his coffin. They were all telling each other stories and giggling slightly in a way of which Reg would have entirely approved. Then suddenly the thought occurred to me that they looked just as if they were waiting to go in to bat. Which, since they were all well into their eighth decade, was a not unreasonable thought, even if depressing.

In his seventies he had his two presidencies – of Middlesex and the Cricketers – to sustain him; he belonged to other clubs such as the Saints and Sinners and Denham Golf Club and he liked to sit with old friends and yarn about the past while contemplating the not very glorious present. In some ways he was a slightly sad figure by then, though in my company he always seemed cheerful even if stricken.

I also felt that the writing of the book that I produced with his help gave him something of an Indian summer both in its researching, for that meant that he was free to reminisce about a past he had so enjoyed, and also after its publication when he was able to bask in a renewed approbation including that of a generation who had previously known little or nothing about him. He enjoyed it when his old friend the *Times* writer John Woodcock said that 'like his batting it is essentially felicitous', when Lord Griffiths, another MCC president, referred to its 'obvious affection for its subject' and when David Frith in *Wisden* said that for 'anybody not familiar with the Compton story reading this book will be a voyage of expectation, amusement and absorption'. He liked the idea of giving pleasure.

After publication he said to me quite often 'Bloody good book, old boy' and yet I suspected that he had never actually read it, even though I had submitted a manuscript for his perusal, quite apart from the finished presentation copies. When I asked, playfully, what made him say so, he used to look mildly embarrassed and say that one of his friends had said so. That was good enough for him.

Taxi drivers looked on him with awe, even as he struggled to get in and out of their cabs. At the Travellers' Club one day the entire central table of former diplomats stood as one when he walked past and one of them thanked me afterwards for bringing him to lunch because 'it does honour to our club'.

Other occasions were less satisfactory. There was, for instance, a bizarre event at a Hilton hotel somewhere near Watford where Denis and I were one half of the bill and the playwright Lynda La Plante was the other. This meant that half the audience were middle-aged men in tweed while the other half were slightly aggressive feminists who Denis immediately decided were lesbians. Proceedings were, inevitably, bifurcated.

On another occasion his old fan the playwright Ronald Harwood asked me if I could inveigle Denis into having lunch with him. Ronnie, as we have seen, had grown up in Cape Town and had first become a Compton fan watching MCC and England play in South Africa in the 1940s. I replied that Denis was keen on lunch but not always reliable, so we agreed that I would come as well and be responsible for getting him to the Garrick Club on time.

The day arrived and we turned up to find Ronnie in paroxysms of pride and excitement. His friend and fellow cricket enthusiast Harold Pinter had wanted to join us but Ronnie had told him, kindly, to get lost. The same with Albert Finney. Denis smiled but looked bemused. 'It's just the three of us,' said Ronnie, leading the way into the dining room.

There at the end of the central table was the actor Anthony Hopkins, newly knighted, newly Oscared and fresh from his triumph as Hannibal Lecter in *The Silence of the Lambs*. He was, at that moment, one of the most famous and familiar faces in the world.

'Tony,' said Harwood, triumphantly, 'I'd like you to meet my lunch guest, Denis Compton.'

Hopkins smiled, went rather pink, started to stand, thought better of it, then changed his mind and shook Denis by the hand, just managing to blurt out 'Mr Compton, I think you've given me more pleasure than any man alive.'

Then, brushing a tear from his cheek – or so I recall, for Denis was adept at making grown men such as Hopkins and J.J. Warr cry – he sat down again and the three of us moved on to our table.

There Denis turned to me and said 'What a nice man! Who is he? What does he do for a living?'

CHAPTER FIFTEEN

I spent some time with Denis in the early 1990s and saw him in public at Lord's and in private in Buckinghamshire. These glimpses of the old Compton are first-hand, authentic and while not the same as seeing the young athlete in his pomp they are, I believe, sightings worth preserving. They are portraits of an old man near the end of his life with echoes of the young hero he once was.

Like many people in his life I spent a lot of time waiting for Denis.

I remember, in particular, the Saturday of the Lord's Test match when England were playing Australia in 1993. It was 19 June.

An Ashes Saturday at Lord's is just about the highest and holiest day in the cricketing calendar, and even though England had wilted before an Australian batting onslaught and were about to capitulate to a bowling ditto, there was still an atmosphere and an elation barely emulated anywhere, whether in sport or the rest of life. I wanted to record a stately progress around the scene of former triumphs but not for the first or last time, Denis was late.

I was reminded of Robertson-Glasgow's elegiac description of the greatest of all cricket grounds, of how 'inside the W.G. Grace gates I saw the same spectator whom I always see on my first day at Lord's. He was waiting for his brother; who is always late.'

I was waiting for Compton; who was always late. Everybody else seemed to have arrived.

I arrived by the tradesmen's entrance, round the back at the Nursery End, having come from the Tube at St John's Wood. There was a sea of cricket lovers surging slowly towards the ground carrying lunch boxes and binoculars, bananas and pork pies.

Inside the ground I walked past the Nursery and the nets and stood for a moment's reflection before the new twin stands at the eastern end. On the left the Edrich, on the right the Compton. There had been a fuss about these stands just as there nearly always seems to be when any sort of change takes place at Lord's. I remembered sitting in the pavilion one day with the *Observer's* Michael Davie, compiler with his son of one of the best of all cricketing anthologies, and watching men at work. In other words men very obviously not at work. We both agreed that almost anywhere but England if a project had gone behind schedule the labourers would have been scuttling about desperate to make up for lost time. Not here.

Now, however, on that crisp, sunny June morning in 1993 both stands looked functional yet elegant, unobtrusively raked to compensate for the pronounced slope from one side of the ground to the other which is one of the features of Lord's. It was good to see the twin terrors of Middlesex batting commemorated in that way.

Hard by them was a bar. 'The Compton Bar' said the sign. 'Food and Drink'. Pause for wry grin. Both Denis and Bill were fond of a jar. Bill had died a few years earlier, apparently after a night on the tiles. Denis was still going strongish but would be unlikely to make it past the Compton Bar without a pause.

It was a low period in English cricket and a high one in

Australian. Alan Border's side was already being compared to Bradman's 'Invincibles' of 1948. That team had rampaged through England unbeaten, and the England side had included Compton and Edrich, both fresh from their record-breaking triumphs of 1947. Over the previous few days the first three Aussie batsmen – Taylor, Slater and Boon – all made centuries and the fourth, Mark Waugh, only fell one short. By the time the Australians declared on 632 for 4 the England opening bowlers, Caddick and Foster, had bowled 68 overs and taken no wickets for 214. No wonder he was late. Denis was inclined to blame the England captain. He didn't approve of England being captained for the 32nd time by Graham Gooch. 'Great batsman,' he conceded, 'but as a captain, a disaster.'

This view, widely held in the cricketing community, did not extend to the selectors, who waited until Gooch had led his side to a comprehensive and arguably embarrassing defeat in the first Test and then confirmed him as captain for the rest of the series. Compton was not pleased with English cricket in June of 1993 and he laid much of the blame on Gooch and his captaincy.

Denis and I had arranged our rendezvous the day before and under the circumstances it would not have been surprising if the great man had forgotten. He had been in John Paul Getty's box in the Mound Stand and the circumstances were convivial. The Veuve Clicquot flowed.

At about quarter past eleven I passed Colonel Stephenson, then Secretary of MCC, clutching a mobile telephone.

Denis thought highly of the Colonel. 'Nice chap,' he said.

In old age Denis tended to like people and gave them the benefit of the doubt. Two adjectives summed up what he didn't like in people: 'pompous' and 'phoney'. Neither, in his opinion, applied to the Colonel although Denis, as President of the Middlesex County Cricket Club, was, in a sense, the

Colonel's tenant and the relationship between the county and the club has always, by tradition, been supposedly scratchy.

A man called Bob emerged from the Middlesex office and asked if I were me. It appeared that Denis had not forgotten but had been delayed.

Everyone was there. David Frost, the broadcaster scuttled along the tunnel under the grandstand; Field Marshal Lord Bramall, haughty in his I Zingari tie, strode into the pavilion. I spotted Swanton, Tim Rice, the Bedser twins, Bobby Simpson, Ray Illingworth, Bob Willis, Richie Benaud, Peter Parfitt, Henry Blofeld and the Nawab of Pataudi, who was the match referee.

Still no Denis Compton until – finally – he arrived. He was limping heavily and wearing a suit with the same vivid red, green and blue striped tie that he had worn the day before in John Paul Getty's box. The tie of the Lord's Taverners.

Compton was seventy-five, had had a hip operation six months earlier, had shed over three stone, and looked like a man who had done a lot of living. As his old acquaintance the Queen Mother once said apropos of a flattering portrait, 'I would not have it thought that life had passed me by.' It was clear at once that life had not passed Compton by. But even in battered and arthritic old age he retained some of the buccaneering, swashbuckling qualities he had in youth. Despite the greyness of his hair and the bags under the eyes he seemed irrepressible, even up against the massed autograph hunters whose offerings he signed with the familiar flourished signatures, great rolling loops for the 'D' and the 'C'. You couldn't, I felt, keep a good man down. It never occurred to me that he would never see the Australians at Lord's again.

'Hello, old boy,' he said – his usual greeting – 'You didn't get the second message.'

I didn't get a second message.

'I asked Daphne in the Middlesex office to tell you to come

round to Ingleby's house for a glass of fruit juice.'

She can't have seen me.

Fruit juice was, of course, a euphemism for something stiffer. 'Ingleby' was Denis's old mate Colin Ingleby-Mackenzie, who captained Hampshire to their first-ever County Championship in 1961. Ingleby lived close to the ground and on match days Denis parked his car in the drive. He was godfather to one of the Compton daughters.

Their approach to the game and to life was always characterised by the same *joie de vivre*, and they both had a lifelong fondness for the horses. Hence the ritual 'fruit juice' before play at Ingleby's house just outside the ground.

Later that day Ingleby recalled his first meeting with Denis. As an 18-year-old fresh out of Eton he was a debutant in the Hampshire team against Middlesex. He was a newcomer, wet behind the ears, and distinctly overawed when Compton and Edrich arrived in the dressing room. These were men he had worshipped from afar.

After a while Compton came over to ask who he was.

'Ingleby-Mackenzie, sir.'

'Well, good luck,' said Compton. 'Have a good game. Enjoy yourself. And just two things. First, it's not sir, it's Denis. And second' – motioning to the paper under Ingleby-Mackenzie's arm – 'would you mind if I borrowed your *Sporting Life*?'

'Of course, sir,' said Ingleby-Mackenzie, and the two were boon companions from that moment on. It was a job getting Compton through the autograph hunters. He made a point of never brushing them aside, and when I made a disparaging remark about their nuisance value that Saturday he replied that it was a jolly nice nuisance to have to put up with. Nevertheless it *was* tiresome and you began to see why so many of the famous names did tend to seek refuge in the privacy of the boxes, the Pavilion or the committee room.

Compton signed for everyone and took his time and

although he did so because he was an essentially kind and considerate man I sensed an echo of the days of his pomp. This was an old man being nice to people but it was also an old man remembering his earlier triumphs and basking in the reflected glory of his former days. He wouldn't have been lionised like this if it hadn't been for the achievements of his youth and part of this ritual was an act of remembrance.

Not that it was all anonymous requests for scribbles. There was the man from Clontarf who said he remembered Denis playing for a Brylcreem XI against an Irish team of his grandfather's. There was Tom Graveney, his old England team-mate, reminiscing briefly about the old days and the gin and tonics, especially the gin and tonics. They both laughed about the booze.

From even further back there was a dapper, twinkling little man called Laurie D'Arcy who had been on the ground staff with Denis. 'Fifty-nine years ago,' he said, 'we were selling match cards over there just like them.' There were two blazered youths, the descendants of D'Arcy and Compton, selling the same sorts of card though the price had increased. Would either of them go on to be a Compton? Or a D'Arcy? This was a poignant coincidence of past and future. It was also salutary because although D'Arcy had been on the ground staff here at Lord's, he had never played for the county let alone England.

The Australian team manager, white-haired and green-blazered, paused briefly for a chat, and Compton asked him about Craig McDermott. McDermott, the Australians' main fast bowler, was whisked off to hospital suffering severe stomach pains. The manager had just come from the hospital where McDermott had undergone surgery to sort out a twisted bowel. He seemed to have come through all right but his tour was over.

'Send him my regards,' said Denis, sounding as if he meant

it. He knew only too well what it was like to miss matches because the body lets you down. He had also always enjoyed contests against Australia and played hard both on and off the pitch, becoming great rivals and best mates with men like Miller. So wishing the wretched McDermott good luck was not only genuine but entirely in character.

Clive Radley the Lord's coach, stocky and nut-brown from days in the nets, thanked him when Denis complimented him on the class of his twelve-year-old son. Denis had seen the boy play at Wormsley, John Paul Getty's ground, and without knowing his provenance had marked him down at once as a cricketer of rare potential. Radley, paternally proud and embarrassed at the same time, accepted the compliments.

Then, as a Parthian shot, Compton said, over his shoulder, 'Don't go coaching it out of him.'

A joke, certainly, but not just a joke. Compton himself was lucky in his own coaches, who harnessed his natural talent and gave it a context and a discipline in which to bloom instead of snuffing it out by forcing him to play like a guardsman doing drill by the book. Overcoaching *can* snuff out natural ability and flair. Or so Compton believed. And if ever there was a case in point he was it. A stern coach would have eradicated his trademark sweep. He didn't want that to happen to little Radley.

Eventually we made it to the sanctuary of the Middlesex Board Room, where Daphne brought us both a reviving 'fruit juice' and Denis reminisced about Gubby Allen and Paul Getty. Then we went out again to the Middlesex room in the Allen stand, up to the top of the Pavilion, past the old Middlesex and England dressing room and on to the bar at the top of 'Q' stand. Here Denis met Ronnie Harwood, his lifelong South African fan. Ronnie kissed him on both cheeks and said, apparently unembarrassed, 'I worship you.' Denis appeared startled, but over a lifetime of playing out other men's dreams he had become used to such adulation. Or at least accustomed to it. Such gestures always seemed to perplex him, but not to worry him unduly.

Soon it was time for lunch and we went our separate ways. We had arranged a rendezvous for early afternoon by the Grace Gates where Denis was meeting his wife, Christine, but deep down I sensed we wouldn't make it. Sure enough we didn't.

It was strange seeing him there at Lord's that day a living legend, affectionate adulation greeting his every step.

On a quieter day at his old home ground that summer of '93 we did manage another meeting, part of an afternoon and a gentle lunch. His old county Middlesex were playing Leicester and we wandered round relatively unmolested and checking those things that had stayed the same and those things that had not. Lord's, his home ground, had changed in a number of important physical respects since his youth. But just as his outward appearance was greatly altered while the inner man remained true to himself, so you felt that Lord's, his spiritual cricketing home, retained its soul no matter what.

What struck me most in that fleeting glimpse was that, though age had wearied him a little and the years condemned, there was still in Compton a spirit of fun and braggadocio, of cavalier impudence, a generosity of spirit and even little-boy naughtiness which was sadly lacking in 1993's professional game of cricket and lacking too, perhaps, in the public life of the day . . .

While he was characteristically late for the Saturday of the 1993 Test it was a different and unusual story on the first day of the Middlesex versus Leicester game that same year. Denis had said noon outside the Middlesex office but when, courtesy of the usual recalcitrant London Underground system, I arrived well past the hour I was told that Compton had been and gone long ago. He was 'probably' now in the committee room. And so he was.

The committee room in the Pavilion is a holy of holies just across the corridor from the Long Room. Denis was sitting in a high wooden chair in the front of the two rows, gazing out of an open window at the field of play where Haynes and Roseberry were looking comfortable against the Leicester opening bowlers. To his right was the host of the day, D.B. Carr, formerly of Derbyshire and England. Lurking in the background was Fred Titmus, who had come into the Middlesex team in the twilight of Compton's career and had gone on to win 53 England caps. Expected shortly was Mike Brearley, most cerebral of all Middlesex and England captains.

'I'm not used to being kept waiting like this,' said Denis, sitting me down beside him, digging me hard in the ribs and chuckling. The Middlesex Secretary, Air Commodore Hardstaff, son of Joe, the Nottinghamshire and England batsman, had telephoned requesting Compton's presence an hour earlier. He had been at the ground since eleven. Presently D.B. Carr took orders for drinks, which seemed to be an almost universal white wine. To be sitting thus was surely any civilised Englishman's idea of virtual Elysium.

Denis was here in his capacity as Middlesex President, a stalwart of the county set-up, though until three years before he had been too preoccupied with journalism and advertising to take the time off even to serve on the Middlesex committee. I sensed that the post had been worth waiting for. Here he was, at the core and the apex of the county team he had once adorned. Here he was afforded real recognition more than sixty years after he had first scored a hundred on this cricket ground of cricket grounds as a fourteen-year-old elementary schoolboy.

Here he was, being a Grand Old Man on one hand yet one

of the boys on the other. The atmosphere was quite unlike the almost feverish frenzy of the Test match Saturday. This was almost lazy.

It looked an easy wicket to bat on, just as it was in the summer of 1947. Yet it was not always thus. For years Lord's was supposed to have an infamous 'ridge' at around about a length at the Nursery End of the wicket. The theory was that if a bowler pitched a ball onto the ridge it would leap off at any one of a number of unpredictable, not to say lethal, angles. The 'ridge' was one of the cricketing clichés of a generation.

I asked Denis if he had found the ridge a problem. He pondered a moment. Then he said, 'Throughout my career I never noticed it.' This seemed extraordinary, so we sought corroboration from Titmus. He had never been aware of the ridge either. 'There was a dip in the middle,' he said. 'You could see the water gathering there when it rained, but I don't remember anyone saying, "Cor, how do I cope with the ridge?"' The ridge, it seems, was something of a media invention, or so it was according to Compton and Titmus.

Typical, I thought, that something over which the pundits agonised so knowledgeably should have been a matter of almost total unconcern to those who actually played on it. But then you wouldn't have expected Denis to have much time for 'experts', then or now.

A much more meaningful idiosyncrasy for both men was the slope. You could see it quite distinctly looking from the Pavilion towards the Compton and Edrich stands. The grass at the foot of the grandstand is six foot three inches higher than at the bottom of the Tavern. Compton said it definitely affected his leg-spin bowling.

In the old days there was no sightscreen at the Pavilion end. They installed the present, rather irritating movable screen in the 1970s. In fact Compton said he never found any great problem batting with the unshielded Pavilion behind the bowler's arm. He was more often unsettled facing the Nursery end, when sometimes there would be a sunny glare off the trees which still poked up above the top of the stands. The new stands were the same height as the old, so the trees were still visible, giving the ground an agreeable *rus in urbe* feeling. Good landscaping, though not necessarily to the advantage of the batsmen.

'There'd have been ten thousand people here in my day,' said Denis, peering round at the pathetic few hundred souls dotting the stands. And in the afternoon there would have been city folk and actors standing with pints of beer on the concourse outside the old Tavern. They'd blocked it out and put in seats, most of which were empty and usually are except during Test matches and the one-day finals. But the atmosphere generally was much as it was when he played himself. The grandstand was exactly as it was, with the print shop in its bowels still turning out the scorecards and updating them as play proceeded. And under the clock at the Nursery the boys of the ground staff still changed into cricket gear.

'Did you find it difficult batting with the helmet, Compo?' called Titmus from the back of the room.

Joke. He'd heard the President reminiscing and he was taking the mick.

Denis grinned and shrugged. He was off in a fortnight to Australia for the eighty-fifth birthday dinner of Sir Donald Bradman. His wife Christine thought it a long way to go for a single meal and had asked, 'What if the food's no good?' He expected Paul Keating, the Australian PM, would be there to honour his greatest living fellow countryman. Not that Denis knew Keating well. He had known Sir Robert Menzies, that staunch Anglophile and cricket lover who always took a suite at the Savoy and entertained his favourite cricketers, including Denis Compton. Denis might stop off en route in South

Africa to see his sons and also Ali Bacher, Mr South African cricket. Compton was on Christian-name terms there with Prime Minister Vorster, who had been a great friend of Eric Rowan the former South African cricket captain.

Denis had a whole host of peculiar grand friendships. Perhaps the oddest connection with the world of politics was the late General Zia of Pakistan. He had had word of him a few years ago when an England touring party called at the Presidential Palace. 'How is Denis Compton?' asked the general. 'He was my weapons training instructor during the war.'

Compton shook with mirth and we went off to lunch in the committee dining room. The famous Nancy Doyle was in charge, and there was smoked salmon, roast lamb, Spotted Dick and Stilton, Beaujolais and port. The four former England players talked tactics, hands and wrists demonstrating googlies and flippers. They bemoaned the state of English cricket, told tales and jokes. It was a bit like watching former fighter aces chatting about the Battle of Britain.

Afterwards we wandered over to the museum, past the diamond of grass where Denis and the other boys used to stand and wait of an afternoon as members of MCC came up to choose which one of them would bowl at them in the nets. In the corner of the lawn lurked the old heavy roller which the boys used to pull up and down the wicket. Neither he nor Titmus could remember seeing a heavy roller like that on the pitch at all in recent years.

In the museum he asked if his 1947 bat was on display. It was. A man said he had seen Denis using it all through that summer. We contemplated a portrait of a stubbly Graham Gooch which we both agreed was a fright. More to our taste was the conversation piece by the royal portrait painter Andrew Festing, son of Field Marshal Sir Francis, showing Denis and a room full of his peers alive and dead. The dead were shown in full cricketing pomp. The living were as they were when they sat for Festing. We didn't ask to see Denis's infamous kneecap, preserved upstairs in its unpretentious biscuit tin.

Outside Gatting had come to the wicket and was making merry with some pretty trundling Leicester bowling. Compton watched with satisfaction and remembered an adage of Wilfred Rhodes: 'You'll never cut me and you'll never pull me.' The Leicester men were feeding both shots by doing what the great Rhodes never did. They were bowling short.

The mention of Rhodes brought on thoughts of the writers Robertson-Glasgow and Cardus. Cardus always had a soft spot for Compton. 'He used to seek me out,' said Denis. 'Cardus always used to say to me, "You make me feel young."'

It may seem an odd thing to feel about a man of seventy-five who is distinctly dodgy on his pins on account of all the desperate things that had been done to his knees over the years, but he still had the knack of making one feel young. I suspect it was what made him such an adored cricketer and footballer in his youth and prime. There was an endearing and enduring impishness about him which did fill you with the joys of spring. He had a real zest for life and so managed to bring a zest to the lives of those around him.

Seeing him enjoying his Grand Old Man status I was struck by his innate modesty and sense of wonderment that so many good things had happened to him. You felt that he still couldn't really believe his luck. He suddenly turned to me and with a mischievous schoolboy twinkle in his eye he said, 'Let's go and have tea with Paul Getty.'

A man from Mars or even the average American tourist might just have seen an old man with a limp. Believers thought they had seen the next-best thing to God.

In one of our earlier conversations Denis had said to me

that his old friend and adversary Keith 'Nugget' Miller used to say that on the Saturday of a Lord's Test it wasn't possible to walk round the ground more than once and stay quite sober. Denis thought Nugget had it wrong. He thought it was only once.

Later in the afternoon of the Lord's Test Saturday I bumped into 'Ingleby' and asked if he had any news of Denis.

'Denis is lying down,' he said.

That was Denis in public, and his son Patrick believes that public life was where his heart lay.

I've always felt, almost from my first memories of him, that he was a public, not a private man. In other words, his status as a cricket and soccer legend gave him iconic standing among the people, a situation that was maintained and nurtured in the public world of the English media. In that sense, he belonged to England, not to me.

He was not, in truth, a good father, though he was not an actively bad one. In sporting parlance, most of his matches were played away. His priorities, as you can imagine, were his work in the media, and with Royd's. Young people are complicated creatures, with needs of their own, and it was not easy for him to operate on that level.

Having said that, he was one of the most charming, charismatic, modest 'superstars', with a marvellous sense of humour and an ability to get on with just about anyone. People adored him, certainly when I was living with him, and it was extraordinary how long this adulation lasted, many years after his actual feats on the sporting fields had come to an end.

He was also never bitter – another huge plus for me – about the fact that he'd been born at the wrong time to have made big money out of his talents. Yes, he was the Brylcreem Boy, but he would have been a seriously wealthy man in the modern era.

One day that summer of 1993 I took the train from Paddington to see the private man away from the public gaze.

He met me at the station, driving his Peugeot, suited and wearing one of his vivid striped ties. I had said I'd get a cab but he insisted on coming himself. The rain was bucketing down, the visibility was not good and his steering had the same panache as his running between the wickets – mildly unnerving to the man at the other end or in the passenger seat – even if its eccentricity was sometimes exaggerated.

He had been in Ireland the previous week to make an after-dinner speech. The Australians had been playing the Irish. The hospitality had been wonderful. The Australian Neil Harvey, his old mate and adversary, had been there. Denis spoke from a rostrum for about twenty minutes. Not from a written text but just a few notes. He liked being with the Irish, they were so relaxed and convivial, and the chairman who introduced him seemed to know more about him than he knew himself. On the way home the stewardess had given him Bollinger for breakfast.

We were in leafy commuter Bucks, half an hour by train from Paddington and about the same by car down the M40. It was a prosperous neighbourhood, classic commuter country, though in between the garden suburb streets there were bands of farmland, old walled estates and the great woods of Burnham Beeches. Denis had lived here or hereabouts since he moved out of London with the second Mrs Compton in 1951. It's not far, as the crow flies, from working-class north London Hendon where he grew up but in terms of social mobility it was a good number of rungs up the ladder.

His house, grandly designated 'The Little Manor', turned out to be a black and white Tudorbethan construction set back from the road and shielded from its neighbours by trees and shrubs. On the way from the station he pointed to one of the neighbouring houses and said that it was lived in by an airline pilot. That seemed about right. These were seriously expensive houses, and you would guess that most of the inhabitants were upper-middle executives. Not quite the managing director class, at least not of major companies, but just one rung below. It seemed a long way from 47 Alexandra Road, Hendon.

There were neat baskets of flowers hanging from the porch, and through the rain I could see a large back garden with well-tended flowerbeds, a pool, a barbecue and a table with half a dozen or so chairs grouped round it. I asked him if he was the gardener.

'I'm fairly incompetent,' he said, 'and if you're blessed with that sort of incompetence you should stay away. You only do damage.' Mrs Compton – Christine – was the gardener. She was good at flowers and also at vegetables. Denis said he did not discourage her. He said this with a mischievous smile, the same smile he wore when he said that he would mow the lawn but that unfortunately the old knees prevented him. 'The knees are very bad at the moment,' he said. 'They always are when the lawn needs mowing.'

The Compton household consisted of Denis himself, Christine, their two daughters, a dog and sundry cats. Christine was dark, attractive, and still seemed wryly amused by Denis's haphazard ways. She was at Cheltenham Ladies' College with Jeffrey Archer's wife, Mary, but was a year ahead of her. That made her a great deal younger than Denis: forty-something to his seventy-something. When they married in 1972 she said that she wanted two daughters, and she duly had them. In 1994 Charlotte was seventeen and Victoria almost ten. They seemed to regard their father with the sort of fond exasperation daughters reserve for fathers.

Charlotte had just finished her GCSEs and was debating whether to go to Beaconsfield High or to Chesham High. Denis seemed to favour Beaconsfield, but Charlotte wanted Chesham. The reason, it soon transpired, was that 'Beccy' was single-sex but Chesham had boys. Denis laughed at this and did a bit of eye rolling.

Who would make the final decision? 'Mother,' said Denis, glancing towards the kitchen rather like Rumpole gesturing towards she-who-must-be-obeyed. 'And knowing mother, she'll go to Chesham.'

The business of Charlotte and boys was obviously rather a trial. There was also trouble with the telephone, which the girls monopolised to such an extent that the Comptons had installed British Telecom's 'call waiting' so that if Denis was trying vainly to ring home to explain why he was going to be late the girls could be interrupted. Victoria was a promising tennis player and a good eater, though already threatening – to Denis's consternation – to go on a diet. On Sundays they liked to go *en famille* to Denham Golf Club for a serious roast beef lunch.

In addition to the humans there was a fifteen-month-old Old English Sheepdog called Benjy. Denis had been assured that the dog would calm down and become placid when it was two years old, but as he said, a touch plaintively, there wasn't very long to go and the dog was wonderfully but maddeningly boisterous. Its favourite pastime seemed to be putting its front paws on your shoulders and licking your face. And then there were cats.

In other words, despite the fact that he was at the time more than five years beyond the biblical three score years and ten, his family set-up was that of a man thirty years his junior. Charlotte was the same age as my youngest, and at the time I was forty-nine. Men of seventy-five are not supposed to have rollicking Old English Sheepdogs and teenage daughters. Yet Denis did and somehow Denis, being Denis, seemed to get away with it. And you could see that it helped to keep him young.

He had been trying to sort out some paperwork, and the dining-room table was covered in books and letters, contracts and newspaper cuttings. Not much evidence of method, let alone filing. It was a comfortable room. The large sideboard had a family photograph on it and two cabinets were full of china, one of which contained nothing but Staffordshire figurines.

Denis made coffee, getting rather tangled up with the dog and forgetting to provide table mats, which came in later, brought by Victoria, smiling rebuke at forgetful Dad. One of the cuttings was from the *Australian.*

'Johnny Woodcock,' he said. 'Nice, that.'

It was, too. 'The most engaging cricketer I ever saw,' Woodcock wrote. 'What one would have given to see him now, the laughing cavalier of 1947, going out to show Australia's bowlers the magic he brought to the game.'

Denis took his coffee black, no sugar.

He passed over a letter from the doctor who had looked after his diabetes. Denis had organised an autographed cricket bat for a charitable appeal of the doctor's, and the special event at which the bat was auctioned had raised £10,000. This was a thank-you letter.

I had been away for a week and missed some cricket. He was anxious to bring me up to date, particularly on the doings of his beloved Middlesex. Presidency of the county obviously meant a great deal to him. Normally the Middlesex presidents put in a two-year term, but his presidency had been so successful that they were asking him to stay on for an extra three. There had been an extraordinary match against Glamorgan at Cardiff. Glamorgan, going in first, were determined to leave nothing to chance and made over five hundred for only three wickets, Dale and Richards both scoring double centuries. Middlesex started badly but Gatting got a big score, Emburey a rare century, and they finished thirty or so runs ahead. 'Then,' said Denis, 'the most extraordinary thing happened.' Glamorgan went in a second time and Tufnell took 8 for 29. Denis's mouth formed an 'O' of astonishment and he shook his head in disbelief. Glamorgan were all out for 115 and Middlesex, set 88, won by ten wickets.

He seemed as excited about this result as any boy of eight, pointed out that the lads had won their last two games and were eleven points clear at the top of the table. It was easy to see why the county wanted him for another three years. It was more than thirty-five years since he played for them, but he was still on the team.

He threw over another letter. It was from *The Times*, asking if he would be the subject of their question and answer feature 'My Perfect Weekend'. There was a list of questions. 'My perfect destination', 'My perfect companion'. 'What medicine would you take?' There was a PS saying that Venice was banned as a 'perfect' destination because so many people had chosen it already. The girl in charge enclosed some previous examples. One was the 'perfect weekend' of Marina Warner, granddaughter of Denis's old mentor, Sir Pelham. Denis wasn't having any of it.

The phone rang. It was Peter Lawson, boss of the CCPR, the Central Council for Physical Recreation. Would Denis sit on a committee with Sir Stanley Matthews and that girl who had just climbed Everest and whose name none of us could remember? He would. The committee was supposed to encourage more young people to take up active participation in sport. This was an aspiration close to his heart. Indeed how could it be otherwise?

He was not averse to the odd committee and seemed quite pleased that the Middlesex committee met once a month. Joe

Hardstaff, son of the cricketer alongside whom he played, was the Secretary. Sir Ian MacLaurin, then head of Tesco, was also on the committee. Denis was a friend of his, and MacLaurin was an avid cricket fan and player. It was no coincidence that Tesco was a prominent sponsor of the sport. Gaining sponsorships was a bit of a Compton knack. The day I saw him at home he was off to lunch with the marketing director of Nestlé. He was another cricket and Compton fan, and Denis had persuaded him to sponsor his county's one-day match against the Australians.

The lunch was at the offices of McCann Erickson, the advertising agency. Denis still maintained a modest office there, just a small box really with a desk, a chair and a telephone. This was all he needed, since most of his work was best done in more congenial circumstances over a drink or a lunch, perhaps at the Cricketers' Club in Marylebone – an institution he helped keep on fairly tottering feet when it ran into difficulties and which he regularly patronised. He was useful to McCanns, one suspected, as the sort of chap who knew his way around the sporting establishment, could fix things up and make a useful introduction or two. Besides he was a legend in his own lifetime and for an ambitious advertising agency a legend was a useful card to play. Even in his mid-seventies Denis was helping the company acquire new business. In 1993, for instance, it was he, or so he claimed, who hooked the Panasonic account for McCanns.

It was easy to forget, seeing him then, socially at ease, almost grand, that there was a time when doors were closed to him. That morning, surrounded by his apology for a filing system, Denis told me the story of how he joined, with difficulty, his much-loved Denham Golf Club in the middle of the Old Trafford Test in 1948. To that day he couldn't understand why they couldn't have told him over the telephone, but he had been a member for almost forty years.

It is no accident that of the two really great English cricketers of his time it was Hutton who captained his country and who became Sir Leonard, while Compton only had a CBE. There was in Compton a streak of boyishness, irreverence, gaiety and abandon which prevented him ever becoming anything as prosaic as a 'pillar' of anything, let alone the establishment. No matter how many committees he sat on, how many high-powered deals he pulled off, no matter what titles might be conferred, he simply wasn't the stuff of which establishment pillars are made. I asked John Major, one of the most ardent cricketing fans of all post-war Prime Ministers, why Denis had never had a knighthood but although he was full of affection and enthusiasm he ignored my question. Rumour has it that Denis, like his friend Keith Miller, was too friendly with the Queen's younger sister, Princess Margaret, and that it was this which scuppered his chances of the knighthood which went to Len Hutton and Alec Bedser. I can find no proof of this.

It was entirely characteristic and right and proper to find him at seventy-five exchanging banter with his two young daughters, trying unsuccessfully to suppress the boisterousness of his Old English Sheepdog, failing to reply to letters from *The Times*, agreeing to serve on yet another committee, driving to London at short notice for lunch with the Nestlé marketing director. He was leading life as he had always led it. He was having fun and in the end, shamelessly that is what his life was all about. That life was also often chaotic and I caught more than a whiff of that chaos that morning at the Little Manor in Burnham.

CHAPTER SIXTEEN

He died about three years later on 23 April 1997. St George's Day.

He originally went into the Princess Margaret Hospital in Windsor for what should have been a relatively routine hip operation. His old golfing companion and friend Ted Woodward called in and found him weary and resigned. 'I've had enough,' he said. Joe Hardstaff, his friend, the Middlesex secretary, phoned the hospital daily and was depressed to hear his old friend distinctly down-in-the-mouth over the weekend but on Monday he seemed to have rallied and sounded much more buoyant and optimistic.

Christine confirms this and says that he seemed to have recovered so much that the hospital actually discharged him. This was much too soon however for Denis was obviously running a high temperature and seemed confused and rambling. Christine had him rapidly taken back to hospital, where he was discovered to be suffering from septicaemia. His son Patrick phoned him from South Africa at the hospital. 'The line was not a good one,' he recalls, 'and he was weak and his voice was feeble. I remember ending the call by saying: "Get better soon. I love you Dad." I'll always be glad I said that.'

There still seemed no great reason for alarm so it was a bad shock when the hospital phoned to give Christine the news that he had gone.

On the Tuesday when he phoned the Princess Margaret to check on Compton's progress Hardstaff immediately realised that something was terribly wrong. He was asked politely if he were related to Mr Compton and when he described the nature of their relationship he was told that, sadly, Denis had passed away earlier.

Scarcely pausing, Hardstaff got in his car and drove to Burnham to help Christine with the necessary but burdensome paperwork. Christine herself was deeply shocked, not least because she, like the others, really thought that Denis had turned a corner. Jim Murphy O'Connor, an old family friend as well as Compton's long-standing GP, also expressed surprise and for a while, since satisfactory explanations seemed in short supply, Christine even considered suing the hospital for negligence. In the end, however, there seemed to be more important things to worry about.

She read the eulogistic obituaries. 'Cricketing cavalier who dazzled a nation' said the *Telegraph*; 'Buccaneer who put a smile on the face of two sports' wrote the London *Evening Standard*, adding 'Football and cricket mourn the loss of a real boy's own hero'. *The Times* said:

John Major led the tributes yesterday for Denis Compton, the cavalier of cricket and hero to generations of schoolboys, who died in a Windsor hospital after suffering a leg infection. He was 78.

Compton, who represented England at cricket and football, was an idol for many youngsters because of his supreme talent and flamboyant lifestyle, which often involved him arriving at matches still wearing his dinner jacket.

He was also a pioneer of the commercial era, being the first English sportsman to employ an agent. He became known as the

'Brylcreem Boy' because of his advertisements for the hair lotion.

He played in 78 Tests and, in 1947, his greatest season, scored a record 3,816 runs. He hit the winning stroke at the Oval against Australia in 1953 when England regained the Ashes after 19 years. He also won 12 caps for England in wartime football internationals and played outside-left in Arsenal's FA Cup winning team of 1950.

Cricket grounds across the country observed a minute's silence before their county games yesterday.

Later Christine and Denis's five children attended the homely funeral in Fulmer, the grand memorial at Westminster Abbey and the scattering of the ashes at Lord's. Then the three sons returned to South Africa and Christine settled down to bringing up Victoria and Charlotte and rebuilding her life.

Her husband left behind memorials as well as memories. There was already the Lord's Compton Stand alongside the Edrich at the Nursery End which Christine Compton once said was the best and perhaps the only necessary memorial. However as she also said, 'It seems there is an awful lot I don't know about.' For example there was an Item No. 8718394056 on eBay, described as: 'A fine Limited Edition wall plaque in relief sculpture of cricketer Denis Compton'. The plaque looks like a cross between a death mask and a Madame Tussaud waxwork. It's head-only and does its subject less than justice.

'I have no recollection of them being done,' commented Christine. 'I thought the subject was given one with limited editions as was the case with a figurine which I have. Maybe Denis was paid a fee instead . . . all very interesting.'

Another memorial Christine knew little or nothing about was the Compton-Miller medal. David Collier, Chief Executive of the England and Wales Cricket Board, told me that the idea was first voiced at Keith Miller's memorial service when Cricket Australia proposed a 'Miller medal'. The ECB 'suggested – and it was totally accepted by Cricket Australia – that it would be wonderful to celebrate two great cricketers and friends in the same award and hence the Compton-Miller medal was born'.

The Royal Mint struck some solid gold medals and in 2005 Andrew Flintoff was presented with the first of them as player of the Ashes series of that year. He was chosen by David Graveney and Trevor Hohns, the Chairmen of the England and Australia selectors. The launch of the medal took place at Lord's that summer but unaccountably Christine and Denis's daughters were not invited though his son Richard was flown in from South Africa and his grandson Nick, playing for Middlesex alongside Ben Hutton, grandson of Len, was also present. Richard said that it was 'a really special few days. The ECB were so generous and wonderful in the manner they entertained Mrs Miller and myself. It helped that the representatives of the ECB and others present were terrific company too.'

He added, in reflective mode: 'It is rather extraordinary that dad was celebrated with his face on the Compton-Miller medal. So much has transpired since his glory days that I was forced to reflect again on what he really meant to the country and the cricketing world. A number of wonderful and popular English players have followed him but clearly this was another reminder that dad had something special and that he represented a personality that has endured fondly in people's minds. In a world of political correctness and suffocating structure and legislation I was rather pleased to hear that the name of Denis Compton could still be held up to the light. I'm pleased that his charisma, good sportsmanship and unorthodoxy can still be celebrated in the 21st century.'

The first Christine knew about all this was when she read it in the paper. Understandably hurt, as much for her daughters as herself, she wrote to remonstrate and was told that every effort had been made to locate her. As she still lives in the house she shared with Denis and which is less than an hour's drive from Lord's she found this a bit hard to take though the ECB argued, not unreasonably, that having been in touch with Richard they assumed that the family would all have been informed. Christine has been invited to the Lord's Test in 2009, a date which in 2005 seemed disconcertingly far off. Denis's old team-mate Trevor Bailey, who had succeeded him as President of the Cricketers' Club, took up the cudgels on behalf of his widow and daughters.

The annual Denis Compton Awards do however involve Christine's active participation partly because they were started in Denis's lifetime. The genesis was at John Paul Getty's ground at Wormsley in Buckinghamshire. One member of the Getty XI was Neil Burns who had played first-class cricket but was now in semi-retirement as Director of cricket at minor county Buckinghamshire. Denis was impressed with Burns's batting and afterwards went into the pavilion to ask him why he was no longer playing in the first-class game. During the course of a prolonged natter Burns declared that part of the problem with the English game, then at an unprecedentedly low ebb, was the lack of practice. Burns said that the sports management company he ran with his father Roy was trying to set up a scheme to send promising young cricketers to Denis's beloved South Africa to get some serious cricket in during the English winter. Denis was enthusiastic and told Burns that he would like to be involved.

The result was that on 27 August 1996 (Don Bradman's eighty-eighth birthday) Denis officially launched the Denis Compton Awards. A panel of Dickie Bird, Ian Botham, John Emburey, David Graveney, Christopher Martin-Jenkins, Clive Radley and Micky Stewart got together to choose the most promising players in each of the eighteen first-class counties.

They chose pretty well for among the first batch of winners were Marcus Trescothick of Somerset, Ashley Giles of Warwickshire and Ben Hollioake of Surrey, later so tragically killed in a road accident. Roy Burns told me that of the team that won the Ashes back in 2005 no fewer than seven were former Compton Award winners. 'It would have been eight,' he remarked laconically, 'if they'd chosen the right wicketkeeper.'

Sadly Denis was too ill to attend the initial dinner at the Lord's Long Room in April 1997, fifty years after those stirring deeds of 1947. The menu included a tribute to him and his career which concluded with the words 'Denis is delighted to be associated with this Scheme and it is sincerely hoped that – in future years – recipients of these Awards will go on to reproduce the quality of entertaining cricket synonymous with the name of Denis Compton.' Denis died just two weeks later.

His Awards continue, however, presented by Christine every year at the 'Jonners Club' annual dinner. There is also a Compton Memorial Trust set up by Denis's son Richard and his friend Tony Bradshaw. Bradshaw lives in East Sheen in South-West London and the main test-bed for the Trust's activities is his local club, Sheen Park. 'The primary focus of activity,' he says, 'is in the area of club-school links where we endeavour to marry schools to clubs. I fear this is the only way many children in the state system can expect to make progress as cricketers. The charity is very small – income over the last five years has been in the region of £50,000 – but it has a role to play – in Middlesex at least – and the great name lives on!'

Memorials such as these are a testimony to one of the great cricketing careers but they pall besides the memories of what Compton cricket was really like. There are still, as I write, many who can actually recall the magic. At the Swindon Literary Festival recently, for instance, I was mesmerised as a member of my audience rose to describe a single shot he had seen Denis play at the Oval in 1947. It was, I reflected, more than half a century since Denis executed the stroke, and the enthusiastic fan took at least ten times as long to describe the stroke as it would have taken Denis to play it.

In February 1999, less than two years after his death, I was lecturing on the *QE2* off the south coast of Australia and had spent a session chatting away about cricket in general and Denis in particular. Afterwards a man came up to me with an embarrassed-looking wife in tow.

'Thank you very much,' he said. 'After World War Two I emigrated from the Old Dart and came out to Australia where I met this Sheila here and we married and soon had a son. I have been trying to explain to her ever since why it was essential that we christened the boy Denis.

'Now at last I think she understands.'

INDEX

Bedser, Alec, (*cont'd*)
140, 146, 157, 186, 191
Bedser, Eric 84
Bell Lane Elementary School
9–10, 14
Benaud, Richie 94, 184, 204,
246
benefit matches 28
Benson, Charles 220
Bestwick, Bill 30
birth of DC 7–8
Black Horse pub (Fulmer)
215, 216
Blackpool football club 78–9
Bolton Wanderers football
club 168–9
Bond, James 9–10
Border, Alan 253
Botham, Ian 65–6
bowling skills of DC 16–17,
111
Boycott, Geoffrey 226–7
Bradman, Don 58, 96, 97,
98–9, 100, 102, 103–4,
139–40, 143, 149, 150,
205, 261
Bradshaw, Tony 278
Brearley, Mike 259
British Empire XI 84
Brooke-Taylor, Tim 3
Brown, Bill 80
Brown, Freddie 96, 181, 185
Brown, George 19
Brown, Sid 119

Bruce, Nigel 51–2
Brylcreem 135–7, 153, 172
Buccaneers cricket club 84
Buckley, Frank 169
Busby, Matt 81
Butler, Frank 83

Cambridge University 125–7
Cardus, Neville 2, 56, 70, 109,
224–5, 263
Carlisle, John 238
Carr, D.B. 255
Carr, Wesley 2–3
Carruthers, Frank 81, 83
Cavaliers cricket club 211
Chapman, Herbert 15, 37, 38,
39, 44
Charles, John 169
Charlton Athletic football club
76
Chelsea football club 170–2
childhood of DC 8–9
Clarke, Osmond 197, 206
Clay, J.C. 127, 150
Close, Brian 50
coaching of DC 16–19
Collier, David 271
Compton, Brian (son) 86,
159–60
Compton, Charlotte
(daughter) 216, 266, 267
Compton, Christine (wife) 218,
225, 258, 265, 266, 273,
274, 275, 276–7, 278

Fingelton, Jack 98, 99, 100, 140–1, 145, 149–50, 192
Fishlock, Laurie 84
Flintoff, Andrew 272
Flynn, Errol 187–8
Fowler, Archie 16–17, 18
Frith, David 141, 145, 245

Gatting, Mike 18
Gilchrist, Roy 231
Giller, Norman 25, 29, 77, 221, 223
Gladwin, Cliff 157
Glamorgan cricket club 127, 150, 264
Glanville, Brian 75, 167
Glasgow Rangers football club 39–40
Gloucester cricket club 200
Goddard, Tom 133, 207
Gooch, Graham 249, 262–3
Gordon, John 227
Gover, Alf 120–1
Gower, David 241
Graham, Clive 220
Grant, David 96
Graveney, Tom 3, 33, 188, 190, 200, 231, 256
Green, Benny 15, 74, 78
Green, Michael 181
Green, Stephen 196, 240
Greene, Richard 136
Griffiths, Hugh 126
Guinness, Edward 216

Guise, J.L. 28

Hagan, J. 80
Hain, Peter 237
Hall, Wesley 231
Hallows, Charlie 231–2
Hammond, Walter 50, 59, 65, 91, 95–6, 97–8, 104
Hampshire cricket club 113, 114
Hapgood, Eddie 39, 80
Hardstaff, Joe 55–6, 92, 101, 104, 128, 273–74
Harvey, Bagenal 135, 221
Harvey, Neil 260
Harwood, Ronald 151–2, 153, 158, 187, 248–9, 258
Hassan, Khalid 190
Hassett, Lindsay 58, 88, 139
Hayes, Douglas 198
Haynes, Johnny 136
Hayter, Reg 123, 129, 134–5, 152, 154, 246
Headingley 129
Hearne, J.W. 27, 48
Hendren, Patsy 12, 23–4, 28, 47–8, 56–7, 93
Hennessy, Peter 107, 108–9
Heyhoe–Flint, Rachel 212–13
Hill, Jeffrey 220
Hill-Wood, Peter 2
Hobbins, Sid 76–8
Hobbs, Jack 12, 122, 133
Hollies, Jack 93